Policing Yesterday, Today, Tomorrow

Policing Yesterday, Today, Tomorrow

The View from South Wales

Edited by Martin Innes, Trudy Lowe and Gareth Madge

UNIVERSITY OF WALES PRESS

2023

www.uwp.co.uk

British Library Cataloguing-in-Publication Data
A catalogue record for this book is available from the British Library.

ISBN 978-1-83772-084-2
eISBN 978-1-83772-085-9

The rights of the Contributors to be identified as authors of this work have been asserted in accordance with sections 77 and 79 of the Copyright, Designs and Patents Act 1988.

The University of Wales Press gratefully acknowledges the support of the Higher Education Funding Council for Wales in publication of this book.

Typeset by Marie Doherty
Printed by CPI Antony Rowe, Melksham, United Kingdom

CONTENTS

ACKNOWLEDGEMENTS

Martin Innes, Trudy Lowe and Gareth Madge

The original concept for this book first began to take shape as South Wales Police approached its fiftieth anniversary in 2019. The idea of the then Chief Constable, Matt Jukes, was to explore how the anniversary might be commemorated with the production of a volume that not only celebrated the force's history but also drew upon it, to reflect the changing role of the police in society more generally over a time of rapid social change. Building on a longstanding collaboration with the Universities' Police Science Institute at Cardiff University, a small team of staff from both organisations convened to look at how that might be achieved. Together they devised the innovative concept of blending both practitioner and academic authors to give the book a blend of 'real world' grounding and insight based upon South Wales Police as an analytical unit. The result, we hope, is a volume which is at its heart commemorative and celebratory but also open, reflective and challenging. We are indebted to Matt Jukes for his original idea, drive and enthusiasm, and to Huw Cogbill for his significant contribution to the early development and shaping of the project.

By the autumn of the anniversary year, a publishing contract with the University of Wales Press had been agreed and potential contributors had been approached, with individuals signing up to author or co-author chapters in areas of their substantive expertise. In January 2020, a workshop enabled them to start the process of writing together, learning from the skills and experience of each other to co-produce their contributions.

But little did we know what lay around the corner. Just as work got off the ground, the UK went into the unprecedented public health crisis of the Covid-19 pandemic. For South Wales Police, as across the country, operational issues changed and ballooned overnight as successive periods of national and regional lockdowns brought in new legislation and policing challenges resulting from social distancing regulations. Academics too were impacted by the 'work from home' guidance and the need to adapt quickly to a new way of working, not least the move to online student teaching. This book might have been derailed there and then, had it not been for the commitment to the project from all of its contributing authors, and we cannot thank each of them enough for their dedication, support and forbearance throughout the much longer than anticipated process of bringing their work together and getting it to print.

Throughout that process, Jeremy Vaughan and Umar Hussain have provided support and direction to help us achieve the vision we set for the project, despite numerous challenges along the way. And we are also grateful to Sir Denis O'Connor and Alun Michael for giving their time to review the finished manuscript and to pen their insightful introduction and preface respectively, which frame the volume perfectly.

Our book has grown from a unique exercise in collaboration between the force and Cardiff University, and it owes a great deal to those who have driven, consolidated and developed the concept of the Universities' Police Science Institute over its sixteen-year history. Among the many to whom we owe a debt of gratitude for their foresight and support in this respect are former South Wales Chief Constables Barbara Wilding and Peter Vaughan, together with Bob McAllister, Dave Francis and Mel Jehu, who were important early supporters of the Institute, and Emeritus Professor Jonathan Shepherd.

Last but by no means least, we thank the University of Wales Press for recognising the potential value of this volume to a number of audiences, and for their unwavering patience with all involved with its creation.

LIST OF CONTRIBUTORS

Cheryl Allsop is a Senior Lecturer in criminology at the University of South Wales, where she teaches and researches major crime investigations, missing people, miscarriages of justice and cold case investigations. She is the author of the first ethnographic account of a major crime review team entitled *Cold Case Reviews: DNA, detective work and unsolved major crimes* published by Oxford University Press and is the co-editor of the *International Handbook of Homicide Investigations* soon to be published by Routledge.

Stephen Carr is transformation strategy lead for the Home Office. He was formerly programme manager for the Welsh Government's Safer Communities Programme – aimed at refreshing and reinvigorating community safety partnership working across Wales – following his work leading the Welsh Government's Working Together for Safer Communities Review. As head of community safety for Cardiff between 2006 and 2012, he led the Safer Capital community safety partnership and the development and implementation of the 2010 Tilley Award-winning Transforming Neighbourhoods model of multi-agency neighbourhood management programme and is now a judge for the National Problem Solving programme and annual Tilley Awards.

Lorraine Davies has over 28 years' investigative experience serving as a Detective at every rank within South Wales Police. She retired as Detective Chief Superintendent and Head of Specialist Crime with an extensive portfolio including: Public Protection,

Major Crime Investigations, Serious and Organised Crime, Force Intelligence and the Forensic Scientific Unit. She worked closely with Welsh Government and the Police and Crime Commissioners Office on strategic issues including Violence Against Women and Girls and the provision of Sexual Assault Referral Centre Services. She led on developing and delivering public protection training to police and partner agencies including the International Leaders Development Programme comprising Senior Officers from Ambulance, Fire Service and Police.

Jonathan Drake is a former Director of the Wales Violence Prevention Unit, where he led a multi-agency team with a mission to prevent violence in Wales through applying a public health approach. In his earlier policing career, he was an Assistant Chief Constable for South Wales Police, having also served in Staffordshire Police. His responsibilities included serious and major crime and he was the National Police Chiefs Council Lead for Intelligence.

Adam Edwards is Reader in Politics and Criminology in the School of Social Sciences, Cardiff University. He is interested in comparative urban governance, policing and security and co-edited *Policing European Metropolises: the politics of security in city-regions* (Routledge, 2017). Currently he is working on the security implications of smart cities and the growing interrelationship between online and offline crime and victimisation. He is co-editor of *The SAGE Handbook of Digital Society* (SAGE, 2023).

Jenny Gilmer has been a police officer for over twenty years and, having served previously with British Transport Police, is currently an Assistant Chief Constable with South Wales Police. At the time of writing, she has responsibility for Local Policing and in that capacity oversees the police officers and staff who provide service to the communities of South Wales including response, neighbourhood policing and investigators.

Wendy Gunney is an Assistant Chief Constable with South Wales Police. She began her policing career in 1997, working for both

Thames Valley Police and South Wales Police. She has a varied background having worked in covert policing, intelligence, the regional organised crime unit, and local operational policing, predominately in Cardiff. Wendy is an accredited firearms commander and public order commander.

Umar Hussain is the Chief Financial officer of South Wales Police. He has extensive financial experience in both the private and public sectors, including with Gwent Police and Lincolnshire Police. His current role involves providing strategic direction, control and advice on all financial matters affecting the force. He also has chief officer responsibility for a wide range of support services. He has also played a leading role in developing collaboration between Welsh police forces. In 2015 he was recognised for his services to policing by being appointed MBE in the Queen's Birthday Honours.

Martin Innes is a Professor in the School of Social Sciences at Cardiff University, where he also leads the Security, Crime and Intelligence Innovation Institute. He is the author of four books and a large number of articles and book chapters. Innes has achieved international renown for his work on police murder investigations, counter-terrorism and neighbourhood policing. He is a trustee of the Police Foundation, and has advised governments across Europe and globally about issues of police innovation and reform.

Matt Jukes joined South Wales Police as an Assistant Chief Constable in 2010 after fifteen years of police service in communities in South Yorkshire, similarly affected by the decline of their coal and steel industries. In South Wales, he went on to lead a conclusive phase of action concerning several miscarriage of justice cases from the 1980s and 1990s. He was promoted to Deputy Chief Constable in 2013 and Chief Constable in 2018. After leading the force's initial response to the Covid pandemic, he transferred to the Metropolitan Police where at the time of writing, he is responsible for national counter-terrorism policing. He is the holder of the Queen's Police Medal for services to policing.

Catherine Larkman joined South Wales Police in 1989 after graduating from Swansea University. She served over 31 years, mainly in operational policing roles, before retiring as a Superintendent. Cath was one of the founders of the Female Police Association and was named as an influential female in the force 'Breaking the Glass Ceiling' exhibition. Community and police relationships have always been important to her, and she received a Special Recognition Award in 2020 for her leadership of the Unity Shield, a pan-South Wales sporting tournament, an event that built bridges between female minority communities and the Police.

Catherine Llewellyn-Roberts is the Head of Communications at South Wales Police. The principal communications advisor to the Chief Constable and the Police and Crime Commissioner, she is responsible for co-ordinating strategic communications across the organisation. Catherine leads a communications team which consists of marketing, internal communications, media relations, digital communications, social and visual media.

Trudy Lowe is a criminologist and former Research Fellow at the Universities' Police Science Institute, Cardiff University. She has worked on numerous police science research projects for South Wales Police, and other forces nationally and internationally, across a diverse range of policing activity. Her primary foci have been Neighbourhood Policing, Counter-Terrorist Policing and Prevent, and Vulnerability.

Gareth Madge is a retired solicitor and former chief officer in South Wales Police where, in addition to legal services, he also had responsibility for corporate development and liaison with Welsh Government. He was a member of the Board of Directors of the Association of Chief Police Officers and helped establish its successor body, the National Police Chiefs Council. Since his retirement he has been actively involved in raising awareness of South Wales Police's history and heritage. He was appointed OBE in the Queen's Birthday Honours of 2015 for his services to South Wales Police and policing.

Rt Hon Alun Michael is the incumbent Police and Crime Commissioner for South Wales, having been first elected in 2012 and then for a third time in May 2021. Alun was the Labour and Co-operative member of the UK Parliament for Cardiff South and Penarth for twenty-five years from 1987, before he stepped down to stand as the Police and Crime Commissioner. During his time in Parliament he held a number of ministerial positions, including as Deputy Home Secretary, and as a member of the Cabinet as Secretary of State for Wales. He was for a time also a member of the then National Assembly for Wales and was the first First Secretary (First Minister) of Wales.

Sir Denis O'Connor is the former Chief Inspector of Constabulary 2009–2012. Denis served in Surrey Police and Kent Police, before being appointed as an Assistant Commissioner in the Metropolitan Police in 1997. He was Chief Constable of Surrey Police between 2000 and 2004. He was appointed Commander of the Order of the British Empire in 2002 and was knighted in 2010.

Mark O'Shea is a Detective Superintendent with South Wales Police. His police service began in 1995, predominantly serving in CID and the Major Crime Investigation Team as an SIO in 2015. Since that time he has led a range of complex enquiries, including numerous category A homicide investigations. He is a qualified PIP 4 SIO, Kidnap and Extortion SIO and a Senior Identification Manager for disaster victim identification. A graduate of the University of Glamorgan, at the time of writing he is studying for a Master's Degree in Strategic Leadership and Management at the University of Wales.

Kath Pritchard is a retired Detective Superintendent and an accredited trainer on the National Senior Investigating Officer Development Programme for Major Crime and Serious Organised Crime. She was also a National Crisis and Hostage Negotiator. Kath led on strategic programmes such as European Diversity in Policing, the NPCC Policing Sex Work Guidance (2015) and chaired and presented at an Economic and Social Research Council Conference on Understanding Sex Offender Disclosure in

Wales. Kath supports the WRU (Welsh Rugby Union) as an independent Safeguarding Panel member, referee, and coach, striving to break down barriers, promoting inclusion through sport.

Amanda L. Robinson is Professor of Criminology in the School of Social Sciences and co-Director of the Security, Crime & Intelligence Innovation Institute at Cardiff University. Her research specialisms include multi-agency responses to domestic and sexual violence, policing, specialist courts, and the criminal justice system. She was directly involved in producing the Welsh Government's White Paper proposals that were passed into legislation as the Violence against Women, Domestic Abuse, and Sexual Violence (Wales) Act 2015. Amanda has published nearly 100 research articles and technical reports as well as chapters in high-profile edited collections. At the time of writing, she is an Editor of the *British Journal of Criminology*.

Colin Rogers is Professor of Policing and Security at the University of South Wales. A former South Wales Police officer of 30 years' service, he has conducted research on many policing and crime topics, both nationally and internationally, as well as publishing widely in academic and practitioner journals. He has been asked to advise policing agencies and government departments on policing and community issues in such countries as Uruguay, Brunei and Australia. His current research interests include police education, the future of the police workforce and the use of volunteers in policing.

Jonathan Shepherd is a surgeon, criminologist, and professor at Cardiff University. Prompted by his discoveries and his patients' physical and mental injuries he developed the prototype community safety partnership and violence prevention unit – Cardiff's violence prevention board. To boost police research, he initiated the Universities' Police Science Institute. He pioneered the Cardiff Model for Violence Prevention, an established UK export which the WHO promotes globally. His advocacy for police and probation professional bodies mirroring the Royal College of Surgeons resulted in the College of Policing and the Probation

Institute. He is the first UK winner of the international Stockholm Criminology Prize.

Jeremy Vaughan started his policing career in 1996 and has worked all over Wales. He has a background in both operational policing and criminal investigation, as an accredited senior investigating officer; hostage negotiator; firearms commander; public order commander; and counter terrorism commander. He has led nationally on police counter corruption, use of facial recognition technology, pay and conditions of service and the emerging biometrics programme. Having served South Wales Police as an Assistant and then Deputy Chief Constable, he became Chief Constable in 2020, leading the Force through the global health pandemic.

Peter Vaughan was appointed Chief Constable of South Wales Police in 2010 and retired at the end of 2017 after thirty-three years police service. As Chief Constable he was vice president of the Association of Chief Police Officers (ACPO) and vice chair of the National Police Chiefs' Council (NPCC). He is currently the Director of Policing and Security at the University of South Wales. The department is partnered with the South Wales, Gwent, Dyfed Powys, Devon and Cornwall, Gloucestershire, Wiltshire, and Dorset police forces delivering the police degree apprenticeship and graduate diploma programmes. Peter is the Lord-Lieutenant for the County of Mid Glamorgan and holder of the Queen's Police Medal for services to policing.

PREFACE

Alun Michael

Policing is a unique profession. It requires a body of people who are organised and disciplined for specific operations but who are personally and individually proactive (a recent screensaver reminded every individual in South Wales Police that 'You are a Leader') while caring about the needs of vulnerable individuals and being sensitive to the concerns of whole communities. Policing is frequently the 'last service standing', expected to show the expertise in which others have been trained when they have gone home for the night or the weekend. Over 80% of calls to the non-emergency 101 service have nothing to do with crime or the wider responsibilities of policing and the number of calls goes up inexorably year after year. And there has been increasingly a return to the Peelian expectation that officers will intervene early to prevent harm and to 'nip things in the bud' rather than just responding.

At one extreme the job of a constable is simple – keep the peace and stop bad things happening – while at the other extreme it is uniquely complicated, involving an incredible range of things that he or she is expected to deal with, instantly and according to the law, on a daily basis. Bad enough for the individual, but as the chapters in this book show, the range of specialisms is equally mind boggling, from detection and forensic science to the challenge of online crime, the amazing sophistication of some lawbreakers and the myriad reasons that people commit crime or harm others. Officers have to understand the relational issues that lead to domestic violence and abuse or sexual harm as well as the causes (such as adverse childhood experiences) that we know lead too often to becoming a perpetrator of violence, a victim of violence, being drawn to drugs or excess alcohol and to the destruction of hope and opportunity that comes from time in prison.

The police service is small in numbers (fewer than one to four hundred of the population in South Wales) and the number keeping the peace in the centre of our great cities at night are very small, so they depend on having authority in a vast variety of circumstances and in every community. As a society we invest significant powers in these civilians and expect them to exercise those powers with perfect discipline because the key word is 'trust' and when trust is lost or damaged the powers still exist but the authority has gone.

That is no small challenge when you want each police officer to be perfectly disciplined, highly trustworthy, someone to be looked up to as a paragon but also 'someone just like us', the boy or girl next door, rooted in our communities and representative of every part of society. Recruitment from all sections, including Black and Asian communities, as well as eradicating racism and unconscious bias, are seen as essential rather than 'nice to have'. We have seen what happens in countries where the police are seen as 'other' – an occupying force, 'not like us', not to be trusted. Indeed, that has happened in South Wales, at some times and in some communities, when policing, has departed from the highest principles and standards that we expect to see.

I have been privileged to follow its history from a variety of perspectives since South Wales Police was formed in 1969. At the start, I was a young newspaper reporter and trade unionist, later a youth worker working with young offenders, a magistrate, a city councillor and for 25 years a local MP (which included a period as Deputy Home Secretary then Secretary of State for Wales and First Minister) before my ten years as Police & Crime Commissioner. In the 1980s, I saw how the Miners' Strike stretched relationships in every mining community, and one wise decision by the Chief Constable was not to seek the assistance of the Metropolitan Police and to insist that in South Wales, it would be policed only by Welsh officers. He knew that on either side of the picket line were brothers, cousins, fathers and sons of those on the other side. Many who worked through that period to become senior officers had developed a wise recognition of the need for the police to be neutral even in the most polarised situations. It is crucial for the police always to be the police of the public not the police of the state or of any faction.

In South Wales we have had times when standards of integrity and collective excellence have fallen short. That is illustrated starkly by the Lynette White case when one white man was seen running from the scene of a murder and yet three black men were convicted and sent to prison. For a time, police leaders seemed to be in denial about the impact of such a miscarriage on trust and the importance of leadership was shown when Chief Constable Tony Burden articulated the need to 'follow the evidence wherever it leads – however painful that may be for us'. That approach has been followed with the same integrity by the subsequent four Chief Constables and their leadership teams, but that case and others showed how toxic it is when even a few abandon the highest standards and how complex, time-consuming and messy it is to deal with the aftermath and fallout from such a case. Events like the murder of Sarah Everard by a serving police officer cast a shadow from the Metropolitan Police across the whole of British Policing. While glaring examples of misuse of police powers for personal gain or personal gratification may be small in number, they show the fragility of trust and confidence on which policing depends and the importance of challenge and intensive scrutiny. 'The price of liberty is eternal vigilance' – and that is nowhere more relevant than in the constant challenge to demonstrate the highest standards of integrity within the police service at the same time as maintaining the 'ordinariness' that is its hallmark.

It is also important not just to look inward. The complex range of expertise illustrated by the chapters of this book is impressive but cannot hide the fact that on their own the police can only respond to harm rather than preventing it. But prevention is 'the first responsibility of the Police' according to Sir Robert Peel. That is why co-operation and partnership working have now become such a key element in policing – illustrated through Community Safety Partnerships and a range of more specific local examples of formal and informal teamwork. Again, it's a lesson learned early in South Wales where the work of Professor Jonathan Shepherd showed the value of using NHS data to understand and reduce violence and the work of Public Health Wales showed with absolute clarity the impact of Adverse Childhood Experiences (ACEs), giving a clear focus for the Police & Crime Plan and the 'and Crime' element of the Police and Crime Commissioner role.

It is the reason why the role of the PCSO is now central to neighbourhood policing and community safety. When I first stood for election as Commissioner in 2012, the most frequent question on the doorsteps was 'Now then, Mr Michael, if I vote for you, you won't take away our PCSO will you?' Originally seen as 'nice to have', the additional numbers funded by Welsh Government have been crucial to maintaining and enhancing neighbourhood policing.

It is also worth celebrating the commitment of the 'Specials' in South Wales Police, the volunteers who are now fully integrated and respected alongside full-time officers, recognised in 2022 with the Queen's Award for Volunteering. Volunteering is the essential act of citizenship, and these very special citizens give extraordinary service to their communities.

The Police also play a central and vital role in the even more complex network of Criminal Justice that serves Wales. Our team in South Wales Police has played a significant leadership role in the way that network has matured and developed over the past decade and continues to accelerate, something that probably provides more than enough material for a second volume.

But as well as trying to understand the complexity and challenging nature of the whole range of demands on the police, it is probably important to keep it simple starting with those two key principles set down by Sir Robert Peel. Police in this country have sometimes lost track of them – notably when the arrival of the Panda Car took officers off the streets, out of the communities and onto wheels – but in South Wales today I would argue that those key principles are pursued as vigorously and clearly as at any time in the past two hundred years. Of course, they constantly have to be interpreted afresh, but the two central principles are as crucial today as they were when he established the Metropolitan Police in 1829.

- The police are the public and the public are the police.
- The first responsibility of the police is to prevent crime.

That is often framed as 'Success in policing is demonstrated by the absence of crime not the presence of activity' and while neither of these key principles is reflected in the myriad thriller stories told through television and film, that makes them no less vital to success in policing in our real world of South Wales.

As the annual force awards evening demonstrates year after year, there are numerous extraordinary examples of bravery, leadership, imagination and vision as well as the ordinary day-to-day committed service provided by the vast majority of officers and staff. And as the chapters in this book demonstrate, there is an enormous amount of complexity that must be coped with by the police. But at the end of the day perhaps the central responsibility of all of us – from Chief Officers and every leader to those of us who work with the police or hold them to account – is to focus on supporting the delivery of the Oath of Office sworn by every new Constable and to always keep it in mind, the promise to serve '… with fairness, integrity, diligence and impartiality, upholding fundamental human rights and according equal respect to all people'.

Responding when bad things happen as well as 'keeping the peace' and preventing crime and harm are central to the day-to-day business of South Wales Police, and the essays in this book show the complexity and intensity of work that is needed to deliver those basics of a decent society.

Rt Hon Alun Michael
Police & Crime Commissioner for South Wales

INTRODUCTION: WEATHERING CHANGE OR SHAPING REFORM?

Sir Denis O'Connor

The value of this book's perspective on South Wales Police (SWP) is that it provides a glimpse of where policing as a whole has come from, over time, rather than the more familiar lens of a particular development, failure, or crisis, associated with a component of policing, or a specific event. Conventional introductions outline what follows chapter by chapter, but this one is deliberately framed as an interpretation of what the chapters collectively amount to in relation to change. What emerges is a more three-dimensional picture where social norms, the political environment, and the police organisation are evolving simultaneously across the decades. There is a lot of noise across the years, but there are signals for the reader to extract from the SWP experience, and the result has the potential to elevate our view on change (making things different) and reform (making things better) in policing in the round.

The big story is that policing in SWP has profoundly changed, as a telling comment from Chapter 5 suggests:

Within a few generations, the locally resident bobby was replaced by a Neighbourhood Policing Model, involving beat officers reporting to geographically based stations (based on demand) to change into uniforms, receive an

operational briefing, pick up appointments and transport
to patrol their area (Hussain and Lowe, Chapter 5).

During that time, the local service received by the public shifted
from being firmly rooted and situationally aware of local sensibil-
ities, to a more 'expeditionary' model of policing. A case is made,
in the book's chapters, that it is a model with a heart. But notice
is served early on, that we are on the cusp of highly disruptive
change, the question being raised at the outset as to "whether the
police, with its structural roots in the nineteenth century, can ever
really encompass and accommodate the dynamics and mechanics
of digital harms" (Innes and Vaughan, Chapter 1).

South Wales Police (SWP) offers a full spectrum of police
services dealing with everything from local anti-social behaviour
to capital city policing and terrorism. SWP, whilst 'on point',
like many in British policing, in a sea of political, social, and
economic change over these years, has learnt lessons and adapted.
Along the way, worthwhile reforms are exemplified on a range
of issues including positively addressing discrimination (Madge,
Chapter 2), increasing rigour in investigation following miscarriages of justice, exploiting forensics (Allsop and O'Shea,
Chapter 7), expanding accountability for performance, and
acknowledging changing norms around protecting the public
from harm (Robinson et al., Chapter 9).

Looking at this police force as a unit of analysis across time,
it soon becomes apparent that whatever change has occurred,
there hasn't been a grand strategy to guide leaders in developing policing. There may have been many motives at play in the
development of SWP, however, I suspect that much of the halting,
but identifiable progress charted in the chapters herein, has been
tethered by leadership with sense of the significance of local identity and attachment to the core consent and discretion elements
of the British Policing Model (Innes and Vaughan, Chapter 1;
Jukes, Chapter 3; Vaughan, Chapter 11) by individuals inside
and outside SWP.

A sense of identity was clear during the 1984/85 miners' strike,
when the then Chief Constable insisted that, 'the local strikes
should be policed by Welsh officers' (Madge, Chapter 2). Decades

later attachment to South Wales as a 'place' with its 'proximity, and often, familiarity between key Welsh public servants and politicians', enabled a genuinely coherent collaborative 'government' approach during Covid-19 (Jukes, Chapter 3). We are reminded that across the decades, despite pressures across the spectrum of services, SWP have sought to, 'keep a balance between community policing, crime prevention and specialist crime" (Larkman and Rogers, Chapter 6). Pioneering work on both public protection and protecting the public, especially in relation to violence against women and girls, is a source of pride (Robinson et al., Chapter 9). Neighbourhood Policing was stripped out in many police forces in England during the austere noughties, but not to the same degree in SWP. The relative balance and significance of community policing in SWP retained a real degree of substance. In 2004 SWP had 1.7% of the total PCSOs for England and Wales, but by the tail end of austerity in 2019, they accounted for nearly 4% of the total. An ex-Chief puts it this way:

> There is clearly a sense of a community policing tradition and almost a 'brand' in terms of how South Wales Police conceives of the relationship to the citizens it polices, that is in some ways passed from one Chief to another (Jukes, Chapter 3).

Policing by consent requires finding a sometimes uneasy balance between values and priorities, the classic being liberty and security. As Isaiah Berlin pointed out, some in political and leadership roles want to assure us that they can always follow all good ends, but police officers who deal with victims know that 'total liberty for the wolves is death to the lambs' (1998, p. 10). Unless resources are infinite, police constables and leaders must make choices and trade-offs between what is valued most, whether this relates to enforcement or delivery of services.

The fundamental issue then, is what trade-offs are made and are they recoverable? By way of example SWP retained a balanced 'policing by consent' based relationship, despite the urging of some politicians to 'get tough' during Covid-19, by spending a lot of effort on persuasion. This was made possible by a doctrine of 4 E's which was agreed by chiefs in England and Wales. This tempered hastily conceived UK regulations, where the resort to enforcement by the police, generally came only once engagement, explanation and encouragement had been exhausted.

But trade-offs associated with cost reduction, in services heavily dependent on people (NHS, teaching, policing), as some economists have noted, quickly touch service delivery and only slowly, if ever, recede. Police resources are sticky and not easily sliced and diced, the result too often, is as a colleague described it, 'robbing Peter to pay Paul'. This was evident in SWP in the seventies where a financially driven substitute for local policing, 'unit beat policing' (Larkman and Rogers, Chapter 6), failed to impress the public. Again, financial crisis in the 1990s led to police officers being diverted to cover support staff functions and a predictable litany of 'a freeze in recruitment; reductions in transport costs including fuel and maintenance; as well as station closures' (Hussain and Lowe, Chapter 5). As for the most recent decade, central government had been advised to limit cutbacks in 2010 (Welsh Audit Office 2010) but pressed on. It is therefore not surprising that SWP could not escape the consequences of financial cuts that 'narrowed service provision to being largely reactive' (Jukes, Chapter 3).

Cutbacks from central government, unanchored by a purpose beyond cost reduction, have been a recurring feature of policing in England and Wales across the decades. But at least in SWP some comfort can be taken from the recognition of the issues and a determined effort to recover by the local leadership. Thus, local beat officers were restored after the unit beat policing phase. After protracted protestations and negotiation, SWP received an enhanced budget later in the nineties, enabling recruitment and avoiding station closures. There is pride too in local successes against the odds, whether raising victim satisfaction from 'the lowest to amongst the highest' during austerity and the survival and advances of innovative research and evidence-based policing partnerships with the Universities' Police Science Institute (UPSI) and the Cardiff Model for Violence Prevention (Innes and Vaughan, Chapter 1; Shepherd et al., Chapter 8). Again, after a decade of austerity, Matt Jukes (Chapter 3) describes the effort invested in 'trying to shift more services back to a "preventative" disposition', in accord with Peel's historic objectives.

This book illustrates that there has been a lot of change, and some reform, largely reliant on local leadership. There has been room for some progress and pride for developments that go with the grain of consent, and the safety needs recognised by local people. But use of technology to pro-actively rather than reactively protect, has been trickier. For instance, the implementation of facial recognition technology as proposed by SWP was ruled unlawful by the Court of Appeal in 2020. Given the question raised at the outset regarding digital transformation, can policing in SWP as elsewhere in the UK, change enough? A police reform dilemma emerges. Is reliance on local leadership for transformation on digital operations sufficient, when central Government itself struggles to position itself on liberty, freedom and protecting the public on this territory?

The consent-based model of policing introduced in the early 19th century, relied heavily on central democratic leadership, a careful mapping of boundaries on what police could do in public space, together with reassuring communications. The public were wary then of intrusiveness and the Peelian ethos was that the police would follow the public, rather than lead them. With the result that the British policing model has always been tacitly predicated upon a relatively minimalist preventative disposition and not just reliant upon the use of force. The premium on reassuring communications can hardly be overstated. As the police instruction book of the time put it; 'be particularly careful not to interfere idly and unnecessarily' but, 'when required to act, they should do so'. The SWP technology case study illustrates that there is room for progress and pride that goes with the grain of consent and the safety needs of local citizens, but there are limits when they encounter 'structuring influences' (Hussain and Lowe, Chapter 5).

Technology has driven an explosion of communication and demand, good and bad, in policing. The rise in calls for service in SWP moving from 81,483 (1969) to 703,703 (2019), with roughly the same population, tells a stark story. Insightfully we are reminded of the maxim that 'first we shape the technology, then the technology shapes us' (Innes and Llewellyn-Roberts, Chapter 10). The brave attempt by SWP to innovate and introduce facial recognition is highly instructive about the route to reform, where the threat may not be evident, the benefits may not be obvious to everyone, and the police try to lead. The public may accept use of CCTV to recover missing persons or tackle homicide, which had a national mandate. They appear content to support undercover digital operations to respond to and capture suspected paedophiles. But technology proactively scanning all our faces, rather than behaviour in public places is a different ask. It shifts the balance between liberty and security. There is a lot at stake here.

The potential is that with technology and associated algorithms, the police can, as Robert Mark a great Commissioner and communicator put it, stay 'on point' for public expectations of service, protection, and justice. As importantly, it may enable them to attempt to retain consent through an ability to rapidly conduct a larger dialogue on police action on social media. Without technological capacity and capability fitted to the information age, police relevance will wane. But the construction of public permission for such technologically mediated innovations in the conduct of policing do not yet appear settled. It will be important that such matters are worked out if the notion of policing by consent is to remain meaningful in the near future.

The case for use of facial recognition in public space and other interventions in digital space, needs clarity on the benefits, the boundaries around it and reassurance on the balance of liberty and security that remains. Presumably it needs a degree of engagement, explanation, and encouragement as employed in Covid-19, to a degree that hasn't been mobilised yet. The genius of the original British Policing Model was not just the preventative orientation, but the realisation that success for a new form of policing depended upon winning trust and legitimacy as a primary rather than secondary consideration. There was a lot of change then, but there was also a nationally supported mandate for police reform to deal with the consequences of the industrial revolution. That great reform wasn't undertaken in a piecemeal fashion. Should a national mandate be developed to enable the police to play their proper role in protecting people during the digital revolution? In essence, do we want the police to do their best to weather digital change, or be informed by a democratic debate and steer about the balance to be struck to keep the public safe in this era?

References

Berlin, I. 1998. *The proper study of mankind : an anthology of essays.* London: Pimlico.

Welsh Audit Office. 2010. *Sustaining value for money in the police service.* Audit Commission. Available at: *https://www.audit.wales/sites/default/files/Sustaining_value_for_money_in_the_police_service_in_Wales_English_2010_14.pdf*

1

REFORM, REINVENTION AND RECURRENCE IN POLICING

Martin Innes and Jeremy Vaughan

Historically, the 'invention' of the police as a social institution was intimately connected to how modernising societies sought to navigate and negotiate the social forces and tensions unleashed by the Industrial Revolution, and its accompanying processes of urbanisation. Although the innovations in thinking and practise that occurred in the early nineteenth century and coagulated into the bureaucratic organisational form of 'the police' were to prove especially influential and long-lasting, they did not occur in isolation. For the establishment of the police institution was just one of a number of significant governmental interventions that transformed the systems and processes of regulation and governance, in terms of how the state sought to maintain order and prevent and protect its citizens from an array of harms. The state progressively assuming responsibility for policing was part and parcel of a wider shift in reconstructing the role and purpose of government institutions, across the domains of public health, safety at work, the built environment, as well as security in public spaces.

Whilst it has become commonplace in academic commentaries to assert 'policing' stretches 'before' and 'beyond' the police as a formal institution, because they are one component (albeit an especially significant one) in the state's regulatory apparatus designed for the delivery of social control and order maintenance, such considerations have become especially apposite in the contemporary moment. For as multiple commentators on the trajectories and dynamics of the information age have asserted, many of our key interactional and institutional formations are being profoundly disrupted and changed by an array of digital information communication technologies (Marx 2016; Zuboff 2018). Indeed, some commentators are starting to ask whether, if the information revolution is going to be as deep and profound as the industrial and urban revolutions were in terms of social, economic and political consequences, then might we need similarly dramatic revisions to the ecosystem of social control. This might involve considering whether the police, with its structural roots in the 19th century, can ever really encompass and accommodate the dynamics and mechanics of digital harms.

If this were not complex and challenging enough, and layered on top of the above considerations, we are writing at a moment where the Covid-19 global health pandemic has disrupted and displaced rhythms, rituals and routines of social life in ways that would hitherto have been almost unimaginable and inconceivable. Almost overnight, officers from South Wales Police and their colleagues across the UK, as in many other countries, found themselves deployed as part of a new public health surveillance network. This involved trying to secure behavioural compliance with citizens as social and economic life was rapidly 'locked down' as part of desperate efforts to interrupt the viral transmission pathways and reduce Coronavirus' reproduction rate. Furthermore, it also saw the Welsh forces, for a period, being asked to police the border between England and Wales on behalf of the public, to restrict all but essential travel between the two nations.

The pandemic has been a rapidly evolving situation that has necessitated a degree of improvisation and innovation, as new policies and procedures have had to be rapidly designed and delivered to respond to the unfolding emergency. At the time of writing, there had been at least 29 different iterations of official coronavirus guidance and regulations issued by the Welsh and English governments, not all of which were consistent or coherent with one another. As such, negotiating the pandemic has also opened a window into how the police view their own mission. For example, from some quarters, there were calls for police to become centrally involved in enforcing new regulations associated with the initial 'lockdown', assertively ensuring the maintenance of 'social distancing'. But many senior officers publicly demurred from such suggestions on the grounds that they were neither feasible, nor desirable, and certainly incompatible with the idea that the British policing model proceeds, for the most part, on the basis of 'policing by consent'. Instead, the UK police's involvement with policing the pandemic alighted on a four stage model of: 'engage; explain; encourage; enforce'. As the periods of lockdown stretched on and infection rates rose, there was some re-balancing towards increasing the use of enforcement actions against egregious instances of breaching lockdown guidelines. More generally, the urgent need to try and regulate public health behaviours brought many members of the middle classes into contact with police, which were far less likely to happen pre-pandemic. These points notwithstanding, what is intriguing about this basic escalatory dynamic is that it represents a highly condensed analogy of the broader policing system. The majority of police work is predicated upon negotiating order and compliance, rather than resorting to legally endowed enforcements.

So, whilst at first glance aspects of the current situation feel unique and unprecedented, they may actually fit within a broader and deeper pattern. Notably, Egon Bittner (1974), the American sociologist of the police, once famously opined that the defining quality of the police is that they are called upon to act in circumstances where 'somebody is doing something that somebody needs to do something about right now!' Thus although 'law enforcement' is often centred in political and public discussions of the police function in society, this is only part of what police do. As Keith Hawkins (1992) perceptively concluded, law is frequently an instrument of 'last resort' where most problems get resolved through negotiating order. But what the police do uniquely provide is a rapid response, generalised capacity and capability to secure and enforce social order. This has proven important as states across the world have scrambled to innovate responses to coronavirus, with police getting involved in various public health measures

In this chapter, what we want to do is show how, by adopting a 'wide and long' analytic lens to examine policy and practice development in policing, it is possible to distil and discern some recurring patterns. In essence, this involves continual and ongoing efforts to improve the services provided to the public, either in terms of their quality or efficiency. At the same time, these reform efforts repeatedly gravitate around a recurring set of challenges and problems. What we intend to do, coherent with the focus of this book as a whole, is explore these through a particular focus upon South Wales.

STRATEGIC REFORMS AND 'STRUCTURES OF FEELING' IN POLICING

One of the recurring motifs of academic studies of the police has been to show how particular issues and episodes in police work can be located within broader and deeper patterns of behaviour and organisation (Reiner 2010). For example, across a number of empirical studies, Peter Manning (2010) has repeatedly sought to excavate how, despite revisions to the 'surfaces' of how policing is represented to the public, there are some more ineluctable pressures that fundamentally determine core elements of the police function in democratic societies (see also Sparrow 2016). Likewise, Loader and Mulcahy (2003) attended to the police role in symbolically performing otherwise invisible facets of how liberal democratic states orient to the citizenry. And Robert Reiner (1978) has shown how key facets of police occupational culture and the working personalities of police officers as they interpret and make sense of the world that they are moving through, in terms of their decisions about how, why, when and against whom to leverage their legal authority and powers, typically transcends individual organisations and specific roles.

This longer-term perspective is in tension with the fact that we are writing this book against a more immediate backdrop of what feels like repeating disruptions to the organisation of contemporary social life, that are 'laminating' one on top of another. The aforementioned Covid-19 pandemic has brought forward new challenges for policing, co-occurring with a revived interest in police-community relations triggered by the Black Lives Matter movement and associated specific calls to 'defund' some police departments in North America. More parochially, such challenges are imbricated with the potential consequences of Brexit, which will undoubtedly have constitutional impacts upon the relations between British police forces and their European counterparts, but might also induce increased risks of community tensions. Laminated across these and becoming an increasingly influential social and political movement are the groups protesting for climate justice, amongst the most visible and radical of which is Extinction Rebellion. Framing all of which are the changes to the media ecosystem and information environment, wherein a range of increasingly sophisticated information communication technologies are altering how and what we know. In the process, inducing significant changes to the institutional and interactional ordering of society. This includes the array of demands for service from the public, as new forms of behaviour come to be defined as criminal harms, and also how police engage with the public and their partner agencies.

Mapping these longer-term trajectories of development as policing adapts to deeper shifts in social ordering is more typically the kind of work undertaken by academic outsiders to the 'social world of policing', whereas the interests of police 'insiders' focus more upon how the organisational rhythms and routines are driven by a 'conveyor-belt' of new incidents, cases, emergencies and calls for service, which have to be 'triaged' and in some instances responded to. Over the years, there have been repeated attempts to break the organisational focus of incident driven demand, through strategic reforms. For example, Community Policing has argued for a more situated conception of the police role, where officers are embedded within particular community contexts, using the deeper situational awareness this affords them to shape local interventions (Alderson 1979; Fielding 1995). Problem-Oriented Policing urges police organisations to focus upon 'problems' as opposed to incidents, where the former are defined as series and clusters of events with shared underlying causes (Goldstein 1990). By implementing diagnostic processes such as the 'SARA' model of problem-solving (scan, analyse, respond, assess) it has been asserted that police can influence the causes of crimes and disorders, and thus aggregate patterns of prevalence and distribution. Although adopting a slightly different language and logic, the doctrine of intelligence-led policing has advocated broadly similar reforms, but steered more towards criminogenic people than places (Sparrow 2016).

Across its fifty years, at different points in time, and in different operational units, all of these concepts have been tried and tested within South Wales Police, with varying levels of impact. Experiments with community policing, large-scale training programmes trying to instil problem-solving methodologies across the organisation, and using the disciplined approach to collecting and processing information associated with the National Intelligence Model, have provided the basis for the stories that South Wales Police has told itself about itself, and about the imperatives for reform. And yet, the fact that such attempts have had to be repeated and layered upon one another, tells us something about the limits of the traction achieved in terms of influencing organisational routines and officer behaviour.

That this is so is an indicator of how the emergency-response function of policing exerts a profound and deep influence upon the 'structures of feeling' that are seemingly integral to the working personalities of police officers. The concept of 'structures of feeling' was first introduced by the historian Raymond Williams (1961) to capture how different ways of thinking emerge at different points in history. He preferred the notion of 'feeling' to denote that such matters may not be fully worked out or articulated, but nevertheless shape and guide how and why things get done in particular ways. This seems a useful idea to import into discussions of policing and police occupational culture.

Relatedly, and as intimated in the preceding passage, academic studies of the police have identified how the kinds of values and worldviews constitutive of 'cop culture' that were originally surfaced in the pioneering ethnographies conducted in the 1960s and 1970s, continue to shape and influence the practicalities of how police work gets done. For example, Bethan Loftus's (2009) observations of police talk and action in English police forces in the years following the millennium, resonate strongly with the themes highlighted by scholars such as Bittner (1974),

Skolnick (1966) and Reiner (1978; 2010). For what they all point to, and it is a theme replicated across many similar studies, is how police decision-making about how, when and why to intervene, is a highly discretionary act that depends significantly upon the situated interpretations of the officer 'on the ground'. Indeed, the presence of discretion in terms of how the 'law in books' gets translated to 'law in action' seems to be an irreducible and defining feature of the Office of Constable.

A necessary and important counterpoint to accenting the importance of discretion in shaping police actions is that, in certain situations and when responding to certain types of problems, there are modes of policing defined by the exercise of command and control. Most obviously this applies to public order situations, where the efficacy of police authority and power depends upon acting collectively, rather than as individuated officers. But it also appears in more 'team' based endeavours such as major crime investigations, where the basic operational unit is a group blending a number of specialist functions, rather than single detectives. The defining characteristic of this mode of policing is officers responding to the direction and control of senior decision-makers. The reason for stressing this is that many of the seminal and most influential depictions of police work have centred the activities of street policing, and then used this focus to generalise a set of ideas about what policing is and how it is conducted. However, if we think about the many varied types of task that a police organisation performs on a daily basis, distributed across its many departments and units, we begin to gain a sense of the complexity that attends to contemporary policing when viewed in a holistic manner. Every day, whilst some officers in South Wales are operationalising their discretionary powers, their colleagues are simultaneously acting in accordance with tightly defined orders issued by their senior commanders. How these different operational modes of policing articulate with one another, and the frictions induced, is an under-explored dimension of contemporary police work and probably warrants further attention.

How then should we think about and conceptualise such issues? For there does seem to be a tension between highlighting a series of strategic reform programmes intended to reconfigure elements of the design and delivery of policing, and a recurring set of 'deeper' structuring influences. One way to reconcile this is to understand the process of police reform as a continuous dialectic of permanence and change. Framing the issues in these terms helps to articulate the ways policing, as the principal state institution for managing social order, frequently finds itself at the forefront of navigating and negotiating how society responds to social, political, technological and economic transformations. In this sense, the concept of dialectic is supremely useful because of how it accents the 'hybridised' ways in which policing responds to societal changes, and in the process, is partly changed itself.

It is precisely because of these conditions that research and evidence has become so important to processes of police improvement. Indeed, over the past decade or so, the discourse and logic of evidence-based policing has become one of the principal motors for reform. It is fair to say that South Wales Police have been at the forefront of this agenda. In 2007, they invested funding into setting up the Universities' Police Science Institute (UPSI) in partnership with Cardiff and Glamorgan universities, the same year that the Scottish Institute for Policing Research was established. But what was unique about the UPSI concept was the direct relationship between a police force and their local Higher Education Institutions, collaboratively engaging in basic and applied research, accompanied by multiple channels for knowledge exchange. So where other evidence-based policing initiatives were highlighting the importance of quite complex randomised control trial research designs, in South Wales a series of projects were relatively quietly implemented to deliver operationally useful insights and evidence.

Over time this approach has inevitably matured and altered, but it has proven sustainable. Every year for the last fourteen years (at the time of writing), and spanning the agendas of four separate Chief Constables, some form of funded collaborative research has been undertaken involving South Wales Police and its university partners. The importance of this approach is how, over time, the evidence deriving from individual projects starts to mosaic together. It builds understanding, that aggregates into more than can be gleaned from a single research study, no matter how well designed. The arrangement of having direct local relationships between Higher Education Institutions and police forces has become far more commonplace over the past couple of years, but it was not always so.

This is not to say that there hasn't been a long-standing interest in research as an aid for police improvement. Contemporary students attending to some recent discussions of the evidence-based policing movement could be forgiven for thinking this was a wholly new agenda. It is not. Indeed, one of the most interesting and insightful discussions of how and why research is critical to the business of police reform and improvement is to be found in a series of lectures by Sir Robert Mark, one of the most celebrated Commissioners of the Metropolitan Police, published in 1977 as a book entitled 'Policing a Perplexed Society'. What is striking to the contemporary eye is just how familiar a number of the themes he addressed are. Notably, given the focus of the current discussion, Mark stresses at length just how important good research is, as officers and the organisations to which they belong wrangle with increasingly complex and fluid societies.

PLACE, POLITICS AND THE PAST SHAPE POLICING

The issue of recurrence highlighted in this chapter is important. The contemporary moment is one where, induced initially by the Global economic downturn of 2008, but now being amplified and reinforced by the pandemic, we are seeing socio-economic inequality and disadvantage reappearing in ways not experienced for a generation. But again, this is not entirely new. There may be different immediate causes, but fundamentally similar challenges to be managed and negotiated. For instance, the Black Lives Matter protests of summer 2020 are the most recent iteration of how police-community race relations are a long-standing issue, as attested to by the race riots that took place in Cardiff in 1919. Similarly, the miners' strikes of the 1980s and the police role therein, continue to exert a profound influence upon the collective memories of some communities in South Wales.

In Wales, a post-industrial legacy still shadows aspects of how and why police and communities interact in certain ways. The South Wales Police area covers a significant geographical footprint, that includes a diverse variety of community settings. These range from the major urban conurbations of Cardiff and Swansea, through the now deprived former mining towns located in the South Wales Valleys, and on to some fairly isolated rural villages dotted along the coastline in the Vale of Glamorgan. Indeed, from a policing perspective it is this 'mixed economy' that is especially interesting. For where some police forces in England and Wales are clearly 'urban' forces, and others can be defined as engaged principally in 'rural policing', South Wales is one of a select number that integrates elements of both. As a consequence, it maintains a full range of operational services and departments, collaborating closely with its neighbours on matters such as firearms units, public order and major crime units, where other forces have to 'lean' on their neighbours to support the delivery of such services. It is also noticeable that this diversity of contexts means that policing acquires certain 'local flavours' in different parts of the South Wales area. The police presence in towns like Merthyr Tydfil or Pontypridd is distinct from how it presents in more rural places like Llantwit Major, or in relatively affluent settings such as Penarth.

South Wales Police is the largest of the four police forces in Wales, providing services to around 1.3 million citizens over an area of approximately 810 square miles. Although the numbers of staff fluctuates, it consists of around 3,000 police officers and 2,200 police staff (including PCSOs). This gives an average number of around 3.96 officers per 1,000 population, which is slightly above the average for England and Wales as a whole. Located within the force area are 63 out of the 100 most deprived areas in Wales. Based upon 2018/19 data, on an average day the force:

- receives 553 emergency 999 calls;
- 1,375 non-emergency calls;
- deals with 1,027 occurrences;
- and makes 107 arrests.

There is also an important set of political influences that derive from Cardiff being capital city for a devolved nation. As later chapters in this book describe in more detail, the complex webs of accountability and governance that are growing up around the administration and regulation of the police is creating new issues to be navigated in terms of understanding how police services are designed and delivered. South Wales Police, for example, is responsible to UK central government and the Home Office, whilst simultaneously the Chief Constable is held to account by the local Police and Crime Commissioner. But it is also influenced by the public service agenda of Welsh Government, reflecting how key partner agencies such as health and education are devolved responsibilities, falling under the purview of the Welsh First Minister. The latter influence has become especially demarcated by the response to Covid-19, and how Welsh policy has demonstrably parted ways from its English counterpart, leading to slightly differing political expectations about the contribution of the police.

As yet this represents a minor fissure, but in time, it may be freighted with more significance. For rumbling away in the background, for some years now, has been a political claim that Wales ought to seek legal powers to devolve policing and criminal justice. In part, this is framed as seeking parity with the situation in Scotland, but the case has also been made more pragmatically on the grounds that increased joint-agency working is eased if all concerned are accountable to the same political regime. Enmeshed within these negotiations are a need to clarify what the proper objectives of policing are, and where their responsibilities end in relation to the outcomes being sought by them and their partners.

Acknowledging these layers and complexities is important for understanding the organisation and orientation of policing in South Wales. For whilst there has been a general disposition towards community policing style modes of delivery, it would be misleading to suggest that police-community relations are wholly aligned. There are tensions and antipathies. There are scars also, inasmuch as long-running infamous miscarriages of justice such as the Lynette White murder case have tarnished the confidence of some segments of the community.

SURVEILLANCE AND 'ASSISTED' FACIAL RECOGNITION

The preceding section highlighted the 'added value' extracted from the accumulation of research insights and evidence, built up over time, through a series of studies. The most recent exemplar of this has been a focus upon assessing and evaluating a new biometric surveillance technology that represents the state-of-the-art in terms of policing. Facial Recognition Technology (FRT) systems use artificial intelligence algorithms to produce a new instrument for police surveillance of people 'at risk' and posing 'a risk'. Coherent with the overarching theme of this chapter though, conducting surveillance of criminogenic persons and places is a core task of the police mission, that is now potentially being reinvented through the application of technology.

Surveillance is about identifying and locating persons of interest (Marx 2016). As Simon Cole (2002) excavates in his history of fingerprinting as a forensic technology, the ability to connect a person to the bureaucratic records held about them and their past behaviour has been a foundational challenge of policing. It is one that continues to this day and is an area where South Wales Police have been leading nationally (and internationally) in terms of their use of facial recognition surveillance technologies.

Reflecting its status as the capital city of Wales, Cardiff was selected to host the 2017 football Champions League Cup Final at the Millennium Stadium. In no small part, the success of the bid to host this event was down to the fact that South Wales Police could point to significant public order experience of managing major sporting events through the regular series of rugby internationals, and the presence of two football teams with an occasional presence in the Premier League. This experience notwithstanding, hosting the Champions League posed particular challenges. Foremost amongst which was an intelligence challenge. Because both finalists were non-UK teams, the availability of intelligence about potential troublemakers and risky individuals was more limited than it might otherwise have been.

Meanwhile there had been growing interest, within central government and parts of the police service, in the advances in automated facial recognition systems and their potential policing applications. Notably, such systems were becoming more commonplace in borders and customs environments, and whilst there had been some very limited trials of facial recognition by police in the UK and other jurisdictions, no-one had yet seriously tested how such technologies could be integrated into the tactics, techniques and procedures of street policing. Consequently, a decision was taken to use the occasion of the Champions League Final to do just this, to be followed up by a longer-term application across a range of policing issues. Importantly, provision was made for these trial deployments to be carefully evaluated.

Facial recognition technology involves real time and/or post-hoc biometric[1] processing of video images of an individual's facial features for the purposes of matching to a database and identifying individuals. The system is based upon a 'watchlist' of enrolled 'probe' images of the faces of individuals who are defined as being 'of interest' to police. The reasons why these persons are 'interesting' can flex and change. During a deployment, faces of members of the public are scanned as they pass fixed and mobile camera points, with the resulting images analysed by a facial recognition algorithm. This calculates the subject's facial dimensions, usually focusing on the size and relationship between individual features (such as shape of the eye socket, distance between eyes, shape of the jaw and so forth). More advanced algorithms integrate digital modelling that compensates for low light, lens distortions or faces tilted away from cameras. The measurements extracted from the processed image are then encoded and cross-referenced with a watchlist database of similarly processed images, attached to which are further bureaucratic data including, for example, ethnicity codes and warrant information. When the algorithm establishes a 'possible match' an alert is sent to a police operator for review. If the operator confirms the likelihood of a match having been made, this may trigger an attempt by other officers to engage the individual concerned.

Cardiff University's research design for the evaluation of South Wales Police's use of facial recognition technologies was configured to generate an evidence-based picture of the affordances and challenges associated with police deploying such technologies across a range of settings and situations. In so doing, a key feature of the research was testing both the accuracy of the algorithm and technology, as well as the socio-technical issues that arise when it interacts with police operating procedures and routines. A key conceptual innovation and insight that resulted from the research was the idea that the technology functioned more akin to 'assisted' rather than 'automated' facial recognition. The latter being the descriptive label applied to it prior to the evaluation results being published. The key point being that the algorithms were operating in such a way as to frame and enable decision-making conducted by the police operators by furnishing them with better information, as opposed to the technology autonomously making such judgements with no human input. In effect then, how the facial recognition system was being used by police, was very different to how it was deployed by UK Border Force staff at airports, where it is much more clearly a fully 'automated' identification process.

This sense of there being complex interactions between the interpretations and decisions made by human operators, and the technological affordances of the system, in terms of how, when and why it was used by police, was a key narrative for the evaluation. It was definitely not a 'plug and play' system from the perspective of street policing, and its practical implementation required 'edits' and amendments to make it useful. Thus, in terms of generating useful policing outcomes (such as identifying possible 'persons of interest') the performance of the system was found to depend upon three key sets of factors:

- *Organisational performance* – covered how the standard operating procedures and organisational routines of the police are both shaped by and shape the results produced.
- *System performance* – reflects how there were multiple decisions about hardware and software configuration that were taken, that impacted upon how many faces could be scanned and the number of alerts triggered.
- *Operator performance* – is focused upon how behaviours and decisions taken by individual operators further structure and influence how matches are made, and which are acted upon effectively.

The importance of these themes and viewing assisted facial recognition as a socio-technical system, rather than just an algorithmic technology, was foregrounded in August 2020 in a judgement from the Appeal Court that found against South Wales Police's use of the system. As a high profile, politically contentious innovation in policing, the South Wales deployments of facial recognition technology had been subject to intense scrutiny and legal challenge. Although a judicial review had originally found facial recognition to be a lawful policing application, the appellant tested this finding on 5 key grounds. The Appeal Court concluded that whilst they were broadly satisfied that it could have legitimate and proportionate policing applications, they nevertheless expressed two key concerns. Firstly, that not enough had been done to establish whether the algorithm was compatible with the Public Sector Equality Duty to ensure non-discrimination in the delivery of public services. Second, the judges were concerned by the level of discretion available to officers in terms of determining the composition of the 'watchlist' database of images that shapes who might, or might not be picked up by the cameras, and also similarly in deciding where the cameras might be deployed.

Limitations on space do not permit us to discuss such matters in detail. But what is of direct relevance to the line of argument propelling this chapter, is how even a pioneering state-of-the-art technology's deployment by police, pivots around the discretionary power that fundamentally inheres in the office of constable. And then, more broadly, this fits within a pattern where police have long sought to harness new technologies to assist them with their core recurring functions, such as, for example, monitoring and identifying 'risky' citizens (Ericson and Haggerty 1997). However, what empirical studies of reforms driven by policing technologies have repeatedly demonstrated, is that they induce a number of complex effects, not all of which are anticipated.

This was, for instance, the story told by Sparrow, Moore and Kennedy (1990), in their analysis of the introduction of panda cars and the '999' emergency response telephone number. Both of these reforms were conceived as harnessing the affordances of new technologies to configure a style of 'professional policing' that would be more flexible and responsive to citizens' calls for

service. According to Moore et al., however, what wasn't anticipated by the authors of such strategies was how, in reducing the
role of uniformed foot patrol, the social impacts of these reforms
increased the sense of distance between the police and policed.
Thus, opening up a gap that various community policing models
have been striving to recover ever since.

The reason for including an extended discussion of facial
recognition technology here is because of how it encapsulates and
integrates some of the key themes that underpin this book. For on
the one hand, it showcases an example of police trying to harness
leading-edge technologies, and the ethical and practical dilemmas
and controversies that such efforts induce. Equally however, this
particular instance conveys how we should not be beguiled and
our attention misdirected purely by the 'surface' issues associated
with the involvement of new technologies. Because at a 'deeper'
level, the story of facial recognition and identification systems
is about police trying to harness technological developments to
perform and reform one of their long-standing, recurring basic
functions.

CRISIS AS A CRUCIBLE FOR REFORM

Developing the point initiated in the previous paragraph,
although the term surveillance tends to connote notions of
technologically mediated mass observation, the principles underpinning this approach to managing social problems and governing
populations have a long history. In a fascinating discussion whose
contemporary relevance is undoubtedly revived in an era of coronavirus, the philosopher Michel Foucault (1977) describes how
public health surveillance as an instrument of governance has
its roots in the systems devised for managing highly contagious
plague pathogens in rapidly urbanising societies.

This signals an important point, that has just as much resonance for contemporary policing as it does for disaggregating
some of the base systems of social control. That is how social,
political and economic crises have repeatedly functioned as a
stimulus for reform and improvement. It is, for example, no accident that Community Policing was 'invented' in the late 1970s,

just as social tensions were becoming especially acute, as symptoms of a blend of the liberalising of social identity and relations, and the neo-liberalisation of political economy.

In the midst of the global economic crisis following the collapse of economic markets in 2008, it became commonplace to hear public sector leaders, including senior police, talk about 'not letting a good crisis go to waste'. Reviewing the history of police reform and improvement, it is evident that there is a kernel of truth to this phrase. Many key innovations in police processes and systems have been triggered by the perception that there is an emergency situation that needs responding to, where established standard operating procedures are neither necessary, nor sufficient.

Given the moment we find ourselves situated in, as rehearsed towards the start of this chapter, a global health pandemic has been laminated on top of a series of social stresses and strains deriving from other sources, it seems highly likely that there will result some serious and dramatic revisions to the organisation and conduct of the police function. We do not necessarily know what these are, nor can we accurately forecast them. At the time of writing, the available data do seem to suggest that an impact of the pandemic lockdown has been to increase the number of crimes that occur in private spaces, such as domestic violence and the kinds of offending targeting vulnerable children, as well as some digitally enabled forms of offending such as cyber-frauds, whilst suppressing other more traditional crime types. But it remains to be seen whether these patterns persist and thus what implications they may have for the organisation of policing.

What we can say with more certainty is that having an awareness of how policing has responded to previous crises, and what worked and what didn't, could be extremely helpful. This notwithstanding, the potential to realise any such benefits is circumscribed by the fact that policing has generally tended to neglect its own history. Unlike say the military, where considerable intellectual investment is directed towards understanding past campaigns and operations, and researching them in detail, the education of police officers is itself framed by the ethos of 'presentism' referred to earlier in this chapter. Obviously precise circumstances do not exactly replicate each other at different points in history. Nevertheless, when it comes to managing crises, there are usually parallels and resonances meaning that there are useful lessons that can be learned.

It is for precisely this reason that the current book is intended to blend a contemporary analysis of the work of South Wales Police, with a touch of forecasting about how current patterns and trends might shape what comes next, and in turn, how the policing of South Wales today is framed by the legacies of what has come before. For at an earlier juncture in this chapter, we invoked the title of Sir Robert Mark's 'Policing a Perplexed Society' to articulate how previous generations have been alert to, and struggled with, the challenges of reforming policing to cope with the onset of new social, political and economic arrangements. Viewed through a current lens, it would seem to us that society has grown no less perplexed than when Mark was writing. Indeed, if anything, the extent and intensity of the 'perplexity' has grown and is accelerating. Consequently, it is imperative that opportunities are taken to reflect, learn and share analyses of what works, what doesn't and what it is promising, which leads us on to the design of this book.

THIS BOOK AND THE 50TH ANNIVERSARY OF SOUTH WALES POLICE

Unprecedented is one of those words that is routinely and regularly over-used in contemporary political commentary. It is invoked by authors to signal to their readers that an issue or occurrence is both out of the ordinary, but nevertheless significant. But if used accurately and with conceptual precision, that something is unprecedented means it is an original, devoid of a historical forerunner. Framed in this way, at the time of writing, where some base institutional and interactional patterns of social organisation are being reconfigured to manage and mitigate the social, political and economic impacts of the Covid-19 global pandemic, our situation is properly described as unprecedented.

In the spirit of 'not letting a good crisis go to waste', we have encouraged our fellow contributors to assess and reflect upon the implications of coronavirus for the conduct of policing in their essays, given the volume's overarching concern with mapping the past, presents and futures of police work. But equally, this is not intended to be a collection defined by these recent events. For in formulating the conceptual design for this book and its purpose, we had three principal ideas that we believed would make it different and original when compared with all the others that have been published on the subject of the police and policing:

- *A single organisation, but with multiple policing disciplines* – The vast majority of published works are organised around specific policing disciplines, for example focusing upon community policing; public order; major crime etc. Instead, this volume takes the South Wales Police as its base unit of analysis. The idea being that by looking at the range of policing issues and challenges that a single policing organisation routinely has to engage with, and that have to be regularly balanced and negotiated, a different and innovative perspective on the organisation of policing can be illuminated.

- *The police have tended to neglect their history* – A second guiding narrative for the volume is to ensure that a sense of organisational history is threaded through the analysis. This reflects how academic policing history is a relatively neglected topic, something that constrains our ability to understand how and why contemporary arrangements are as they are. Certainly when compared with say, military studies, far less attention has been directed towards policing's institutional development over time. By addressing this neglect, we think there are both lessons to be learned and mistakes that can be avoided.

- *Co-producing knowledge between practitioners and academics* – The idea for this book has grown out of a long-term pioneering innovation undertaken between South Wales Police and Cardiff University that stresses the importance of dialogue between science and practice. Building out of which, a third key feature of this volume is that the majority of the essays are authored by a blend of academics and practitioners. It is this commitment to co-production that has stood at the heart of the long-standing collaboration between Cardiff

University and South Wales Police, and it is anticipated that this approach will infuse the book with 'real world' grounding and analytic purchase.

These three themes were distilled out of the original idea for the book that grew out of this longer-term partnership, and a series of conversations and dialogues about the state of policing, and the state-of-the-art in policing research. These exchanges were brought into sharp relief by a desire to commemorate the fiftieth anniversary of the formal establishment of South Wales Police in 1969, through the amalgamation of several smaller organisations.

But we think the adoption of this focus has wider resonance and applicability. For where a number (possibly the majority) of the more significant book length empirical studies of policing have been based in major urban forces, locating the analysis in South Wales means it is a situation and setting that is more representative of the mix of policing services that most citizens across Europe experience, and most police organisations are seeking to deliver. It is our belief that it is the covering of this spectrum and diversity of issues, that range from national to neighbourhood security, that affords this book its particular value. After all, most policing does not occur in the global cities that have tended to provide the backdrop for so many seminal accounts in academic policing studies.

Accordingly, this volume reflects upon the role of the police in society, and the ways this changes, but also stays constant. By focusing in 'high resolution' detail upon events and developments in South Wales, it seeks to use these as a way of valuing the old and embracing the new, to illuminate broader patterns and trends in society and how it is policed, to ground the discussion, whilst also engaging with wider currents and trajectories.

Note

1. The EU GDPR and companion EU Law Enforcement Directive both define facial images as biometric data.

References

Alderson, J. 1979. *Policing freedom*. Plymouth: Macdonald and Evans.

Bittner, E. 1974. 'Florence Nightingale in pursuit of Willie Sutton: a theory of the police'. In: Jacob, H. ed. *The potential for reform of criminal justice*. London: Sage.

Cole, S. 2002. *Suspect identities: a history of fingerprinting and criminal identification*. Cambridge, MA: Harvard University Press.

Ericson, R. and Haggerty, K. 1997. *Policing the risk society*. Oxford: Clarendon Press.

Fielding, N. 1995. *Community policing*. Oxford: Clarendon Press.

Foucault, M. 1977. *Discipline and punish: the birth of the prison*. New York: Vintage.

Goldstein, H. 1990. *Problem-oriented policing*. New York: McGraw-Hill.

Hawkins, K. 1992. *The uses of discretion*. Oxford: Clarendon Press.

Loader, I. and Mulcahy, A. 2003. *Policing and the condition of England: memory, politics and culture*. Oxford: Clarendon Press.

Loftus, B. 2009. *Police culture in a changing world*. Oxford: Clarendon Press.

Manning, P. 2010. *Democratic policing in a changing world*. London: Routledge.

Mark, R. 1977. *Policing a perplexed society*. London: George Allen & Unwin.

Marx, G. 2016. *Windows into the soul: surveillance and society in an age of high technology*. Chicago: Chicago University Press.

Reiner, R. 1978. *The blue-coated worker: a sociological study of police unionism*. Cambridge: Cambridge University Press.

Reiner, R. 2010. *The politics of the police*. 4 ed. Oxford: Oxford University Press.

Skolnick, J. 1966. *Justice without trial*. New York: John Wiley & Sons.

Sparrow, M. K. 2016. *Handcuffed: what holds policing back, and the keys to reform*. Washington D.C.: Brookings Institution Press.

Sparrow, M. K., Moore, M. H. and Kennedy, D. M. 1990. *Beyond 911: a new era for policing*. New York: Basic Books.

Williams, R. 1961, *The long revolution*. London: Chatto & Windus.

Zuboff, S. 2018. *The age of surveillance capitalism*. New York: Profile Books.

2

A BRIEF HISTORY OF SOUTH WALES POLICE

Gareth Madge

The purpose of this Chapter is to frame the thematically organised chapters which follow by providing a chronological account of how South Wales Police has adapted to a range of social, political, legal, economic and technological developments over time.

This historical background is important as a means of understanding how and why key policing services have come to be configured in particular ways. This will include considering the part played by some key events in influencing the delivery of policing. As will be seen a number of recurring internal and external themes emerge.

The narrative is presented under the following headings:

- Policing in South Wales before South Wales Police;
- Amalgamation: Four into One;
- Chief Constables and their times;
- Governance and oversight: from a Police Authority to a Police and Crime Commissioner;
- Conclusion.

The narrative takes account of developments and events up to 31 May 2020, being the end of the first fifty years of South Wales Police.

POLICING IN SOUTH WALES BEFORE SOUTH WALES POLICE

South Wales Police, or South Wales Constabulary as it was then called, came into being on 1 June 1969. However, if the historical developments since then provide a framework for understanding the organisation as it is today, it is equally important to consider what policing was like before it was created.[1]

Up until the early years of the nineteenth century, policing was a very localised activity based on communities regulating themselves through watchmen and parish constables, with magistrates exercising their centuries old powers of local administrative and legal oversight.

By the early nineteenth century such arrangements were increasingly perceived to be haphazard and ineffective. The catalyst for change came in London with the formation of the Metropolitan Police in 1829 after Sir Robert Peel was able, as Home Secretary, to withstand opposition to the introduction of what was termed 'the New Police'.

The early success of the new arrangements in London was followed by the Municipal Corporations Act 1835 which provided powers for the boroughs in England and Wales referred to in the Act to establish their own police forces. As a result, in 1836, police forces were formed in Cardiff, Swansea and Neath (Merthyr Tydfil was policed by the Glamorgan Constabulary until 1908 when it became a county borough and thereby acquired its own police force).

As far as the counties were concerned, the County Police Act 1839 enabled magistrates in counties to establish police forces, and the Glamorgan magistrates took advantage of this to appoint a superintendent and six constables to cover only a part of the county in Lower Miskin and Lower Caerphilly.

The second Marquess of Bute,[2] as Lord Lieutenant, was a keen advocate of extending these arrangements and put forward a scheme which was accepted by the magistrates in 1841 resulting in the formation of the Glamorgan Constabulary with responsibility for the whole of the county. Captain Charles Frederick Napier, formerly of the Rifle Brigade, was appointed chief constable along with four superintendents and 34 constables.

Over the ensuing years the borough and county forces developed their own identities. Some of this reflected the difference in status between them. The county forces were always regarded as having a different social status exemplified in many instances by the connections which existed between county chief constables and the local landed gentry.[3] Captain Lionel Lindsay, chief constable of Glamorgan from 1891 to 1937, is a case in point. He was the grandson of Lord Tredegar, and the Lindsay family itself had its roots among the landed estates of the south of Ireland.

The governance of these forces also reflected differences, with the borough forces being part of the administrative structures of their borough corporations. It was they who appointed the chief constable, or head constable, as he was for many years referred to, and had powers over their force's terms and conditions, including in respect of discipline.

In the counties there was a more arms-length relationship between the justices in quarter sessions[4] and the chief constable and his officers. In particular, day to day control of county forces rested with chief constables. Under Section 6 of the County Police Act 1839, he was responsible for the appointment and discipline, including dismissal, of members of the force.

In addition to these broader issues, the police forces of South Wales reflected the socio-economic developments in the area during the nineteenth and twentieth centuries.

The period from the middle of the nineteenth century to the outbreak of the First World War in 1914 was one of immense change in the county of Glamorgan. This is reflected, for example, in the demographic changes in the valleys of the Rhondda where the population in 1851 was 951 but had grown to 55,000 by 1881 and reached a high point of 167,000 in 1924 (Davies 1994, p. 402). It was a period of considerable inward migration, not only from English counties such as Gloucestershire and Somerset, but also from the rural areas of Wales.

As the nineteenth century progressed there was a relative decline in the ironmaking industries of Merthyr, which had been at the forefront of the early developments of the industrial revolution, whilst the coal mining areas of South Wales-steam coal in the eastern valleys and anthracite in the west-saw immense growth and other industries also prospered.

The Glamorgan Constabulary, as the police force responsible for policing the coal mining areas, responded by, for example, the building of police stations in the communities which depended on coal mining (many of these stations were inherited by South Wales Constabulary in 1969) and the attaching of police officers to coal mines to assist with security.

This connection with coal mining was put under great stress during the unrest in the coalfield in the period before 1914 as seen in the disturbances in the Rhondda and Cynon Valleys when Captain Lindsay was a prominent and, at times, controversial figure.[5]

There were also important developments in Cardiff which grew from the size of a small town in the middle of the nineteenth century to being the biggest coal exporting port in the world by the start of the First World War. It also developed a significant role in local and Welsh affairs with the construction of the buildings of the civic centre in Cathays Park including the National Museum of Wales. The increased status of Cardiff was reflected in 1905 when it was a made a city and its police force's name changed accordingly.

The development of the docklands of Cardiff led to the growth of multi-ethnic communities, particularly in the area of Butetown. Whilst there had been some tensions there before the First World War, they came to a head in June 1919 when, following riots in other places such as Liverpool, there were riots in Cardiff[6] caused by a mixture of racism and employment problems arising from the end of the war. The city's police force had a difficult task to keep order and three people died during the riots.

Swansea too saw growth as a commercial centre with the development of metal industries in its hinterland building upon its longstanding connection with the copper industry.

In the period between the end of the First World War and the beginning of the Second World War, the Glamorgan Constabulary, in particular, had to deal with the protests against the economic conditions of the time, including the miners' strike of 1921 and the general strike of 1926.

After the Second World War, there were a number of developments. For the Glamorgan Constabulary there was, in particular, the re-location in 1947 of the force headquarters from Canton in Cardiff where it had been since the nineteenth century, to the site of the former Royal Ordnance Factory in Bridgend, which remains as the headquarters of South Wales Police. In 1947 too, following a post war review of police forces, the Neath Borough force merged with Glamorgan.[7]

The 1950s and 1960s saw developments in crime investigation with increasing use of fingerprint evidence as an example, whilst the use of radio communication and mobile patrols also increased, and a police dog section was established in the Glamorgan Constabulary in 1960.

The Cardiff City Police acquired a new headquarters building in 1968 in Cathays Park close to the other important civic buildings mentioned earlier.

By the 1960s, however, there were more fundamental changes on the horizon. In 1960, in response to concerns, including the relationship between borough chief constables and watch committees, a Royal Commission on the Police was established under the chairmanship of Sir Henry Willink.

Although the Commission had been set up by a Conservative Government, which followed it up with legislation in the form of the Police Act 1964, it was the Labour Government elected in October that year which took the matter forward. In particular, the Act established what became known as the 'tri-partite' governance relationship between chief constables, police authorities and the Home Office.

Another issue which had caused concern was that there were believed to be too many police forces in England and Wales. The Act, therefore, enabled the Home Secretary to compulsorily amalgamate forces if voluntary arrangements were not forthcoming.

The outcome of this in the years ahead was to see a steady reduction in the number of police forces. It was against this background that the South Wales Constabulary was formed in 1969.

AMALGAMATION: FOUR INTO ONE

> The debate on the amalgamation of the borough forces in one huge South Wales Constabulary was especially fierce at Cardiff, prompting questions in parliament and an official inquiry. In Swansea, where the long history of crime and policing had often been a source of pride, there was some regret and a little bitterness, but ultimately an acceptance of the inevitable. At the Guildhall lunch in May 1969, to mark the last meeting of the watch committee, the voices of protest, including that of the retiring chief constable, were muted (Jones 1990, p. 273).

The initial step in the proposed amalgamation of the police forces of Glamorgan, Cardiff, Swansea and Merthyr was taken by Labour Home Secretary Roy Jenkins when he wrote to each police authority on 17 May 1966 inviting them to agree to a voluntary arrangement.

There was, in essence, a positive response from Glamorgan, Swansea and Merthyr but Cardiff indicated that it could not agree as it was of the view that it should, as a reflection of the city's status, retain its own police force.

There then followed exchanges of correspondence and the holding of meetings involving the City Council, its Watch Committee, and the Home Office as a result of which agreement was reached with the other authorities regarding amalgamation and a shadow combined police authority was established.

Such agreement was, however, soon undermined when discussion took place regarding the detail of the amalgamation. There were three key issues: (a) the representation of the individual authorities on the new combined police authority; (b) the name of the combined force; and (c) the siting of its headquarters.

Whilst agreement was eventually reached on membership and on the name as 'South Wales Constabulary' (despite some reluctance, it seems, from Glamorgan which inevitably proposed that it should be the 'Glamorgan Combined Constabulary'), it was the matter of where the new force's headquarters should be situated which caused the most serious disagreement and led to the breakdown of negotiations.

Glamorgan believed that it should be at its Headquarters in Bridgend whilst Cardiff were of the view that it should be in the new headquarters of the city's police in Cathays Park. The decision of the shadow police authority that it should be in Bridgend led to Cardiff re-stating its opposition to the amalgamation in its entirety.

As a result, on 14 March 1968, in the absence of a voluntary scheme of amalgamation, James Callaghan, who had replaced Roy Jenkins as Home Secretary, gave notice of his intention to compulsorily amalgamate the forces. Cardiff maintained their objections, and an inquiry was then established under the provisions of the Police Act 1964 to consider the proposed scheme and the objections to it.

The Inquiry was conducted by Stephen Brown QC[8] who heard evidence in June and July 1968 from those supporting Cardiff's objection[9] together with that of Her Majesty's Inspector of Constabulary who supported the proposed scheme and that the headquarters should be in Cardiff.

After considering the evidence and the submissions from lawyers representing the various interested parties, Brown concluded in his report of October that year: (a) that there was no reason why Cardiff should not be included in the amalgamation scheme proposed by the Home Secretary; (b) that the headquarters of the new force should be in Cardiff with Bridgend being the communications and training centre; and (c) the new force should be called 'South Wales Constabulary'.

The question of the siting of the headquarters, however, continued to cause friction with James Callaghan also expressing the view that it should be in Cardiff.[10] It also arose during a debate on the Amalgamation Order,[11] held in the House of Commons on 26 March 1969, which largely repeated what had gone before regarding objection to the scheme and especially the matter of the headquarters.[12]

Despite all opposition, the Order was made the following day, 27 March. It established a police force called South Wales Constabulary, to come into being on 1 June 1969, and a combined South Wales Police Authority made up of 39 councillor and magistrate members representing the four previous force areas.

There is little doubt, however, that Glamorgan's influence on the new force had held sway. The chief constable was to be Melbourne Thomas, formerly chief constable of the county, the headquarters was to be in Bridgend and key positions for the Authority also came from the county, including the chairman, Councillor Smith. There was some consolation for Cardiff as Gwilym Morris, Cardiff's chief constable, became deputy chief constable and the Cardiff City Police headquarters was to have a special role as 'support headquarters'.

Whilst the political controversy had raged in relation to the amalgamation, the forces affected had been busy preparing for it with a number of joint working parties and there appears to have been good co-operation notwithstanding the understandable concerns of some staff as to the future. As Melbourne Thomas put it in a letter of 1 May 1969 to all members of the new force: 'there will undoubtedly be many initial problems and difficulties, but with the co-operation and combined effort of all members we can overcome them'.[13]

Such co-operation between the forces was nothing new in the operational sphere. A Regional Crime Squad had been formed in 1965 and operated from Cardiff. It, and the forces of Cardiff, Glamorgan and Swansea, had readily gone to the aid of the Merthyr Police on 21 October 1966 when a coal tip engulfed a school and houses at Aberfan killing 144 people, including 116 children. A joint Criminal Records Office had also existed for several years.

However, notwithstanding such co-operation between the previous forces, the creation of the new combined force was seen by its advocates as heralding a new era. It would be one of the biggest forces in England and Wales with a strength of over 2,300 police officers and over 500 civilian staff to police a population of over one and a quarter million people (nearly half the population of the whole of Wales).[14]

The new force had little time to settle down, though, before it was faced with challenges. Just a month after amalgamation, on 1 July, there was the Investiture of the Prince of Wales at Caernarfon Castle. This required support from police across Wales and there were also demands resulting from the requirements of policing Royal visits to South Wales in the wake of the Investiture.

Then, in the autumn, the visit of the South African rugby team prompted a wave of anti-apartheid demonstrations at matches including one held at Swansea where there was much violence and there were severe criticisms of the policing and stewarding of it.

Nevertheless, and despite the lengthy political controversy which had preceded amalgamation, Melbourne Thomas in presenting his first annual report[15] for the period up to 31 December 1969, ended his introduction on an optimistic note:

> … the new force … is progressing daily towards the integration and efficiency desired from amalgamation. Twelve months from now it will be possible to look at the progress made from a much better perspective point. The general sense of progress now is quite encouraging.

CHIEF CONSTABLES AND THEIR TIMES: MELBOURNE THOMAS (1969-71) AND SIR GWILYM MORRIS (1971-9)[16]

Melbourne Thomas remained as chief constable until 1971 when he retired and was succeeded by his deputy, Gwilym Morris, who had been chief constable of Cardiff from 1963 to 1969, following 29 years' service in the Metropolitan Police.

After amalgamation, a great deal was done to create new structures for the force in terms of its divisional boundaries and command and management arrangements.

A constant issue was that of recruitment. Efforts were made to increase the establishment of the force but, especially towards the end of the decade, difficulties were encountered resulting from the financial pressures then affecting the police service. Police staff levels, in particular, suffered and had to be reduced notwithstanding the desire for them to take up roles which had previously been performed by police officers.

However, the review into police pay by the Government and chaired by Lord Edmund-Davies, which reported in 1978, did much to improve the position regarding the recruitment and retention of officers.

The development of Unit Beat Policing, where police officers increasingly patrolled in vehicles, had implications for the way in which the police interacted with the public. Its advocates considered it a better and more efficient use of resources than the traditional foot patrol of 'the bobby on the beat', whilst its critics lamented the perceived loss of personal contact with the public.

A programme of modernisation was undertaken, which saw new police stations being built in Port Talbot, Bridgend and Porthcawl, which replaced old buildings, and an entirely new police station was built at Cockett in Swansea.

In addition, computerisation began to play a bigger part in the work of the force with, for example, the records of police officers being transferred from manual to electronic systems.

As a result of the Sex Discrimination Act 1975, the separate women's police section was abolished, and women began to be integrated more fully into policing.

Women had first become involved in policing in a limited way during the First World War, and during the Second World War a Women's Auxiliary Police Corps was formed to provide administrative and clerical support.

Progress in relation to the employment of women as warranted officers was, however, slow. It would be many years before more substantial advances in the role of women were to be achieved in line with the expectations which underlay the 1975 Act.

Also, at a national level, the development of the Police National Computer was to create a profound and lasting improvement to the delivery of police services.

CHIEF CONSTABLES AND THEIR TIMES: SIR JOHN WOODCOCK (1979-83) AND DAVID EAST (1983-8)

Gwilym Morris, who had played a key role, first as deputy chief constable, and then as chief constable, in the amalgamation process and the force's first decade of existence was awarded a knighthood in 1979, the year in which he retired after 46 years' service as a police officer.

He was replaced by John Woodcock, formerly chief constable of North Yorkshire who was to be influential in the further development of the force. After leaving it in 1983 he played an important part in policing policy throughout England and Wales, first as one of Her Majesty's Inspectors of Constabulary, and then as the Chief Inspector of Constabulary in which role he was knighted.

Following the departure of John Woodcock, David East, formerly chief constable of Devon and Cornwall, was appointed as chief constable.

The 1980s again saw continued financial pressures which had an effect on training but the force was, nevertheless, able to maintain recruit levels to enable it to be close to its full establishment. There also continued an emphasis on civilianisation in order to release warranted officers for operational duties.

The programme of improvements to the force's infrastructure continued with new divisional headquarters in Pontypridd and Norbury Road in Cardiff and the creation of three area control rooms to deal with police communications and telephone calls from the public. This was facilitated by the development of a computerised command and control system.

The growing importance of the media in policing was recognised by John Woodcock when he established the force's first public relations office, soon after becoming chief constable in 1979.

1981 saw the 150th anniversary of the Special Constabulary (tracing its roots to the Special Constables Act 1831), which was marked with a parade at Police Headquarters. It reflected the important part that volunteers play in the policing of South Wales.

There were, however, several challenges.

The riots in Brixton in London, and elsewhere, in 1981, had resulted in wide ranging criticisms of the way in which police forces dealt with the unrest, especially in minority ethnic communities. Lord Scarman's report into the riots made many recommendations aimed at improving relations between the police and communities. South Wales Constabulary increased its efforts in this area by establishing community consultative groups and engaging widely in community projects.

The Police and Criminal Evidence Act 1984 signalled fundamental changes to the way in which crimes were investigated and suspects dealt with. Gone were the inadequate Judges' Rules to be replaced by a comprehensive statutory scheme which included several Codes of Practice which officers were expected to follow.

The following year saw further substantial changes to the criminal justice system with the passing of the Prosecution of Offences Act 1985. The police would no longer be responsible for the conduct of criminal proceedings in the courts. This role was to be transferred to a new body, the Crown Prosecution Service, which came into being in 1986.

There were too other, operational, challenges.

The visit of Pope John Paul II to Cardiff in 1982 which attracted huge public and media attention, required the force to put in place the biggest policing operation for a public event since its formation. The visit was a great success and reflected well on the City of Cardiff and on the policing arrangements.

In different vein, the national strike of coal miners which lasted from 1984 to 1985 caused great upheaval in the coal mining communities of South Wales. There was picketing throughout the area and especially at the steelworks in Port Talbot. These events put a great strain on policing resources when, on several occasions, up to 1,000 officers were deployed. However, other than on two days (when assistance was provided by the Gwent and Dyfed Powys forces) the strike was policed entirely by officers from South Wales.

There were also high-profile murder cases during the 1980s which in later years were shown to be miscarriages of justice, notably the murders of Sandra Phillips in Swansea in 1985, Phillip Saunders in Cardiff in 1987 and Lynette White in Cardiff in 1988. The cases became protracted in the complaints, criminal prosecutions of police officers, civil claims, reviews and investigations which resulted. Subsequently a great deal of effort was invested into learning from them through, for example, development courses for senior investigating officers. The force also established a major crime review unit to re-examine unsolved cases and in the case of Lynette White a re-investigation led to the conviction of the true culprit, Jeffrey Gafoor, particularly as the result of enhanced DNA analysis.

CHIEF CONSTABLES AND THEIR TIMES: ROBERT LAWRENCE (1989-96) AND SIR ANTHONY BURDEN (1996-2003)

The early 1990s saw significant financial difficulties for the force which resulted in a halt on recruitment and training and other stringencies. Ultimately, there was a significant injection of money from the Home Office which eased the situation and enabled the force to move forward.

There was great sadness when Robert Lawrence, who had been the deputy chief constable of Staffordshire and had been appointed chief constable of South Wales in 1989, following David East's retirement, died on 21 May 1996, at the age of 53.

Whilst he had been ill, Donald Elliott, formerly chief constable of Devon and Cornwall and a retired Inspector of Constabulary, was appointed as temporary chief constable for a short period. In due course, Tony Burden, formerly chief constable of Gwent, succeeded Robert Lawrence as chief constable.

The tragic events at the Hillsborough football stadium in Sheffield in 1989 were to reverberate down the subsequent decades. The Inquiry chaired by Lord Justice Taylor was to have a lasting impact not only on football and other sports generally, but specifically on the policing of sporting events. In the context of South Wales, it led to much work being undertaken by the force to help improve safety at rugby's National Stadium in Cardiff, at the football grounds in Cardiff and Swansea, and at other sports venues.

One of the innovations during Robert Lawrence's time as chief constable was the formation of a mounted section. South Wales Police's predecessor forces had had mounted officers at various times in the past but all had been discontinued for many years. The new unit was soon to be seen undertaking patrols in urban as well as rural areas and provided a visible presence at the high-profile sporting events, the policing of which was to become a key part of the force's operational commitments in the years to come, the holding of the Rugby World Cup at the newly completed Millennium Stadium in Cardiff (replacing the National Stadium) in 1999 being a prime example.

The previous year had seen the summit of heads of state and government of members of the European Union being held in

Cardiff. At the same time President Nelson Mandela of South Africa visited the city when he was made an Honorary Freeman. These events again required a substantial policing operation.

If the formation of the mounted unit indicated a return to the past, the creation of the South and East Wales Air Support Unit covering the South Wales and Gwent policing areas meant that the two neighbouring forces were able to share the services of helicopter cover for their areas, thus enhancing their ability to deal with, for example, crimes in action, missing persons, and public events. In later years the unit was replaced by the National Police Air Service.

In 1996 there was a significant change to the force's geographical boundaries when the area comprising the Caerphilly County Borough was transferred from South Wales Constabulary to the Gwent Police,[17] The opportunity was then taken to change the force's name to South Wales Police to reflect a more modern terminology.

As a result of the Welsh Language Act 1993, such a change of name had to take account of the need for bilingual signage of buildings, vehicle markings and correspondence as the force embraced the requirements of the Act and gave a much higher profile to the Welsh language than had been the case in the past.

In addition to changes in its boundaries there were also significant changes to the force's governance. In 1995, as a result of legislation,[18] the Police Authority was reduced in size from the 39 members which it had comprised since its formation in 1969, to 17 members (9 councillors, 3 magistrates and 5 independent persons). Subsequently, the total number was increased to 19.

Following on from the restructuring of police authorities, in 1995 the Police Authorities of Wales was established as a collaborative body to deal with issues affecting policing in Wales and to develop collaboration between forces. The South Wales Police Authority played a full part in its activities.

The importance of health and safety in the police service was recognised in 1998,[19] when the provisions of the Health and Safety at Work Act 1974 were extended to apply to police officers. This had a significant effect on the way in which South Wales Police conducted its operational activities.

Another piece of significant legislation was the Crime and Disorder Act 1998 which introduced anti-social behaviour orders and sex offender orders. It also created a framework for partnership working between local authorities and other agencies, including the police, in order to reduce crime and disorder.

In February 1999 the publication of the Macpherson Report into the death of Stephen Lawrence had a profound impact on the relationship between the police and racial minorities. Chief Constable Burden played a leading role, on behalf of the Association of Chief Police Officers, in responding to the recommendations in the report.

As the twentieth century drew to a close, there was great concern that the change in date would cause serious disruption to computer systems; the so called 'Millennium Bug'. South Wales Police established contingency plans to deal with the matter but in the event no difficulties arose.

Finally, it is worth noting that the central police station in Swansea, which housed the area's divisional headquarters and which had previously served the former borough force from the early years of the twentieth century, was replaced with a modern building on the site of the city's former fire station. It was officially opened by the Prince of Wales in July 2001.

CHIEF CONSTABLES AND THEIR TIMES: BARBARA WILDING (2004-9), PETER VAUGHAN (2010-17) AND MATT JUKES (2018-20)

Chief Constable Burden became President of the Association of Chief Police Officers in 2000 and was later knighted. He retired in 2003, and was succeeded by Barbara Wilding who had been a deputy assistant commissioner in the Metropolitan Police. She was the first woman to be appointed as a chief constable in Wales.

Following Barbara Wilding's retirement in 2009, Peter Vaughan became chief constable. Apart from a period as assistant chief constable of Wiltshire Police, he spent all his service with South Wales Police and in becoming chief constable he was the first officer to serve in every rank in the force.

He later became acting President of the Association of Chief Police Officers and was Vice President of its successor body, the

National Police Chiefs Council, from its inception. He retired in 2017, and Matt Jukes, who had previously served in the force as an assistant chief constable and as deputy chief constable, was appointed to succeed him. He, too, had played a leading role in the creation of the National Police Chiefs Council.

During this time, the demands made on warranted police officers to deal with ever changing patterns of crime, together with the drive for greater efficiencies in the delivery of policing services, led to the introduction of police community support officers,[20] who were seen as a cost-effective way to provide visible policing by patrolling, and engaging with, local communities.

Force structures were also the subject of attention. Following the publication of the Inspectorate of Constabulary's report 'Closing the Gap', the Labour Government introduced proposals for police force mergers which would have seen one police force for the whole of Wales. The abandonment of these proposals was to lead to a greater emphasis being placed on collaboration between police forces.

Another significant development during this period was the introduction of the 101 non-emergency telephone number for the police. South Wales Police played a leading part in its development and it was seen as a means of providing a better service to the public whilst reducing the burden on force control rooms in dealing with the increasing number of calls received.

South Wales Police also led in developing relationships with higher education, including the establishing of the Universities' Police Science Institute in partnership with Cardiff University and the University of Glamorgan (now University of South Wales).

This period saw significant developments in the infrastructure of South Wales Police with new buildings being erected, older ones being refurbished and new technologies introduced. Many of these improvements were achieved despite the period of austerity in public service finances which followed the financial crash in 2008, and which resulted in the force having to reduce the numbers of its police officers and police staff by several hundred. The force followed a determined policy of 'doing better with less'.

As far as buildings are concerned, at force headquarters a new scientific support facility enabled the force to provide modern, well-equipped accommodation to assist in crime investigation, and the main administrative block was refurbished and a new floor added to it.

Also, as part of the changes at police headquarters a new public service centre was established bringing the former three area control rooms together to provide an enhanced emergency and non-emergency call handling service. This has been supplemented by the South Wales Fire and Rescue Service and the Mid and West Wales Fire and Rescue Service co-locating their call handling within a combined service centre where there is also a presence by the Welsh Ambulance Service.

In Cardiff, a well-equipped, modern divisional headquarters was built in the fast-developing area of Cardiff Bay, to replace a police station which had previously existed there and to take over the role of divisional headquarters from the central police station in Cathays Park, which had, prior to amalgamation, been the headquarters of the city's police force. New police stations and modern custody facilities were also opened in Bridgend and Merthyr.

New technologies have included the increasing use of mobile data devices for operational officers with the consequent replacement of traditional paper notebooks, and the introduction of body worn cameras for police officers.

The force has been energetic in its pursuit of new technology solutions to assist with the demands of modern policing and has been a pilot force in respect of automated facial recognition. This has caused concerns in some quarters on human rights and civil liberty grounds and has been challenged in the courts.

In line with the increased emphasis on collaboration between police forces mentioned earlier, a joint scientific support unit has been established with Gwent Police, and a joint firearms unit serving South Wales, Gwent and Dyfed Powys. In 2010, a joint legal service was created between South Wales and Gwent, the first such collaborative unit in the UK.

These units joined two, earlier, important collaborative arrangements: the Wales Extremism and Counter Terrorism Unit (WECTU) and the Southern Wales organised crime unit ('Tarian'), both of which had been created to enhance operational effectiveness in these areas.

In relation to the role of women in policing, we noted earlier the slow progress in earlier decades in the recruitment of women police officers. 2015 was, therefore, significant in that the International Women's Police Conference was hosted by South Wales Police in Cardiff and was a great success.

In the twenty first century the force has dealt with significant operational issues.

The importance of the hosting of major events in Cardiff, and the policing requirements arising from them, were underlined when the FA Cup Finals were held at the Millennium Stadium between 2001 and 2006, whilst Wembley Stadium was being re-developed.

In 2011 the deaths of four coal miners at the Gleision coalmine in the Swansea Valley brought attention from the world's media as efforts were made to rescue them. The ensuing criminal investigation was complex and protracted. It was a reminder that whilst the coal industry of South Wales has all but disappeared, there were still dangers to be found in the old mine workings of the area.

2012 saw the Olympic Games being held in London, which required a significant national security operation to which South Wales Police contributed by policing events in Cardiff and providing support to the Metropolitan Police.

The holding of the summit of heads of government of NATO members at Newport in 2014 gave rise to a massive policing operation involving police forces from throughout the UK. South Wales Police provided support to Gwent Police and also undertook the policing arrangements for associated events held in Cardiff, and in 2017 the European Champions League football final was held in Cardiff which, again, required a substantial policing operation.

From early in 2020 the global Covid-19 pandemic gave rise to significant policing challenges. The stringent measures put in place by the UK and Welsh Governments curtailed public activity in a way not seen since the Second World War. The police service was called upon to enforce regulations prohibiting travel and meetings and South Wales Police sought to do so whilst seeking to interact positively with the public. In addition, the pandemic led to changed working patterns, with many of the force's police staff being required to work from home. The full significance of the pandemic, in social and economic terms, remains to be seen.

GOVERNANCE: FROM A POLICE AUTHORITY TO A POLICE AND CRIME COMMISSIONER

As we saw earlier, in line with the structures set out in the Police Act 1964, a combined police authority for South Wales was established by the Amalgamation Order of 1969. The authority was made up of 26 councillors from the constituent local authorities of Glamorgan, Cardiff, Swansea and Merthyr together with 13 magistrates from the force area, making 39 members in total.

There were subsequent changes in the councillor representation on the authority to take account of the changes in local government in 1974 when the county of Glamorgan was split into three separate counties – South Glamorgan, Mid Glamorgan and West Glamorgan.

As mentioned earlier, further change came with the Police and Magistrates Courts Act 1994 which reduced the size of the authority to 17 members initially although this was later increased to 19. Membership also changed with the introduction of independent members.

The new authority became a stand-alone authority with its own powers to raise money through local taxation, and created its own administrative support separate from its constituent authorities.

However, the Conservative and Liberal Coalition Government formed in 2010, took the view that police authorities were insufficiently visible in their activities and lacked accountability to the public.

The Police Reform and Social Responsibility Act 2011, therefore, abolished police authorities and created police and crime commissioners with responsibility to hold the chief constable to account and also with duties in respect of engagement with crime reduction and the criminal justice system generally.

As a result, the South Wales Police Authority ceased to exist in 2012 and was replaced by an elected police and crime commissioner. Alun Michael, a former UK government minister and former First Secretary of Wales, was elected as the first Police and Crime Commissioner for South Wales and he has subsequently been re-elected to the position.[21]

As part of the revised governance arrangements a Police and Crime Panel was established comprising of councillors and independent members from the force area which acts as a scrutiny body in respect of the Police and Crime Commissioner.

CONCLUSION

Before leaving this journey into the history of South Wales Police, it is worth reflecting, briefly, on three aspects which appear to be of particular significance.

First, it is noticeable how financial and resource issues have regularly formed an important aspect of the challenges facing the organisation from its earliest days following amalgamation, through to its financial tribulations in the early 1990s and, more recently, as a result of the impact of the period of austerity which followed the global financial crash in 2008. The ebb and flow of these financial issues and the force's capacity to recruit police officers and police staff, and to invest in new technologies and buildings, recur throughout. It's against this background that the significant improvements that have been made over the years must be viewed.

Second, the communities of South Wales have, over the past fifty years, seen many changes. The heavy industries which had shaped so much of the lives of their people, their landscape and economy since the nineteenth century have all but disappeared, leaving a legacy of social deprivation in some areas. The ways in which people live and work are changing at pace in a post-industrial, digital age. Cardiff, in particular, has been transformed over the past fifty years with the re-development of the city centre, the Cardiff Bay development, and the city's increased role as a venue for major public and sporting events as well as being the home of the Senedd/Welsh Parliament. The force has had to adapt to these changes within its own boundaries and, at the same time, along with other police forces, had to deal with the increased sophistication of organised crime, which doesn't recognise such boundaries, together with the growth of matters such as on-line crime and offences of sexual abuse.

Third, the governance of South Wales Police has, as we've seen, changed significantly over the years. Arrangements which had their roots in its predecessor forces developed into the structure of police authorities which lasted for 43 years. Their replacement by an elected police and crime commissioner marked a fundamental change in the approach to police governance. The role of the chief constable, although still built upon the principle of operational independence, has had to adapt in response to these changes in governance.

These, and other themes which have been touched upon in this chapter, are considered in greater detail in the chapters which follow.

Notes

1. For the general historical background of policing see Critchley (1967); Emsley (1996). Aspects of the history of South Wales Police and its predecessor forces are to be found in Jones (1996); Hunt (1957); Baker (1965, pp. 40–52); Smith (1989, pp. 71–86). The records of the Glamorgan, Cardiff and Merthyr police forces are in Glamorgan Archives, Cardiff. Those relating to the Neath and Swansea forces are in West Glamorgan Archives, Swansea.
2. For the Marquess of Bute's role in establishing the Glamorgan Constabulary see Baker (1965, pp. 45–56); Davies (1981, pp. 94, 106).
3. The legal and social status of county and borough chief constables prior to 1964 is considered by Reiner (1991, pp. 11–16)
4. The magistrates retained their sole involvement in the governance of county forces until the Local Government Act 1888, which created county councils. Under the Act, Standing Joint Committees of magistrates and county councillors were established. That relating to Glamorgan continued until the Police Act 1964 as a result of which it became the Police Committee of Glamorgan County Council. The Watch Committees of Cardiff, Swansea and Merthyr continued as committees of their respective local authorities but with membership which reflected that of the counties, i.e. two thirds councillors and one third magistrates.

5. The policing of the industrial disputes by the Glamorgan Constabulary under Lionel Lindsay is dealt with extensively in Morgan (1987).

6. The riots and the police response to them are examined in Evans (1980 pp. 5–29; 1983, pp. 76–87)

7. The Police Act 1946 resulted in the abolition of a number of smaller forces. The Neath force had a final strength of 45 officers (Stallion and Wall 2011).

8. His report (Cmnd 3843, December 1968) from which this account is derived, is of particular interest.

9. The extent of the bad feeling which had developed between Cardiff and Glamorgan can be seen in the summary in the report of the evidence of Councillor Gower of Cardiff who stated that the meeting of the shadow authority held in December 1967 had ended in an atmosphere of 'near disorder'. He regarded the whole process not as an amalgamation but a 'complete takeover' by Glamorgan. Brown (1968, paragraph 34, pp. 13–14)

10. Letter dated 5 February 1969 from the Home Office to the Clerk to the Shadow South Wales Police Authority. In it there was, however, a recognition it was a matter for the police authority (Glamorgan Archives, Cardiff, DSWP/29/7)

11. South Wales Police (Amalgamation) Order 1969 (S.I. 1969 no. 484)

12. Hansard (HC Deb 26 Mar 1969 Vol 780 cc 1725–56)

13. *https://glamarchives.wordpress.com/page/12/*

14. According to the census of 1971 the population of Wales was 2,724,275. The 1971 census is available at the Casweb UK Data Service Census Support (*https://casweb.ukdataservice.ac.uk*).

15. This report was effectively a combined report as far as statistics were concerned in respect of the previous forces and those for the South Wales Constabulary between 1 June 1969 and 31 December 1969.

16. The history of policing in general from the 1970s onwards can be found in Brain (2010).

17. See the Police Areas (Wales) Order 1995 (S.I. 1995 No 2864).

18. Police and Magistrates Courts Act 1994 (1994, c29).

19. The change was made by the Police (Health and Safety) Act 1997 (1997, c42). It came into force the following year. Police support staff as employees of the then police authority had always been covered by the 1974 Act.

20. Police Reform Act 2002 (2002. c30).
21. The annual reports of the Police and Crime Commissioner can be found at *www.southwalescommissioner.org.uk*.

References

1831. Special Constables Act. *1831, c.41.* Available at: *https://vlex.co.uk/vid/special-constables-act-1831-808269205*

1835. Municipal Corporations Act. *5 & 6 Will 4, c76.* Available at: *https://vlex.co.uk/vid/municipal-corporations-england-act-808194397*

1839. County Police Act. *2 & 3 Vict, c93.* Available at: *https://www.legislation.gov.uk/ukpga/Vict/2-3/47/enacted*

1888. Local Government Act. *51 & 52 Vict, c41.* Available at: *https://www.legislation.gov.uk/ukpga/Vict/51-52/41/contents/enacted*

1946. The Police Act. *9 & 10 Geo 6, c49.*

1964. Police Act. *1964, c48.* Available at: *https://www.legislation.gov.uk/ukpga/1964/48/contents*

1969. South Wales Police (Amalgamation) Order. *S.I. 1969 no. 484*

1975. Sex Discrimination Act. *1975, c65.* Available at: *https://www.legislation.gov.uk/ukpga/1975/65/enacted*

1984. The Police and Criminal Evidence Act. *1984, c60.* Available at: *https://www.legislation.gov.uk/ukpga/1984/60/contents*

1985. Prosecution of Offences Act. *1985, c23.* Available at: *https://www.legislation.gov.uk/ukpga/1985/23*

1993. Welsh Language Act. *1993, c38.* Available at: *https://law.gov.wales/culture/welsh-language/welsh-language-act-1993*

1994. Police and Magistrates Courts Act. *1994, c. 29.* Available at: *https://www.legislation.gov.uk/ukpga/1994/29/contents*

1995. Police Areas (Wales) Order. *S.I. 1995 No 2864.* Available at: *https://www.legislation.gov.uk/uksi/1995/2864/contents/made*

1997. Police (Health and Safety) Act. *1997, c. 42.* Available at: *https://www.legislation.gov.uk/ukpga/1997/42/contents*

1998. Crime and Disorder Act. *1998, c. 37.* Available at: *https://www.legislation.gov.uk/ukpga/1997/42/contents*

2002. Police Reform Act. *2002, c. 30.* Available at: *https://www.legislation.gov.uk/ukpga/1998/37/contents*

2011. The Police Reform and Social Responsibility Act. *2011, c. 13.* Available at: *https://www.legislation.gov.uk/ukpga/2011/13/contents/enacted*

Baker, E. R. 1965. 'The beginnings of the Glamorgan County Police'. In: Williams, S. ed. *Glamorgan Historian*. Cowbridge: D. Brown & Sons.

Brain, T. 2010. *A history of policing in England and Wales from 1974: a turbulent journey*. Oxford: Oxford University Press.

Critchley, T. A. 1967. *A history of police in England and Wales, 900–1966*. London: Constable.

Davies, J. 1981. *Cardiff and the Marquesses of Bute*. Cardiff: University of Wales Press.

Davies, J. 1994. *A history of Wales*. London: Penguin.

Emsley, C. 1996. *The English police: a social and political history* 2 ed. Harlow: Longman.

Evans, N. 1980. 'The South Wales race riots of 1919'. *The Journal of Welsh Labour History* 3(1), pp. 5–29.

Evans, N. 1983. 'The South Wales race riots of 1919: a documentary postscript'. *The Journal of Welsh Labour History* 3(4), pp. 76–87.

Hunt, W. W. 1957. *'To guard my people': an account of the origin and history of the Swansea police*. Swansea: [Jones, pr.].

Jones, D. J. V. 1990. 'Where did it all go wrong? Crime in Swansea 1938–1968'. *Welsh History Review* 15, pp. 240–74.

Jones, D. J. V. 1996. *Crime and policing in the twentieth century: the South Wales experience*. Cardiff: University of Wales Press.

Morgan, J. 1987. *Conflict and order: the police and labour disputes in England and Wales 1900–1939*. Oxford: Oxford University Press.

Reiner, R. 1991. *Chief Constables*. Oxford: Oxford University Press.

Smith, E. M. 1989. 'Merthyr Tydfil Borough Police 1908–1938, a brief history'. *Merthyr Historian* 4, pp. 71–86.

Stallion, M. and Wall, D. S. 2011. *The British police-forces and chief officers 1829–2012* 2 ed. Police History Society.

Thomas, M. 1969. *Annual Report of the Chief Constable*. Glamorgan Archives. Available at: *https://glamarchives.wordpress.com/2019/06/*

3

LEADERSHIP

Matt Jukes

In their 'General Instructions' to new police officers issued in 1829, the inaugural Commissioners of Police of the Metropolis Charles Rowan and Richard Mayne, quite deliberately articulated the importance of police applying regulations with discretion:

> The following General Instructions … are not to be understood as containing rules of conduct applicable to every variety of circumstances that may occur in the performance of their duty; something must necessarily be left to the intelligence and discretion of individuals.

These are words that have echoed down the ages, continuing to influence the behaviour and conduct of generations of police officers. To a significant extent, it is this accent upon discretion that is one of the defining attributes of the tradition of the British policing model. For as Robert Reiner (1992) perceptively remarked, whereas in most hierarchical, bureaucratic organisations it is the most junior members of staff who are subject to the most scrutiny and surveillance, to a significant degree, in the police service this is inverted. Officers are afforded significant latitude in terms of their decisions about what they do, in respect of whom and why. Indeed, this is enshrined in law with each holder of the office of constable at every rank, being personally legally accountable for the decisions and actions they do or do not take. One consequence of which is that when a police officer is accused of wrongly arresting someone, whilst the chief constable is in civil law terms vicariously liable for the actions of the constable, it is the constable himself or herself who has to justify the decision to arrest.

This accent upon the importance of discretion, also distinguishes policing in a number of important respects from the traditions and styles of leadership to be found in the military, where far more is accomplished through a 'pure' and unfettered use of 'command and control'. Indeed, significant tracts of military strategy and the theory of military strategy are predicated upon the ability of senior officers to be able to issue orders and expect these to be followed, even if they are likely to lead to dire consequences.

One of the intriguing facets of police leadership is that it has to span and oscillate between both these modes. For in certain situations and settings, for example responding to mass public disorder, senior police adopt a command-and-control posture, directly issuing orders to their 'troops'. However, in other moments, where more routine policing tasks are being performed, police leaders are more constrained to influencing and guiding what officers do and why, effectively providing a framework for action rather than directing the action itself. Then, in addition to which, there is the fact that modern police organisations are themselves complex bureaucracies, where demand for services from the public continually outstrips the supply of officers available to service these requests. Thus, there are budgets to be managed to try and limit this demand and supply gap, to make resource allocation decisions between various territorially defined and specialist units within the organisation.

This distinction between what might be labelled 'operational leadership' and 'managerial leadership', and its importance in terms of how policing gets done and why it takes particular forms, has probably been somewhat neglected. For understandable reasons, the majority of the academic work on police leadership, that in terms of volume is itself relatively modest, has focused more on operational matters. But this tendency probably under-appreciates the significance of what happens 'back-stage' in respect of the 'business' of police work.

Framed by such considerations, and the kinds of tensions and dilemmas they signal, this chapter describes, explores and explains some of the key issues associated with senior leadership roles in the police service today. It is an account that is manifestly inflected by the author's personal experience acquired as Chief Constable of South Wales Police, but one that also seeks to draw in and integrate some of the wider lessons and insights from the academic literature.

HISTORIES AND STRUCTURES

There is a vast literature seeking to define and instil the attributes of a good leader. Typically, such contributions describe the ways in which effective leaders are able to establish direction, control and influence on those they are leading. However, an inconvenient truth is that in many leadership roles, the leader does not necessarily get to pick and choose the challenges and tests that will have to be negotiated. This is especially true for policing, where given its involvement in conflicts and adversarial situations, there is a consistent potential for trouble to occur at almost any time. Thus, in some ways, in understanding the key issues for police leadership it is perhaps appropriate to adopt the sociologist Erving Goffman's (1967) apercu that it is "not then, men and their moments. Rather, moments and their men" (p. 3) that count.[1]

To a degree, the extent to which this perspective helps us to unlock some of the relevant issues to considering police leadership 'in the round', is revealed if we trace the legacies of the last few Chief Constables of South Wales Police. So whilst there is clearly a sense of a community policing tradition and almost a 'brand' in terms of how South Wales Police conceives of the relationship to the citizens it polices, that is in some ways passed from one Chief to another, there are inflection points also. These are typically triggered by the ways prevailing social forces and specific incidents intrude into the organisational trajectory of development, demanding attention and oftentimes defining particular eras. It is a process and set of dynamics that was highlighted by Sir Robert Mark, former Commissioner of the Metropolitan Police, when he described how policing was always 'on point' for encountering the consequences of rapid socio-political changes (Mark 1977).

Transposed to a South Wales context, it is possible to trace how these dynamics have played out. For example, John Woodcock as Chief Constable promoted community policing and then subsequently as Her Majesty's Chief Inspector of Constabulary was instrumental in pushing an ethical crime investigation agenda. David East's time was dominated by the miners' strike, which although it posed acute challenges for the force's community focused disposition, nevertheless sedimented the importance of being able to negotiate and co-produce order, by demonstrating what happens when this is absent. Of particular note, was East's insistence that the local strikes should be policed by Welsh officers. This proved to be a seminal decision in 'sedimenting' a particular view of how community relations should be approached and managed by police, that has persisted in the views of subsequent generations of senior officers in South Wales.

The Miners' Strike was itself a symptom of much wider and deeper socio-economic changes and transformations. As part of which, the tenure of Anthony Burden (later Sir Anthony) was, in a similar fashion to what happened in a number of other forces at this point in time, dominated by having to deal with the increasing racial diversity of the British public, and the perceptions amongst some groups that they were being over-policed as suspects and under-policed as victims. Burden's time at the top was also directed at dealing with trying to manage the toxic impact on the force's reputation and the confidence of sections of the public in it, flowing from a series of high-profile legacy cases.

Barbara Wilding was the force's and Wales's first female Chief Constable, and one of the first in the UK. In addition to advancing the role of women in policing, one of her signature achievements was the links she established with local higher education institutions through the Universities' Police Science Institute; arrangements that have subsequently been replicated in many other forces. It was towards the end of her tenure that the impacts of the global financial crisis were becoming evident, meaning that Peter Vaughan inherited a situation requiring significant organisational downsizing as South Wales Police grappled with managing the impacts of austerity. But at the same time, as someone who had grown up in the South Wales valleys, he was determined to reaffirm the importance of communities, being and feeling supported by local policing. At a time when police resources and those of criminal justice partners were under pressure, he can be credited with moving the satisfaction of victims of crime from the worst level recorded in Home Office figures to consistently amongst the highest.

The author's own tenure as Chief Constable was in many ways about both continuity and renewal. Although the overt impacts of public sector austerity were easing, in their wake were revealed a series of suppressed consequences that were the legacy of constraining services over much of the previous decade. Working with the Police and Crime Commissioner and wider partners, this included trying to shift more services back to a 'preventative' disposition, in accord with Peel's historic objectives. This reflected a perception that financial cuts had narrowed service provision to being largely reactive, rather than attempting to get 'upstream' and stem at least some of the flow, through preemptive interventions. Especially important here was the close partnership with Public Health Wales and a shared focus on tackling intergenerational harms, but also establishing a Violence Prevention Unit for Wales (see Shepherd et al., Chapter 8). Like so much in leadership, it was impossible to pursue just one approach. As the Covid pandemic has taught us, public health begins with suppression and this was a period when additional resources and focus were directed to addressing the impacts of 'County Lines' drugs gangs on areas of South Wales, long-affected by chronic substance misuse.

There was also a focus on trust, both within and outside of the organisation. In its public facing aspect, this was about persuading the citizens of South Wales that in an era of rapid social and technological change, the police could be relied on to try and prevent harm and protect them from it. Facing inwards, the discourse was to the staff of South Wales Police acknowledging that there is never any possibility of being able to run a complex and multi-dimensional policing organisation through a model of centralised command and control. Therefore, senior leaders had to trust their staff to do the right thing, and to assure them that if they did and things went wrong (as opposed to wrongdoing), the organisation would back them. Considerable investment was put into engaging with and listening to the concerns of staff for their wellbeing and safety, and trying to respond to them in appropriate ways. Reflecting the focus of this section, however, these themes and trajectories were cast in a new light by the unanticipated onset of the Covid-19 global health pandemic. This is a development we will return to shortly.

Looking across the challenges, accomplishments and legacies of the respective Chief Constables of South Wales Police in this way, and attending to the continuities and changes that are associated with their individual tenures, a couple of features become apparent. First, whilst Chiefs seek to direct and influence the trajectory of the organisation as a whole they lead, they don't get to pick all the battles they have to fight. Indeed, at the very senior levels of police leadership part of the recipe for success seems to necessitate being able to be responsive to crises not of one's own making, and being sensitive and able to divine which issues and episodes possess the potential to activate political concern and/or put at risk the confidence of communities and other critical stakeholders in the organisation.

Layered on top of which is the fact that all of the individuals highlighted above had their own particular leadership styles. The predicates of which have to be negotiated within the traditions and embedded preferences, in terms of policing style, ingrained through the culture and structures of the organisation, that each Chief inherits from their predecessor and then passes on to their successors. After all, typically Chief Constables have a relatively limited 'time at the top', during which they can seek to introduce elements of a vision of how they perceive the organisation needs to evolve and adapt.

Adopting this wide-angled lens, to survey some of the pressures and considerations that shape police leadership across a number of Chief Constables, does though illuminate one further dimension. That is, the extent to which the fundamentals of leadership style have evolved. This is not necessarily about a shift from command and control to influence and persuasion, for as been rehearsed above, these different modes have always co-existed in the precepts of the British policing model. Rather, it is a general pattern of transition, widely observed across other organisations, that might be better described as moving from more autocratic to collaborative leadership.

The 'norms' of leadership and the expectations of those being led have changed over time. This applies as much to policing as it does to many other organisations. Based upon interviews conducted in 1986–7 with 40 out of the 43 Chief Constables, Robert Reiner's book (1991) remains one of the few accounts of senior police leadership and the authority structures in the UK. As he alludes to in the sub-title, 'Bobbies bosses or bureaucrats', the people inhabiting this role see it as an amalgam of several functions. Notably, unlike in other professions such as the military, that recruit an 'officer class', senior police entered the office of constable at the most junior ranks and worked their way up. They were not then recruited for their management or strategic acumen. Although, since Reiner was writing, this principle has been eroded somewhat with the introduction by the government of 'direct-entry' schemes, it is a principle that continues to influence both internal and external understandings of the role.

Unlike say, in a local authority where all staff from the chief executive downwards are employees of the authority and therefore have the same legal status, modern police forces comprise staff with very different relationships to the organisation. There are: police officers, who are technically office holders under the Crown and under the direction and control of the chief constable but they are not employees of the chief constable, other than for certain, limited, purposes such as discrimination law; police community support officers – who are police staff employed under contracts of employment, but exercise some, limited, powers which would ordinarily be described as police enforcement powers; and police staff that are employed under contracts of employment under the direction and control of the chief constable. The position of the latter can be further complicated by the grant to them of limited constabulary powers in certain circumstances. A police leader therefore has to blend these various aspects together to create one cohesive team able to meet the many challenges of modern policing. This is certainly a different world to that in 1969, when South Wales Police was overwhelmingly made up of police officers with police staff employed largely in clerical roles. Today many police staff hold positions of great responsibility in forces.

In keeping with the picture being built across the individual chapters of this book, modern policing is multi-dimensional, multi-layered and involves multi-tasking. This necessarily inflects the challenges that present to senior leaders, and is sometimes something that gets neglected in accounts and reportage of police work. Academic studies typically focus upon a particular strand of policing activity, and in a different but analogous way, media reporting is frequently event driven, focusing upon egregious and shocking events. However, no matter how serious an incident occurs, whilst responding to this crisis, at the same time the organisation has to keep dealing with and processing the thousands of more routine and 'mundane' tasks that make up the bulk of what it is that police do.

For senior leaders, this means that their role spans both the operational and organisational, and the practical and political. All of these dimensions are integral to the conduct of contemporary police leadership. Indeed, some of the most difficult and challenging issues typically relate to organisational and bureaucratic matters. This was especially pertinent, during the recent period of public sector austerity, where officers of all ranks and police staff were being encouraged to leave, including those with considerable experience and expertise, purely for cost reduction purposes. Likewise, the investment that could be made in individual investigations and criminal cases was constrained as much by budgetary considerations as by any more noble ones.

GOVERNANCE AND THE WELSH DIMENSION

Transcending the particular challenges that have confronted individual Chief Constables at particular moments in history, have been recurring tensions between the 'operational independence' of the chief constable and his or her accountability to those charged with overseeing the governance of policing. This stretches across the historic roles performed by magistrates in quarter sessions and standing joint committees, through to police authorities and latterly police and crime commissioners (PCC). The introduction of the latter has had especially important consequences for the constitution and conduct of police governance. For whilst the principle of operational independence remains as a cornerstone of policing and is now recognised through the Policing Protocol issued under the Police Reform and Social Responsibility Act 2011, there are now two corporations sole with the PCC and chief constable each exercising defined legal responsibilities. Whereas in the past, chairs and members of police authorities were relatively anonymous individuals and the chief constable was usually the public face of policing in their area, now PCC's have by virtue of their role as elected public officials, a much greater profile on policing (and criminal justice) issues. Indeed, this can encompass both police policy issues and on occasions operational matters, where there may be public concern or sensitivity, such as a death in custody.

Although the introduction of Police and Crime Commissioners in an oversight role has clarified elements of the political dimensions of police leadership, politics is perhaps more pronounced in South Wales and the other Welsh forces, than is maybe the case for the vast majority of forces in England. The processes of multi-level governance that are being instantiated by devolution, together with the devolved status of most public services with which police collaborate routinely in their day-to-day work, means that senior officers have regular interactions with policymakers in Welsh Government. But concomitantly, the fact that policing is not devolved and remains under the purview of the Home Office, adds an additional wrinkle of complexity. Not least this is because the UK Government in London frequently seems to forget that the arrangements in Wales are somewhat different and a little more complex. So policies that can be relatively straight forward to enact for English forces (because other UK Government departments are already aligned), can involve an additional set of negotiations and reconfigurations when they cross the Severn Estuary, or Offa's Dyke. The positive flip side of this complexity in Wales is proximity, and often, familiarity between key Welsh public servants and politicians. As observed by the HM Inspectorate in its report on pandemic policing, this made for effective, collaborative and consultative relationships when they were most needed (HMICFRS 2021).

In addition to the more common Ministerial interactions that are occasioned by Cardiff being a capital city and the geographic proximity that affords, the 'Welsh dimension' introduces further influences at one level down. This is to do with the slightly labyrinthine qualities of Welsh local government and the organisation of public services. For perfectly valid historical reasons, the key services in Wales have developed very different geographic footprints. So whilst South Wales Police has one Chief Constable, across the same area there are seven local authorities, three local Health Boards, two Fire and Rescue Services and the all-Wales Welsh Ambulance Service, all of which have their respective leadership teams.

This means that whilst a lot of the pan-public service rhetoric in Wales emphasises the value of collaboration and co-production, this is in part because it is a necessity. And whilst for the most part, relationships between the leaders of the respective organisations are amicable and professional, the layers of complexity do, quite understandably, sometimes induce added frictions and multiple negotiations and deals having to be struck. One consequence of this is that the Assistant Chief Constables and BCU Commanders in South Wales play a significant role in maintaining and navigating this network of relationships and partnerships.

THE PANDEMIC RESPONSE

It goes without saying the pandemic has impacted all regions of the country profoundly and in ways that could not have been forecast at its outset. That said, for reasons of socioeconomics, post-industrial legacy and demographics, the consequences of Covid-19 have been felt especially sharply in South Wales. Two-thirds of Wales's most deprived communities are to be found in the South Wales Police area. Somewhat unsurprisingly therefore, for several months in the second half of 2020, two of the local authority areas in the post-industrial Valleys had amongst the UK's highest levels of recorded Covid-19 infections, and the densely populated and diverse communities of Wales's capital were similarly affected.

Responding to this unprecedented situation, necessitated innovations across the board within the organisation. So although it was possible to 'hang' a lot of the response off of established civil contingency protocols, providing tried and tested routines for partnership working and co-ordination, through mechanisms such as the Strategic Coordination Group (SCG) chaired by an Assistant Chief Constable, much had to be invented and reinvented.

In the initial three months of lockdown South Wales Police took over 15,000 Covid-related calls, almost all alleging a breach. This equates to around 1,100 calls each week, and many were grounded in the fact of relationships between families and neighbours being under strain. This caseload translated into around seven complaints each week about the handling of these reports, suggesting that although considerable innovation and improvisation was in play, as police responded to hitherto unique and unprecedented circumstances, the public were relatively happy with the response provided, or at least understanding of the pressures the police were under during this time.

From a strategic perspective these challenges included the need to tailor well-rehearsed civil emergency procedures to the specific demands and issues being surfaced by the pandemic. Not least the need to allow key aspects of the response to be driven by and adapted to evolving scientific understanding of Covid-19; an understanding that shifted as it became apparent that the coronavirus pathogen could not be mitigated and controlled via the kinds of processes and procedures that had been planned and rehearsed to deal with a flu pandemic. But then subsequently, new data and evidence emerged gradually as various experiments were completed, that enhanced understanding of the pathogen and its transmission pathways. This in turn required new behavioural guidelines to be issued to the public. Layered on top of which, was the fact the virus itself mutated into several new variants.

Refracting some of the earlier comments about the 'Welsh dimension' of police governance, these operational policing responses had to be aligned to the Welsh devolved administration and partnerships (the administration of the health service is devolved to Welsh Government), whilst the Ministerial lead for policing matters remained with the UK Government. This is a development that may transpire to have profound symbolic and practical consequences for the future of Welsh policing, inasmuch as the Welsh Senedd was legislating for public health, in ways that meant the Welsh police forces were enforcing distinctively Welsh law.

Not unsurprisingly therefore, a number of operational challenges and tensions were encountered. Most pressing was the difficulty of ensuring that officers on the street were aware of their powers and what they could and could not do to try and secure behavioural compliance with the several iterations of guidance and regulation that were being issued with considerable urgency by government departments. This in itself had a 'downstream' effect requiring new training to be designed and delivered, often in the space of a few days where normally this would take months. These pressures were especially acute given increasing and well-founded concerns that some isolated and already vulnerable people were especially at risk, and that the kinds of safeguarding measures available during normal times were probably being less effective.

At the other end of the spectrum, one of the seen but largely unnoticed consequences of the pandemic and the introduction of new laws and regulations about public behaviour and conduct in social spaces, is that it brought segments of the population who ordinarily have little direct contact with policing, into its ambit. This was freighted with the potential to create disturbances to public legitimacy, although at the time of writing, the available public opinion survey evidence suggests this has not, in fact, transpired (Clements 2020; Office for National Statistics 2020).

All these operational pressures and innovations had to be navigated against a backdrop where the staff themselves were experiencing novel concerns and uncertainties. Like many sectors, these included worries about securing the health and safety of officers and staff as they were performing critical public-facing roles, often inherently involving face-to-face interactions and close physical contact with citizens. Similarly, there was increasing demand for remote and home-working arrangements.

Taken together, the South Wales Police approach to this confluence of issues has been to 'deal with the unusual in the usual way'. That is recognising how policing is at its essential core an emergency response service, where officers react to citizens' calls for assistance, often without knowing precisely what the situation is that they are entering into. In South Wales, this dealing with the unusual in the usual way involved an active effort to try and listen to and respond to the needs of communities, appreciating that this was uncharted territory for everyone.

One feature of the ways in which the response to Covid-19 has developed is the rapid development and evolution of guidance, regulation and law, and the expectation that police will have some role in its application. Indeed, the speed with which such instruments have been introduced and updated has created problems for police, both in terms of knowing the detail of what current control measures they have available, and to which members of the public can be expected to comply. But also, for police leaders in terms of supervising such work and trying to ensure it is proportionate and accountable in its application. Police leaders are accustomed to thinking about possible disproportionalities, especially around poverty and race, that might unintentionally be reproduced through the implementation of new legal instruments.

Reviewing the public discourse on such issues, it might appear that politicians drawn from across the political spectrum have been more enthusiastic about enforcement than senior police officers. In the case of extraordinary legislation, drafted at pace and sometimes misunderstood alongside non-enforceable guidance, police chiefs formed a strategy where in most cases enforcement would be a measure of last resort, to be turned to only once engagement, explanations, and encouragements have been exhausted. That said, it is also worth clarifying that this has not been a static picture, and positions and perspectives on all sides have evolved. Most notably, as the pandemic went on, police placed greater accent on their enforcement powers to tackle the more egregious breaches that were creating epidemiological risks, and threats to the legitimacy of the overall stance. If any was required, this is further evidence of the need for dynamic leadership, responding to events and new information.

FACING THE FUTURE

A theme rehearsed at several points across the preceding sections, has been the need for effective police leaders to be able to reflect upon and adapt to the prevailing circumstances. In this regard, the coronavirus pandemic is likely to imprint a considerable legacy upon policing that stretches forward into the future. For as has been well documented by journalists, many organisations have found that their response to coping with the disruptions induced by trying to cope with the public health measures, has accelerated their investment in and reliance upon technology. This has involved significant shifts in working patterns, with far more people working from home in a more flexible and dispersed fashion. Accompanying which, many of the more routine and mundane activities of organisational life being transacted online and virtually.

These are patterns of life that, if they 'stick' once social distancing requirements decrease in their intensity, will obviously alter the profile of demands for service that police deal with. Not least, because it seems entirely plausible that the post-pandemic society that emerges will be more, rather than less, polarised and riven with social tensions. This is a future that is not simply caused by the virus itself, but rather how the pandemic has accelerated and exacerbated trajectories of development that were already arising. In respect of this particular issue, owing in large part to the influence of social media and structural changes to the media ecosystem.

But equally there are related shifts that apply also to the organisation of policing. Key elements of the police function have always been and will continue to be very 'analogue' in their make-up – preventing harm and arresting people inherently involves physical confrontation. But equally, digital information communication technologies are vital to how policing gets done.

The ramifications and impacts of some of these technologies will be addressed across different chapters in this volume. Here we will restrict ourselves to considering some of their possible potential impacts upon leading police organisations over the next decade or so.

One of the most obvious consequences of the digital revolution is the vast increases in the scale of information that can be routinely collected, stored, processed and disseminated. In policing terms this changes what can be known, and how, about people at risk and posing a risk. It is a very different world from fifty years ago where officers were far more reliant upon the local knowledge they could memorise, the repository of intelligence assembled by 'the collator' and their index card system of 'key nominals'. Today, the police organisation's 'collective memory' has been vastly extended and elaborated. And whilst this undoubtedly brought with it considerable benefits, there are attendant challenges also.

One such is that very often when egregious harms take place, it will transpire that the individual(s) responsible will be known to the police in some capacity and there will have been a history of contacts. As a result, this will often result in difficult and challenging questions for police about whether, given the perpetrators were 'known' entities, their offending should have been prevented. This is a pattern that can be observed across a number of well publicised terrorist incidents over the past decade, but equally tragically in a number of public protection cases.

Such episodes have frequently become important 'litmus tests' for individual police leaders given the ways they are freighted with potential to corrode public trust and confidence in the organisation and institution as a whole. It is vital for the health of democratic norms that officers, and the organisations of which they are a part, are held accountable for the decisions and actions they take, given the power and authority they are 'lent' on behalf of the citizenry. But equally, precisely what the balance is between allowing an organisation to 'learn' from its mistakes and the fact that there needs to be some consequences where understandable, yet unacceptable, failures have occurred, is less settled.

Perhaps more certain is the fact that senior leaders trying to 'cover up' where things have gone wrong or mistakes have been made is not a viable strategy. In today's world where digital records and documents are preserved, the capacity of senior leaders to suppress uncomfortable information, or hope that someone won't find it, is considerably reduced. As such, an important component of leadership today seems to be a willingness to embrace transparency. This is because whilst owning up to mistakes at an early stage can be challenging, it is far less damaging than if the same information is revealed to have been suppressed at a later point in time.

Indeed, this theme of increased transparency and accountability is likely to be increasingly influential going forward. In a world where through the adoption of body-worn video and/or the ubiquity of mobile phone cameras, visual records of interactions between police and the public become the norm, public expectations about the scrutiny that police actions should be subject to are likely to shift.

The question 'who watches the watchers?' that derives from the Latin *Quis custodiet ipsos custodes?* has proven a long-standing conundrum for liberal democratic polities. It is likely that this is to be a defining issue for the current and next generation of police leaders. For we are entering an era where new and emerging technologies are affording unparalleled and unprecedented opportunities for police to engage in surveillance in their attempts to prevent crime and protect from harm. This in itself will raise critical and complex questions about the ethical and public permission frameworks that should govern the data collection and processing activities of policing organisations. But at the same time, very similar technologies will be directed towards monitoring the behaviour and activities of police officers, significantly increasing the visibility and transparency of how policing gets done. It is likely that this process will have positive benefits in terms of public perceptions, but equally it will produce moments of high drama, unveiling scandals with the capacity to rock public trust and confidence in the police service.

CONCLUSION

Leadership in policing is multi-faceted and multi-dimensional. From the response officer who is the first attender at an emergency and must try and take control, and lead and direct what other citizens do to try and mitigate the risk of harm. Through to the officer involved in the delivery of local neighbourhood policing, whose role includes chairing a PACT meeting[2] to enable co-ordination of services provided by multiple agencies in respect of a pressing problem, leadership is intrinsic to how policing gets done.

Focusing more explicitly upon the role of senior leaders, a similar theme can be identified. For some situations and modes of policing, there is a clear command and control imperative, whereas others function far more through influence and persuasion. The latter also applies to the negotiations that must be conducted with leaders in other public services. A lot has been written about the importance of partnership working to the contemporary conduct of policing, but much of this has focused upon operational and fairly tactical issues. Far less attention appears to have been directed to unpicking how leaders with strategic responsibilities negotiate these complexities that involve them seeking to deliver their objectives, whilst also being mindful of the pressures that shape the interests and participation of their various partners.

Such issues and tensions have come to the fore in the context of the coronavirus pandemic. In a cascade of new regulations and legislations, Parliament's authority and policing have been projected into the private lives of people in a manner unprecedented outside wartime. As public confidence was inevitably put at risk, Robert Mark would again recognise how policing remains an anvil on which society beats out its many problems and abrasions. In the author's view, it is a tribute to the women and men of policing that alongside resolve (and despite contested and notable individual events), discretion and intelligence have been evident at a strategic scale.

Notes

1. The gendered language is in the original source and perhaps warrants being adapted given how, over the past decade, a number of members of South Wales Police's chief officer teams have been female. Indeed, this is probably one of the most visible changes in terms of comparing police leadership today with 'yesterday'.

2. PACT stands for Police (or sometimes 'Partners') and Communities Together. These meetings are typically organised by local policing teams as a regular forum at which to listen to local citizens' concerns, but also report on recent policing activities and problems in the area concerned.

References

Clements, J. 2020. *Policing the COVID-19 lockdown – what the public thinks.* Crest Advisory. Available at: *https://www.crestadvisory. com/post/policing-the-covid-19-lockdown-what-the-public-thinks* (accessed: 14 May 2021).

Goffman, E. 1967. *Interaction ritual: essays in face to face behaviour.* New York, NY: Pantheon.

HMICFRS. 2021. *Policing in the pandemic – the police response to the coronavirus pandemic during 2020.* HM Inspectorate of Constabulary Fire and Rescue. Available at: *https://www.justiceinspectorates.gov. uk/hmicfrs/publication-html/the-police-response-to-the-coronavirus-pandemic-during-2020/#foreword*

Mark, R. 1977. *Policing a perplexed society.* London: George Allen & Unwin.

Office for National Statistics. 2020. *Coronavirus and crime in England and Wales: August 2020.* Available at: *https://www.ons.gov.uk/ peoplepopulationandcommunity/crimeandjustice/bulletins/coronav irusandcrimeinenglandandwales/august2020* (accessed: 14 May 2021).

Reiner, R. 1991. *Chief Constables.* Oxford: Oxford University Press.

Reiner, R. 1992. *The politics of the police* 2 edn. London: Harvester Wheatsheaf.

4

POLICING A CAPITAL CITY

Stephen Carr, Adam Edwards and Jenny Gilmer

Compared with most other European capitals, Cardiff is a relatively small capital city. But in common with its counterparts, it regularly attracts major political, cultural and sporting events, which create additional policing demands on top of those associated with any urban area. South Wales Police's own data suggest approximately 40% of their crime demand occurs in Cardiff, with more than 10,000 arrests made every year, an average of 28 per day. The city has one of the highest concentrations of licensed premises in the UK, with 314 premises in a 0.5 square mile area, and prior to the pandemic, had seen more growth in the night-time economy sector than anywhere else in the country (City of Cardiff Council 2021). Over the years the city has hosted the UEFA Champions League Final, international delegations for a NATO Summit, and typically sees multiple international rugby games and major concerts being held annually. It is also the locus of Welsh Government and Senedd Cymru (Welsh Parliament) and consequently the focus for regular protests, rallies and marches, the policing of which attracts significant media scrutiny. There are eleven iconic sites of UK national importance that need protection against strategic threats, and 21 foreign representations in Cardiff (20 consulates and 1 representative office).[1] Unlike for many other capital cities however, these additional policing responsibilities do not attract a funding premium from UK Government, which still holds responsibility for policing in Wales, meaning such services are funded from within South Wales Police's standard budget.

This particular context and set of circumstances render Cardiff especially interesting and instructive to look at, as a way of capturing in a condensed format, the diversity of tasks, responsibilities and challenges that comprise modern policing. In addition, however, there is a second more theoretical reason for looking in detail at the policing of places like Cardiff. This relates to the fact that although urban policing has exercised a clear influence on how police work has been studied and understood over the years, with many of the seminal studies being located in urban environments (Rubinstein 1973), there has probably been insufficient attention paid to how the concept of 'urban' is used as a descriptor for vastly different situations, that vary greatly in scale and intensity. Urban policing as practised in global cities like London, New York, Paris, Berlin and Los Angeles, looks and feels very different to what happens in places like Cardiff. Of note, is that many European cities are closer in size to Cardiff than they are to London or New York (Devroe et al. 2017). Thus, it seems eminently plausible to suggest that evidence and insights into the challenges of organising the delivery of policing services derived from somewhere like Cardiff, might have more immediate generalisability for a greater number of places, than do those emanating from global cities.

Framed in this way, this chapter has three principal aims. First, it interrogates the multi-purpose nature of policing a capital city, in terms of the diversity of challenges and problems that have to be managed and mitigated. Specifically, the chapter draws on the recollections of a number of senior officers, responsible at various times for policing in Cardiff, to place the current pressures in broader historical perspective. This socio-historical dimension identifies several key turning points in policing the Capital allied to the political and economic development of the city, especially since the devolution of statutory powers to the Welsh Assembly, subsequently the Welsh Parliament, and Welsh Government in 1999. These recollections provide a particular perspective on policing the Welsh Capital that emphasises the importance of understanding policing in context and, in turn, stimulates questions for further research into the challenges of policing capital cities. Especially as they pertain to the work of other responsible authorities involved in 'partnership' conceptions of policing 'beyond the police'. This in turn, sets up a particular focus on the police management of public order, as it relates to both political issues, but also major sporting and cultural events. The remainder of the chapter then alights on how these past and present issues are likely to influence and shape the near-term challenges that have to be negotiated by those charged with policing Cardiff into the future.

THE POLITICAL ECONOMY OF POLICING CARDIFF

Political economy is an analytic lens that attends to how inter-actions between political decision-making and economic resources shape the delivery of a particular outcome, decision or service. The particular affordance it offers is that it acknowledges how political options are constrained by available resourcing, but equally, the distribution of these resources impacts upon who has the power to decide what happens (Taylor 1999). A political economy perspective then, typically highlights the ways that specific actions and interactions are structured by a confluence of economic and political forces. Applying these logics to the policing of Cardiff illuminates how profound changes to the infrastructure and demographics of the city have shaped and reconfigured the strategic and operational requirements of policing over the past fifty years since the establishment of South Wales Police. These are patterns of development that are projected to continue.

Elaborating this approach to understanding how the political economy of Cardiff has structured developments in its policing, it is possible to identify four principal themes: (i) the growth and increasing diversity of the city's population, including increasing social inequalities between the wealthier neighbourhoods in the northern arc skirting the city centre and the less affluent neighbourhoods to the south of the centre; (ii) the rapid development of the city centre itself, as a regional, national and international destination for consumption, leisure and entertainment; (iii) the strategic status of the city and its functioning as a venue for political protest and related vulnerability to political violence; and finally, (iv) the reduction of resources available to the police and other authorities responsible for public safety in an era of austere public expenditure.

POLICING POPULATION GROWTH AND DIVERSITY

As the largest city in Wales and the ninth largest city in the United Kingdom, Cardiff currently has an estimated resident population of 357,200 and an urban area population estimated at 474,187. That this figure can only be estimated is in itself, an interesting indicator of the complex dynamics of cities such as Cardiff. For there have been vigorous debates about what is the 'true' population of Cardiff, with its large student communities and high numbers of visitors, and how should this be measured. This matters because such figures provide a denominator for constructing comparisons between different cities – for example in terms of recorded crime – that may have reputational, and thus material consequences. Whatever the 'true' population is, it is projected to grow to 529,536 by 2035, whilst already constituting a population density of 6,400 people per square mile (*www.worldpopulationreview.com*). This rate of growth will be greater than all other local authorities in Wales combined and is expected to grow more than 25% over the next 20 years, faster than any other major UK city, outside London (Cardiff Council, 2018: 10). To accommodate this growth, building work is already well underway on the 42,000 new homes planned over the next decade both in Cardiff and in the city region. In addition to this resident population, it is estimated that 90,000 people commute into Cardiff on a daily basis,[2] whilst the 'What matters strategy 2015/2016 review' estimated that more than 20 million people visit Cardiff each year. The latter is almost double the 1998 figures, which makes it the 6th most popular alternative tourist destination according to National Geographic.

The increased prosperity accompanying the growth of the city has, though, been unevenly distributed. Notably, there is significant social inequality with the southern arc skirting the city centre characterised by substantial indices of deprivation – 35% of children in that part of Cardiff are reported as living in poverty (Pollock 2019). The Cardiff Well-being Plan 2017 indicated that over 25% of dependent children under the age of 20 are living in poverty, ranging from 9% in the relatively prosperous area of Rhiwbina, to 50% in Ely, an outer housing estate that was also the scene of major public disorder in the early 1990s (Cardiff Council 2018). The Liveable City report 2017, highlighted that 25% of Cardiff households are living in poverty.

The population of Cardiff is also diverse, reflecting its history of global trade connections, post-war immigration and the increase in overseas students attending its universities. Currently, it is estimated that more than 54,000 people in Cardiff belong to a non-white ethnic group. There is also a Muslim population of about 4%, which is well above the UK average of 2.7%.[3] Butetown, in the southern Bay and port area of the city, is considered by some as the oldest multicultural community in the UK. There is an annual carnival celebrating this, which first began in the 1960s, and during its heyday, attracted tens of thousands of people, rivalling the more renowned Notting Hill carnival in London.

As in many other cities both large and small, the blend of inequality and tensions triggered by increasing ethnic diversity has meant that police-community relations have not always been harmonious. Sometimes unrest and conflict have been triggered by purely 'local' events. But more often, these have been associated with high profile civil disturbances in major conurbations (London, West Midlands, Manchester, Merseyside etc.) during the 1980s and the series of outer estate riots of the early 1990s, including Ely in Cardiff. Over and above the disorder such incidents involved at the time of their occurrence, they are freighted with a considerable symbolic load in terms of shaping the collective memory of how policing is interpreted and understood over an extended period of time, and the ways pasts, presents and futures are intertwined (Young 1999).

POLICING THE CITY CENTRE

In 2013 Cardiff was voted as the best city for young people to live, reflecting its vibrant nightlife and wide array of daily activities (BBC News 2013). The city's night-time economy has undergone rapid growth and development. By way of example, in 2008,

7 million people visited the city centre night-time economy. Ten years later this had almost doubled to 13.5M visitors and licensed premises had grown 51% from 221 to 333.

Alcohol is well known to be a key driver of policing activity (Edwards 2010). That said, issues with alcohol are not new to the city – the Chief Constable's report for 1982 specifically recorded 3,847 prosecutions for drunkenness alone. Unsurprisingly, the challenges of policing the night-time economy have often been a focus for concern. In 1986, the Chief Constable's report asserted that the 'number of assaults on officers increased "dramatically"', mainly due to incidents around 2am–3am following cessation of late drinking. Serious offences were also seen during this time and a report was presented to the Environmental Service Committee. Similarly, the 1988 report stated:

> One of the most disturbing features seen was the increase
> of spontaneous and unprovoked alcohol fuelled violence
> especially in the city centre. Became increasingly difficult
> to detect because victims and offenders were under the
> influence of alcohol and often from outside the Cardiff
> area.

Such worries and harms notwithstanding, the night-time economy is likely to continue to be a driver of both growth and concern going forward. The City Council and Welsh Government have published ambitious plans for further major developments in the city. One of these is Central Quay, which is to be located in Cardiff Bay, with more than 2.5 million square feet of development planned, including fifty new bars and restaurants.

As intimated above, a vibrant night-time economy brings with it both benefits and costs. It places particular demands upon policing and health services, whilst also supporting significant numbers of businesses and jobs. It plays an important role in attracting large numbers of students to the city, to attend one of the three universities that have premises therein. Combined, these academic institutions attract some 75,000 students from all over the globe.[4] This in itself creates inward investment estimated at around £1B per annum,[5] and prosperity for the city-region.

Of course, safety and security is an important factor in terms of how students decide where to study. That said, the arrival of students each year has a significant seasonal impact upon crime rates. In particular, it is associated with rises in burglaries in their often-shared accommodation, as well as increases in 'assaults with injury' offences related to the night-time economy.

A further surge in visitors to the city, and thus demands on policing, is associated with major sporting events. In common with many cities, Cardiff hosts rugby, football and cricket Internationals throughout the year. Some are very well attended, way beyond the capacity of the relevant stadium, with at times in excess of 250,000 supporters coming into the city to enjoy the atmosphere and watch the games in local public houses.

One unique feature to Cardiff, even amongst other Capital cities, is the central location of the world-renowned Principality Stadium. This means that supporters tend to remain in the city far longer than other comparable events requiring far longer resource deployments of specialist policing assets to ensure a safe and peaceful event – resources that are drawn away from other core duties within wider communities in Cardiff and beyond.

POLICING POLITICAL PROTESTS AND THREATS

As the capital city of Wales, Cardiff is a focal point for protest – local, national and international. When national protests are called in London, there is usually a mirrored event in Cardiff. With the Senedd, Welsh Government and Cardiff Castle there are a multitude of iconic locations (unique to a capital city) ideal for protest and garnering media exposure. With BBC Wales having its headquarters located right in the city centre, there are abundant opportunities for protestors to promote and publicise their causes. The scale of these protests can vary, but all require command assessment and frequently significant resource deployment to the event to facilitate peaceful protest. In turn, this requires South Wales Police to maintain sufficient numbers of suitably trained officers who have undergone expensive initial training and ongoing Continued Professional Development across the appropriate disciplines.

The presence of these major political institutions also requires protection from extremist and terrorist threats. With the current threat level and attacks on parliamentary buildings and politicians in the UK and overseas, there is a necessary requirement for police led security searches and a permanent overt armed deterrent located at the Senedd. Layered on top of which, Cardiff receives a far greater proportion of Royal visits than anywhere else in Wales. As well as traditional Royal functions which are carried out across the Principality, there are unique events such as the Royal opening of the Senedd, Prince of Wales Annual Wales week of events and national ceremonies at Llandaff Cathedral. All of these events require additional armed close protection as well as a Counter-Terrorism Security Coordinator (CT SecCo) assessment and proportionate overt policing operations to provide a robust, yet hopefully reassuring, policing presence.

Additionally, there are major military events involving the parading/changing of the Queens Colours and Royal Gun Salutes. Large Royal Navy ships frequently visit Cardiff and are docked in the Bay where the public have access. With the threat level both nationally and for the military being 'severe', these events require substantial additional security including search and seal, armed policing as well as public order officers to deal with protests.

Aggregated together, these events and issues, coupled with a compact city centre and major international venues adjacent to the city centre, create added complexities and compound the density of demands on policing, as they all contribute to the potential terrorist threat and thus the safety of the public in such environments.

There are very real concerns on this front. The city is the only Prevent priority area in Wales; with Home Office selection based on a range of factors including the terrorist threat and risk picture. This risk has been all too evident with regards to extremism and terrorism linked to Cardiff. On 30 June 2017, Lloyd Gunton was arrested just hours before he was planning to launch a knife and hammer terror attack on a Justin Bieber concert, at what was then a sold-out Principality Stadium in the city centre. He had already prepared a martyrdom letter ahead of this. This followed on from the events of 19 June that year, when Darren Osborne, from the Pentwyn area of the city, had driven a van at pedestrians outside the Finsbury Park Mosque in London, tragically killing one of those he hit. Osborne reportedly had a history of depression and had been rapidly radicalised in the weeks prior to the attack.

Three years previous to which, in June 2014, Nasser Muthana, a 20-year-old medical student, left his home in Cardiff and went to Syria to join ISIS. He subsequently appeared in a recruitment video for the terrorist organisation alongside Reyaad Kahn. Khan, also from Cardiff, was a Grade-A student who left for Syria in 2013. Muthana's younger brother Aseel joined them in Syria in 2014. In 2012, Cardiff brothers Gurukanth Desai, and Abdul Miah, were jailed along with Omar Latif, also from the city, for plotting Mumbai-style attacks in Britain. They had planned a Christmas bombing campaign with targets including the London Stock Exchange, Big Ben and Westminster Abbey.

Cardiff is not unique in this regard. Over the past twenty years, many cities have experienced the shock of having some of their young people deciding to engage in politically motivated violence. The point of including it here is to capture how such issues are part and parcel of the complex web of risks and threats that have to be navigated and negotiated, on an ongoing basis when policing modern capital cities. In the academic literature though, there is a tendency to separate such matters out and to differentiate between street policing and what Jean-Paul Brodeur (2010) labelled 'high policing'. But whilst separating issues out in this manner aids discussion and understanding, it rather downplays the complexities of real-life, in terms of the array of simultaneous risks police in places like Cardiff are routinely having to manage.

For example, one such 'mainstream' policing issue concerns the drugs markets and violence associated with so-called 'county lines' organised crime. This label describes circumstances where gangs from large urban areas travel to county locations to sell heroin and crack. The gangs enforce loyalty through violence, fear and intimidation with low level runners travelling to South Wales on a regular basis to deliver drugs and collect cash. It involves children being exploited to deliver drugs, often using intimidation, violence, debt bondage and/or grooming. Partially related to the developing 'footprint' of this issue, like other cities, Cardiff has seen a rise in knife related incidents. Figures for 2018/19 revealed that Cardiff accounted for 40% of all knife related recorded incidents in the South Wales Police area (South Wales Police figures). In the second half of 2021, as Cardiff (along with all other UK cities) sought to re-establish a greater sense of normality following the extended period of coronavirus pandemic related lockdowns, there was a worrying flurry of incidents involving serious knife related violence in the city.

POLICING AUSTERITY

As rehearsed above, the key point of a political-economic analysis is to draw out how the combination of material economic factors in conjunction with the distribution of political power structures the conduct of actions and interactions as they relate to the policing of organised crime, terrorism, as well as more mundane crimes. In common with other police forces and public services, the imposition of public sector austerity cuts in the wake of the 2008 global financial crisis, have impacted the size and shape of the force. And although these budgetary pressures have been eased more recently, it will take time to recover the real-terms reductions in both officer and police staff numbers. Further to which, any such easing may prove very temporary given the political pressures to start repaying the massive government debt that has been used to underpin the response to the coronavirus pandemic. However, such matters notwithstanding, senior officers from South Wales tend to suggest that the impact on Cardiff of cuts in public expenditure on policing over the past decade have been exacerbated by funding mechanisms that further constrain the resources available, compared to other capital cities in the UK (see Hussain and Lowe, Chapter 5 for more detail).

Of course, it is not just the police who have experienced the consequences of a period of extended public sector austerity. It has impacted also across all of their key operational partners. Indeed, it is cuts to these public services that may prove to be especially criminogenic over the medium to long-term, resulting in 'downstream' increases in demand for policing services. For example, youth services budgets have been especially hard hit, leading to a significant scaling back in the provision of youth clubs, as well as other diversionary activities and services. Such issues notwithstanding, they do indicate just how important partnership working arrangements are to how Cardiff gets policed. Most notably, there was a period between 2007 and 2021, where the City had a legitimate claim that, in terms of community safety, it was one of the best performing in the country. There was a lot of pioneering and innovative work done around this time using multi-agency neighbourhood management tasking and co-ordination and intelligence processes. These processes and systems were used to build 'rich picture', evidence-based assessments of local communities and their priorities, using the data to precisely target key problems for interventions. However, the onset of UK government austerity cuts, saw almost all such activity cease.

Policing within South Wales is increasingly feeling the effect of being a non-devolved service and not receiving the appropriate traction with either the Home Office or Welsh Government to secure increased funding for the unprecedented growth and demand in the capital city over the last decade and into the next. So, whilst Welsh Government and Cardiff Council can create ambitious growth plans in terms of population and the night-time economy, because policing is non-devolved, these documents do not really have to take account of the 'downstream' consequences for policing and public safety. Consequently, there is a significant and growing gap in relation to unfunded security arrangements that, as things stand, will only widen in the foreseeable future. There are, for instance, major infrastructure developments associated with the ten-year, £1.2 billion investment in the Transport for Wales Metro project (HM Treasury et al. 2016) and the electrification of the London to Cardiff rail network. Both will be a major attraction for businesses to relocate to South Wales, with the associated inward investment and job creation to the Capital City region. But such trajectories of development will increase the threat, risk and harm, and the complexities of policing demand.[6]

Recently, the operational policing resource deployed to the capital city has been under considerable strain in meeting the existing, let alone future, predicted demands of both day-to-day policing and the policing of major events. During periods of peak demand these strains have been 'covered' and 'patched' by drawing on resources from other South Wales communities and specialist departments to supplement the existing complement of Cardiff based officers. Unlike other similar sized forces, South Wales Police consciously tries not to draw on policing resources from other forces to supplement its own officers partly as mutual aid is at a premium cost, but also to try and ensure a culturally consistent policing style.[7]

POLICING MAJOR EVENTS

A recurring theme of the preceding sections was how public order and major events plays an influential role in the policing of the city, both substantively, but also in terms of shaping the availability of resources for other activities. Given this, it is worth exploring these issues in a little more depth and detail. Each year, South Wales Police services around 600 major sporting, cultural and political events, the majority of which take place in and around Cardiff. As a consequence, the organisation has built up considerable experience and expertise in this area, and indeed, would consider itself to be one of the most capable in the UK. This reputation has, at times, been hard won, and not without challenges and controversies. But as is the case with policing more generally, sometimes the most profound service improvements have had their origins in the most problematic cases.

Across the decades, South Wales Police would describe their tradition of major events policing, as grounded in an engaging, community style of policing first and foremost, where robust enforcement is introduced only where necessary. Counter-pointed with the approach adopted in London say, you will frequently hear South Wales Officers opine, that their approach is 'less in your face' and less 'assertive'.

It is an approach to major event policing that has been honed and tuned over the years, by virtue of Cardiff being selected as the site for a number of national and globally significant events. For example, the 1969 Investiture of the Prince of Wales on 1 July, at

Caernarfon Castle in North Wales, was watched by millions on television and attracted protests from a minority. It required support from officers across Wales and was followed by several high-profile royal visits to the South Wales Police area. In 1982, Pope John Paul II visited Cardiff. And in 2014, the Celtic Manor Resort in the neighbouring Gwent Police force area, was chosen to host that year's NATO Summit. This was a huge security operation by any standards with 150 Police Support Units and around 10,000 officers in total being deployed over the two-day event to protect the 67 heads of state and government who attended. A number of the key 'set piece' events occurred in Cardiff, attracting mixed crowds of onlookers and protestors with a multiplicity of grievances.

THE ELY RIOTS

Whilst South Wales hasn't seen the volume of public disorder experienced in other capital cities, notwithstanding wider events such as the Miners' strikes in the early 1980s, there have been exceptions. In September 1991, unrest broke out in Cardiff with the so called 'Ely Bread Riots'. What started as a dispute between two retailers, escalated into public disorder with around 500 youths from the locality and further afield participating, and around 175 officers deployed. The days were hot and at the time, the area which is part of the aforementioned 'southern arc' in the city, was suffering from disproportionately high unemployment and deprivation.

During the disorder, stones were thrown, some petrol bombs used and air rifles were fired. Simon Fuller, then an officer recalls how:

> We were later deployed further up Stanway Road, there had been some fighting between local youths in the area and clearly it was an attempt to lure us into a trap but we were reinforced by the 'Area Response Group' and the youths all ran away. We were dealing with that sort of cat and mouse malarkey all night. The media loved it, they were trying to liken it to Brixton, Toxteth and Broadwater Farm. I went up to Toxteth on mutual aid and to St Pauls in Bristol in the early 1980s and Ely was a minor skirmish in comparison.

As indicated in the last two sentences of this quotation, in part the infamy of the Ely riots and their pull on the public imagination, stems from how they fitted into a media narrative at the time, that had been established via similar, but more violent events that had already occurred in other urban areas. This meant that both journalists and their audiences were already sensitised to stories of riot and urban disorder. So when issues broke out in Cardiff, it was reported in fairly sensationalised terms that had quite a stigmatising legacy on Ely and its residents. Overall, the riot lasted for three days and resulted in 22 people being arrested. It has a certain form of 'dark' notoriety, in that it was the first time full riot gear was used in South Wales.

POLICING SPORT AND CULTURE

But the major events profile of Cardiff is not just defined by politics and protest, a considerable amount of effort and resource is invested in policing major sporting and cultural occasions also. In a typical pre-Covid year, Cardiff was the setting for multiple Premiership, Championship, European and international football matches, international cricket, regional and international rugby, and world championship boxing.

Of particular note, between 2001 and 2006, the FA Cup Finals were held at the Millennium Stadium whilst Wembley Stadium was being redeveloped. Fans of Arsenal, Manchester United, Liverpool, Millwall, West Ham and many others made their way to Cardiff to watch their teams play in the finals of various competitions. In those days, before Cardiff City was itself in the Premier League, major clubs bringing with them so many fans were a rarer sight in the city. Whilst commanders from the time recall disorder the night before the first couple of games and challenges around traffic management, policing plans were quickly refined. In total the Millennium (now Principality) Stadium hosted 44 finals and supporters from 48 different clubs. This provided a significant opportunity for South Wales Police as an organisation to develop its experience and expertise in managing large crowds of people.

This experience notwithstanding, Cardiff has experienced its share of football related disorder over the years and significant time, effort and resource have gone into addressing this. Local 'derbies' between Cardiff City and Swansea City in particular, have at times proved particularly challenging, but again this dynamic has evolved with the passage of time. Many factors have assisted this, including legislative initiatives such as the introduction of 'Football Banning Orders', alongside more 'organic' shifts in terms of a changed demographic, with more families attending games. Other developments that have had a positive impact include the evolution of the role of the Dedicated Football Officer and a partnership commitment to work closely with the local Clubs to stamp out disorder.

Historically, these kinds of changes were provided with particular impetus by interventions such as the reports of Lord Justice Taylor following the Hillsborough disaster (Taylor 1989). These had a massive impact on the policing of not only football, but also other major sporting events such as rugby and cricket. They required the establishment of all seater stadia, and the formal delineation of the respective roles and responsibilities of clubs/police/local authorities. South Wales Police was at the forefront of responding to Taylor because of what was then the National Stadium (now the Principality Stadium).

Whilst the Taylor Reports and Safety of Sports Grounds legislation resulted in improvements in safety at grounds so that policing levels within grounds could be reduced, from a police perspective, there has remained a consistent issue with what can be re-charged to the organisers of such events in relation to the policing in the vicinity of grounds. The aggregated impact though is that whilst football disorder is not entirely a thing of the past, it tends to occur now in pockets and to be relatively infrequent.

PROFESSIONALISING PUBLIC ORDER AND MAJOR EVENTS POLICING

Underpinning the evolution of South Wales Police's approach to the policing of major events, as sketched out above, has been a more general process of the professionalising of public order policing. This has been a response to learning the lessons both from what has happened in South Wales, but also elsewhere. As part of which, the Gold/Silver/Bronze command structure was introduced with the nomenclature becoming increasingly commonplace in policing, used routinely way beyond the world of public order.

Training has changed too and developed from being relatively minimal fifty years ago, to being intense and sophisticated, requiring the highest standards of discipline, knowledge and communication. Public order commanders at all levels are now required to demonstrate their operational and occupational competence at the appropriate level prior to deployment and to undergo rigorous continuous professional development throughout their service, in order to maintain their nationally mandated accreditation.

New roles have been introduced over the years also – specialists within this already specialised world. Protest liaison officers receive additional training and are chosen for their communication skills to build rapport with protesters both before and during events to ensure wherever possible, a right to peaceful protest can be facilitated, whilst minimising the impact on affected communities. Police Search Advisors lead trained search teams to ensure venue security is maintained, and actual or potential security breaches can be quickly and effectively dealt with. Additionally, CT SecCos give advice and set standards on security matters, a key role in the run up to any large event. In South Wales, a small dedicated team sitting within Specialist Operations are responsible for resourcing both local events and mutual aid commitments nationally. South Wales Police is effectively the strategic force for Wales as a Nation and as the largest force it is required to maintain a level of specialist response capabilities for both the regional and national security and safety infrastructure.

BACK TO THE FUTURE?

In more recent years, the UK in general and Cardiff and South Wales specifically, have seen a re-emergence of large, organised protest activity. As our society and politics becomes increasingly polarised and fractious, and as public concern about the climate emergency and associated social problems intensifies, we can speculate that many of the patterns and trends in policing mapped out in the preceding sections are likely to continue.

In particular, as protester tactics evolve so too do the counter-measures – both preventative and reactive – employed by the police. There are of course tricky and complex challenges with regards to balancing and respecting the requirements of Human Rights legislation and the interests of those choosing to protest against the interests of the wider community. Extinction Rebellion, Black Lives Matter and others have taken to the streets of Cardiff to seek to express their social concerns. At the time of writing, South Wales along with the rest of the world is in the grip of the coronavirus pandemic. During this period there have been regular anti-lockdown, anti-mask, anti-vaccine protest events in Cardiff. Given the potential of such sentiments to cause wider public health harms, they pose intricate ethical questions about the extent to which they should be facilitated and enabled. In particular, adverse publicity in respect of South Wales Police's approach to such occurrences arose on 24 July 2021, when an anti-lockdown march ended up outside of the home of the First Minister, in the Pontcanna area of the city. It remains to be seen what the longer term ramifications of this might be.

CONCLUSION

Adopting a city as the base unit of analysis for policing, affords a unique way of understanding how a range of overlapping and interacting, yet differentiated, policing services, comprise the police role in an ongoing, day-to-day way. Oftentimes these aspects are separated out and discussed individually, but it is equally interesting to think about how they combine and 'rub up' against each other. Furthermore, it is also intriguing to explore how a basic grounding in the values of community policing can feed through to shape the delivery of other policing functions, such as public order, counter-terrorism and managing serious organised crime threats.

'Seeing like a city' when appraising policing, is an analytic lens that usefully alerts us to some of the complexities of contemporary urban policing and public security management. Significantly, one 'take home' from the preceding discussion is how the delivery of security does not take place in isolation, but rather has to be balanced and reconciled with other competing demands and forces. These might include, for example, the pursuit of economic growth via the night-time economy to support employment opportunities, or a political decision to build more houses. It is sometimes posited that policing and security is a necessary condition for a vibrant and growing cityscape, and whilst this is probably true, its influence should not be over-stated. For the 'realpolitik' of urban governance is that other political, social and economic forces are the shapers of how a city evolves, and policing is required to react to these. In Cardiff, these patterns and trajectories of development have been instrumental in fostering a commitment to cross-sectoral and multi-disciplinary partnership working. A lot of important policing work gets done collaboratively, with South Wales Police both supporting and being supported by their public service partnership network. In addition, focusing upon the city helps to draw through some of the continuities and changes that have characterised the unique admixture of policing challenges in Cardiff since the establishment of the South Wales Police.[8] Everything changes and yet remains the same in that, throughout this time, policing Cardiff has been dominated by the demands of 'major events' spanning sporting, leisure and entertainment themes, including the significance of the weekend night-time economy for the city's development. Yet the scale and complexity of these events has intensified considerably in the two decades since Devolution and the allied, deliberate, promotion of the city as a location for UK and international investment. In turn, the success of this promotion and the rapid growth of the residential and commuter populations it has stimulated, has further exacerbated the challenge of policing more with less resources.

Such inter-dependencies are adding to the already multi-layered pressures upon policing in capital cities like Cardiff. Given this, it is worth recalling the official acknowledgement, first made in 1984, that the police cannot be expected to reduce problems of crime and disorder 'alone' as these are multi-faceted problems requiring multi-agency responses (Home Office 1984). This concept of policing 'beyond the police', and 'in partnership' with other authorities responsible for problem-solving, has been somewhat in retreat over the past decade of austerity, certainly in terms of investment and expenditure on prevention. If, however, the capacity for policing the capital is to be rebuilt, it is a concept whose time has surely come again for an increasingly challenging and complicated era.

Notes

1. Wales Extremism and Counter-Terrorism Unit/Centre for the Protection of National Infrastructure.
2. Source: walesonline, 9th March 2018
3. *www.worldpopulationreview.com*
4. *www.investincardiff.com*
5. Source: South Wales Police Director of Finance.
6. Source: interview with Cardiff BCU Commander.
7. Source: interview with BCU Commander.
8. We have appropriated this phrase from Amin and Thrift (2017).

References

Amin, A. and Thrift, N. 2017. *Seeing like a city*. London: Sage.

BBC News. 2013. 'Cardiff "best city" in UK for young adults says poll'. 2 October. Available at: *https://www.bbc.co.uk/news/uk-wales-south-east-wales-24354835*

Brodeur, J. P. 2010. *The policing web*. Oxford: Oxford University Press.

Cardiff Council. 2018. *Cardiff's well-being plan*. Cardiff: Available at: *https://www.cardiff.gov.uk/ENG/Your-Council/Strategies-plans-and-policies/Local-Wellbeing-Assessment/Draft-Local-Well-being-Plan/Documents/Wellbeing%20Plan%202017.pdf*

City of Cardiff Council. 2021. *Statement of licensing policy*. Cardiff: Shared Regulatory Services. Available at: *https://www.cardiff.gov.uk/ENG/Business/Licences-and-permits/Entertainment-and-alcohol-licences/Documents/Statement%20of%20Licensing%20Act%20Policy.pdf*

Devroe, E., Edwards, A. and Ponsaers, P. 2017. *Policing European metropolises: the politics of security in city-regions*. Abingdon: Routledge.

Edwards, A. 2010. *Working paper 133: evaluation of the Cardiff Night-Time Economy Co-ordinator (NTEC) post*. Cardiff: Cardiff University. Available at: *https://orca.cardiff.ac.uk/78193/1/wp133.pdf*

HM Treasury, Office of the Secretary State for Wales, Rt Hon Stephen Crabb MP, Rt Hon Greg Hands MP and Rt Hon George Osborne. 2016. *City deal: Cardiff capital region.* Available at: *https://assets. publishing.service.gov.uk/government/uploads/system/uploads/ attachment_data/file/508268/Cardiff_Capital_Region_City_Deal.pdf*

Home Office. 1984. *Joint departmental circular on crime prevention.* Home Office, Department of Education and Science, Department of Health and Social Security and Department of the Environment. Available at: *https://depositedpapers.parliament.uk/deposited paper/2201265/details*

Pollock, I. 2019. 'Child poverty: Wales is the only UK nation to see increase'. BBC News. Available at: *https://www.bbc.co.uk/news/uk-wales-48259327* (accessed 29 July 2023).

Rubinstein, J. 1973. *City police.* London: Macmillan.

Taylor, I. 1999. *Crime in context.* Cambridge: Polity Press.

Taylor, L. J. 1989. *The Hillsborough Stadium disaster inquiry, final report.* London: HMSO.

Young, J. 1999. *The exclusive society.* London: Sage.

5

FINANCE, RESOURCES AND THE ORGANISATION OF POLICING

Umar Hussain and Trudy Lowe

On 26 March 1969,[1] during the final parliamentary debate on the South Wales Police Amalgamation Order, Member of Parliament for Merthyr Tydfil S. O. Davies (1950 to 1972) launched an impassioned plea for its withdrawal. He called it 'an atrocity on our well-established police force' being enacted 'with the profound disapproval of the people of Merthyr Tydvil', that would reduce it to a 'crowd of impersonal beings'. A Welsh miner and trade union official himself, his remarks conveyed something of the regard in which policing was held within the tight-knit communities of the post-industrial South Wales valleys, and the profound significance of how local officers were deeply rooted within them:

> I have lived in my constituency for over 50 years. I have known many policemen personally and, on many occasions, I have been able to co-operate with them. Apart from their chief, Merthyr Tydvil's policemen are drawn from the local community which is, because of its industrial history, extremely closely-knit. Our policemen have come through the local primary and secondary schools, they play in the local soccer and rugby teams and they are regarded as friends.

Whilst his plea proved unsuccessful, the recruitment of officers from within communities and their close affiliation to them, has remained a consistent feature of the force over the decades since amalgamation.

The rationale for the merger of four existing forces into one South Wales force cited increased efficiency and effectiveness as key anticipated benefits of the restructure. However, the process failed to prescribe any 'hard' measures against which these aims might be assessed, making it impossible to conclude with any certainty whether the combined force was indeed more efficient and effective, or not.

This chapter assesses how South Wales Police has been organised and re-organised as part of a recurring desire to retain a connection to the communities it serves, in the face of ever increasing financial and resourcing challenges. The story told pivots around several significant strategic moments over the past fifty years, to show how key decisions about finance and resourcing have shaped the services provided to the public. At the same time, these moments of change are shaped by deeper 'structuring' influences. Not least, the increasing role played by a range of information and communication technologies, that have transformed how South Wales Police collects, processes and uses all kinds of information and data. Indeed, a recurring theme throughout this chapter is tracing out the complex interplay and interactions between decisions to invest in people *and* technology, that combine to have a 'downstream' impact upon organisational performance. The overarching conceptual point being to show how the policing services that the public experience directly, are enabled, shaped and influenced by a significant 'back-stage' machinery that has been largely neglected in academic accounts of the police. The first half of the chapter focuses more on the primary resources of policing, before the second half attends more to matters of economics and financial budgets.

THE SOUTH WALES POLICE WORKFORCE

In the lead-up to amalgamation, one potential financial saving highlighted centred upon the provision of force-owned police accommodation for serving officers. For proponents of a community policing type ethos, having officers living in police houses ensured local 'bobbies' became truly established within their communities, had a knowledge and incentive to maintain safety and order within their beat, and was one of the key compensations for the relatively lower pay of a constable. However, for the advocates of amalgamation, this arrangement resulted in less staff mobility and caused a challenge of distributing personnel to meet demand across the new, much larger South Wales policing area. Consequently, there was a general process of disinvestment from the police housing stock, with the number of police houses owned and rented by the force declining from 859 in 1969, to nil today.

This reduction in the police house estate played a role in transforming the mobility of the force. Within a few generations, the locally resident bobby was replaced by a Neighbourhood Policing Model, involving beat officers reporting to geographically based stations (based on demand) to change into uniforms, receive an operational briefing, pick up appointments and transport to patrol their area. In a small way, this is a story of change that encapsulates and condenses the fundamental relationship that exists between the public-facing dimensions of policing, and decisions about how to spend budgets and allocate resources. Intriguingly however, these 'backstage' issues have been addressed only fleetingly in the academic literature on policing studies.

The South Wales Police workforce has undergone constant change over the 50 years since amalgamation. The organisation has shifted from a force of predominantly male, uniformed officers conducting a public facing operational function supported by civilian administration staff, to a much more blended set of roles and responsibilities. Whilst the diversity of the force is still far from representative of the communities it serves, there have been significant improvements in gender balance, with the first female Chief Constable Barbara Wilding, appointed in 2005 and increasing numbers of female officers, as well as more female staff members performing specialised professional and technical civilian roles.

Table 5.1 provides some headline statistics that enable a comparative assessment of how the force has evolved and developed over the period under review.

Table 5.1: Changing profile 1969-2019

	1969	2019	Change
Annual expenditure	£6M	£287M	£281M
Population	1,258,450	1,282,106	23,656
No. of 999 calls received	36,901	201,949	165,048
No. of non-emergency calls received	44,582	501,754	457,172
Total annual calls for service	**81,483**	**703,703**	**622,220**
Male police officers	2,326	2,062	(264)
Female police officers	65	925	860
Police officers	**2,391**	**2,987**	**596**
Police staff	459	1,911	1,452
Police community support officers	–	374	374
Calls for service per officer	34	236	202

Much of this change was a consequence of key pieces of national legislation and amendments to regulations during this period. The Race Relations Act (1965) was the first legislation in the UK to address racial discrimination. The Act outlawed discrimination on the grounds of colour, race or ethnic or national origins in public places. It was followed a decade later by updated legislation (the Race Relations Act 1976) that established the Commission for Racial Equality, banned direct and indirect discrimination, and allowed for complaints to be made to industrial tribunals and courts. A year earlier, the Sex Discrimination Act (1975) similarly afforded protection to men and women from discrimination on the grounds of gender or marital status as it applied to employment, training, education, harassment, the provision of goods and services and the disposal of premises. Together these Acts set the scene for all employers, the police service included, to help address the diversity of its workforce.

Changes to the working hours of police officers in April 1970 reduced the working week from 42 to 40 hours in all officer ranks up to and including Chief Inspector. In South Wales, this resulted in a loss of one duty per month, the equivalent of 126 Police Constables or 5 percent of the establishment, overnight. Towards the end of this same decade, significant improvements to the pay and conditions of police officers were implemented as a result of the 'Edmund-Davies' Committee of Inquiry on the Police.

The introduction of health and safety legislation in the latter part of the century also had a rather different set of impacts on the management of the policing workforce, including embedding such considerations within routine planning and training. Under the Health and Safety at Work Act (1974), all individuals were mandated to ensure, as far as reasonably practical, the health and safety of themselves and others potentially affected by work activities and at workplace premises. When the Act came into force, attested constables were not explicitly covered by its main provisions, although it made clear that police officers should be given the protection afforded to people in other occupations. It was not until the subsequent enactment of the Police (Health & Safety) Act in 1997 that the unique role of officers was addressed. This served to highlight the strong desire of the service to improve standards of health and safety within it, alongside meeting its obligations to implement a series of European Union health and safety directives applying to all workers, including the police.

By the mid-1980s, recognition of a number of other protected characteristics had developed sufficiently to encourage a police force that was more visibly diverse in other ways. Not least, height restrictions for recruits (men 5ft 8 inches and women 5ft 4 inches) were abolished, and individuals who wore glasses or were colour blind were no longer precluded from joining the service.

As the twentieth century drew to a close, the death of Stephen Lawrence and the resulting Macpherson Inquiry in 1999 led to a substantial overhaul of Britain's race relations legislation and a review of recruitment, retention and promotion processes within the police service followed. South Wales Police (in line with many forces) has, despite repeated and ongoing efforts, struggled to attract and retain officers from minority ethnic backgrounds that would allow it to fully reflect the diverse communities it serves.

In addition to the recognised bodies of officer and staff unions, a number of additional support networks have been established to help try and ameliorate this long-standing challenge with becoming more diverse and representative, including:

- A Disability Support Network;
- A Black Police Association;
- A Christian Police Association;
- A Gender Equality Network;
- A Lesbian Gay Bi-sexual Transgender Network.

From the early 1990s onwards, the civilianisation programme transferred many 'back office' functions previously carried out by police officers to police staff roles, not requiring warranted powers. This freed up highly trained (and relatively expensive) officers for public facing operational roles, whilst also opening up a route to advancement for police staff as new career paths were created. This trajectory continued under Section 38 of the Police Reform Act (2002), which created the role of the Police Community Support Officer (PCSO) as non-warranted, uniformed officers to work within neighbourhoods to provide a visible police presence and community reassurance. The first PCSOs were deployed across the South Wales Police area in 2003 with numbers gradually increasing to over 500 by 2013, when direct funding by the Welsh Government created an additional 206 posts.

THE SOUTH WALES POLICE INFRASTRUCTURE

Changes to workforce capability and capacity, were accompanied by and reinforced by alterations and investment in infrastructure, intended to support the delivery of modern policing services and respond to evolving community needs.

One of the most obvious in this regard has focused upon transport and the development of related technology. This has seen very basic patrol cars equipped with a radio and little else, transformed into today's mobile workstations where officers are able to access force intelligence systems in real time en route to the call, thus rendering them better able to anticipate the policing circumstance and respond in a more informed manner.

Self-evidently this becomes especially valuable where the call for service pertains to reports of firearms, violence, or vulnerable individuals. The modern police vehicle fleet has full Wi-Fi booster capability to enable officers to work from citizens' homes, even when they don't have a Wi-Fi connection. They are also fitted with automatic vehicle location systems to enable the control centre to better direct officers to the incident.

THE POLICE ESTATE

For thirty years following amalgamation, the South Wales Police estate was entirely dependent upon Home Office approved capital expenditure, as capital funding was a separate funding stream approved on a case-by-case basis. It comprised more police houses than police stations and progress on modernising the estate was slow, compounded by the financial crises that buffeted the force over the period. The period since 2007 however, has seen a dramatic change as Home Office capital funding declined and a more strategic approach to estate management developed. This included establishment of a 10-year estates strategy culminating in a new Cardiff Bay Divisional Headquarters with a 64-cell complex to respond to the capital city's rising levels of demand, associated with its status as an international sporting venue and entertainment centre. New 'bridewells' were also built in two of the other Basic Command Unit areas, along with a new Serious and Organised Crime intelligence Centre and significant investment in the Headquarters building in Bridgend.

The combined costs of these initiatives were over £100M, paid for via a combination of partnership funding, Home Office Transformation funding, asset disposals and the re-engineering of expensive debt to cheaper longer-term loans. A key aim of the estate strategy being to deliver a modern, more environmentally sustainable and energy efficient, and thus lower annual cost estate. With the savings made available to reinvest in technology and public-facing services. Importantly then, this was not just about fixing and refreshing an increasingly dated set of buildings, important as this was. But rather it was about establishing a physical infrastructure fit for the future, that would support and enable increasingly agile working patterns for police officers enabled by innovative digital technologies and services.

TECHNOLOGY AND POLICING INNOVATION

As intimated in the preceding section, understanding how modern policing gets done in practice is not possible without attending to the role of technology. Much of the political conversation about policing tends to get framed in terms of police officer numbers, but this neglects the extent to which decisions about technological provision and 'back-office' support services are key enablers in terms of how effective and efficient officers actually are. Whilst South Wales police was not initially class leading in terms of its technological engagements, it has made significant strides in this area. In recent years it has acted as a national testbed for a number of leading-edge technological innovations. But given how pervasive and ubiquitous information and communication technologies have become in modern police work, it is instructive to trace back the impacts that specific innovations had on the organisation of policing.

From a South Wales Police perspective, a key moment that fused technological and organisational innovation occurred in 1974, with the implementation of the Police National Computer. Terminals were introduced into the force control room at force HQ and one terminal in each of the divisional control rooms. For the first time, IT training was required and a classroom was set up in HQ with nine terminals to introduce officers on how to make vehicle and people enquiries. Following on from these tentative first steps a decision was taken to develop a computer system to record incidents, despatch officers and to replace the aging teleprinters. The system which would become known as IRIS or Incident Resource Information System was developed by software engineers from Honeywell Bull who went on to design and create IRIS command and control. As part of the implementation process, all the locations within the South Wales Constabulary area were uploaded onto the street index and details of all the burglar alarms were also included, to provide operators and officers with much enriched information. Subsequently, an interface to the Police National Computer allowing for faster access to the national system was integrated to IRIS. The system went on to be used by a number of other UK police forces including Hampshire Constabulary who renamed it Hampshire Operational Resource System (or HORIS), and forces in Australia and Sweden.

For many years, IRIS was the only widespread information technology used operationally in South Wales and became a resilient and trusted part of the force's operational response. One obvious flaw in this regard was that crimes were still recorded and investigated on paper. The FCr.2 crime report form and FCr.3 update were the means by which officers formally recorded crimes and updated their status as detected or undetected. There was no link between the incident created on IRIS and the subsequent actions taken, and often without detailed oversight crimes could get lost in the process. Relatedly, all the intelligence and knowledge of local criminals, their associates and routines were held on card indexes at individual stations across the force. There was little or no cross referencing conducted other than for the most serious cases, or dangerous individuals and even these were not infallible. The need for a searchable intelligence system that provided officers with updated information and intelligence on the community was self-evidently becoming a key issue for South Wales Police.

Developed by Northgate, the South Wales Police Crime Information System went live in 1994. Fairly limited by modern standards, it was a 'green screen' system and did not operate on the POLE (Person, Object, Location and Event) principle that underpins all such systems nowadays. Such limitations notwithstanding it represented a major leap forward for the police, providing access to daily crime recording information, the progress of investigations and importantly, relatively widespread and up to date intelligence from across the South Wales Constabulary area, that could be accessed locally – something not previously possible. It also heralded the introduction of the Crime Information Bureau an early version of a call handling centre focused on recording and updating crime records and investigations. There were significant initial teething problems including long waits to record crimes over the phone with the fledgling CIS

Bureau, followed by a lengthy call to record the relevant information. This did undermine the launch of the system and was an easy target for detractors to point to its flaws, but in time it settled down to become the basis of crime recording and investigation in South Wales until the introduction of the Niche RMS some 13 years later.

The adoption of Niche RMS stemmed from a growing recognition by the late 1990s and into the early 2000s that South Wales Police was falling behind in terms of its digital capabilities. Despite updating the Command and Control system several times, the lack of an integrated end to end system was causing increasing practical and analytical difficulties for the organisation. As such, Niche was purchased as the basis for a new integrated Record Management System (RMS). Significantly, given the particular interests of this chapter, this technological shift had implications for officers and their training. Because the system was intended to replace almost all the operational systems currently in use by the force, it necessitated an ambitious and complicated process of training all officers up to the rank of Superintendent in its use, and also many police staff whose roles involved use of the system or the data likely to be contained in it.

Despite multiple delays and cost over-runs, the 'business benefits' that were leveraged from Niche in terms of enabling improved crime management, reducing harm and supporting victim satisfaction outcomes, induced a profound change in attitude across the organisation as a whole. From this point on, South Wales Police saw technology as an opportunity not a necessary incumbrance and this led to several further innovative uses of technology and data. Limitations on space prevent any detailed discussion of these developments, but include such innovative applications as the increasing use of smartphones as digital assistants and interfaces with force systems.

Bringing this story up-to-date and with an eye to the future, South Wales has established itself as an important global pioneer in its application of biometric identification systems to policing, especially with its early adoption of Facial Recognition Technologies. Faced with the operational challenges of policing the 2017 UEFA Champion's League Final in Cardiff, the force mounted a successful bid to the Government's Police Innovation Fund to partner with the technology company NEC to develop and test the use of facial recognition in public spaces. Several vans fitted with high resolution cameras and the Automated Facial Recognition (AFR) technology were deployed in the run up to and during the event in and around Cardiff.

Although early in its development, the deployment was a great success and resulted in the first ever UK arrest as a result of the live deployment of facial recognition technology The individual arrested had been wanted by South Wales Police on an arrest warrant and had been picked up in the crowds around the event. It is fair to say though that this was an area where the pace of innovation was running ahead of legal thinking and the development of any ethical guardrails for the mainstream use of such increasingly sophisticated technologies. Accordingly, there have been a number of legal challenges to aspects of how facial recognition technologies are being deployed by police. Seemingly the developing consensus in law appears to be that there is no inherent reason why police should not be able to use facial recognition technologies for crime prevention and reduction purposes, provided that due regard is given to establishing levels of necessity and proportionality in terms of its use. For it is certainly a technology with the potential to improve the efficiency of one of the core functions of the police – to identify persons at risk and posing a risk.

FINANCIAL CRISES - THE SOUTH WALES POLICE RESPONSE

From the outset in 1969, the establishment of the force was not accompanied by any significant additional investment, as would normally be the basis of a merger where restructuring and reconfiguration has clear short-term costs. Instead, the expectation was that economies of scale, conjoined with longer-term opportunities for efficiency, would result in substantial and relatively quick cost reductions. The first Chief Constable's annual report to the new police authority highlighted the additional costs of policing demonstrations, sporting events and Royal Visits associated with Cardiff as the capital city of Wales that were not reflected in the budget. This failure to recognise the policing demands of the capital city (see Carr et al., Chapter 4 also) has surfaced a number of times throughout the decades. The financial crises of 1992/93 brought the issue to the fore of both local and national politics, involving the then Secretary of State for Wales, John Redwood; the Home Secretary, Michael Howard; and the Shadow Home Affairs Minister, Alun Michael, who in later years became the first Police and Crime Commissioner for South Wales in 2012.

A MAJOR FINANCIAL CRISIS - 1992/93

The financial difficulties that emerged in full during 1992/93 had started to manifest at the beginning of the decade. In 1990, South Wales Police was facing severe financial restraints. To prevent a predicted budget overspend of £857,000, restrictions were imposed on recruitment, overtime and vehicle mileage. Restrictions on civilian recruitment further aggravated the situation, with 21 constables deployed to force control rooms to cover a shortfall in civilian staff. A review of management and divisional workloads was undertaken to streamline procedures, improve work dissemination and enhance communication and command.

In 1991 the financial difficulties continued, making it difficult to buy new vehicles, improve buildings and fund emerging information and communication technologies. Crime increased substantially in comparison to the previous year with a total of 156,308 offences recorded; an increase of 17.32%. In September, South Wales Police reduced its 8 territorial divisions and 21 sub-divisions to 14 local divisions, saving costs associated with senior officers, support staff, and building work. The new Divisions were led by Superintendents rather than Chief Superintendents, as had been the case previously.

Another difficult financial year in 1993 resulted in the Chief Constable Robert Lawrence signing off a budget plan to prevent the force overspending by £2 million. The possibility of temporarily closing nine police stations across the Cardiff area (Ely, Canton, Cardiff Docks, Roath, Whitchurch, Llanedeyrn, St Mellons, Cathays, and Penarth) was even considered in an effort to save £100,000. However, due to government intervention, the idea was never pursued.

The causes of the 1992/93 financial crises were well documented at the time and can be summarised into three main contributing factors:

1. The force recognised and paid a historic debt (accrued over several years) of police overtime worked but not paid, known as Time Off In Lieu of Payment (TOIL). This debt amounted to £1.2M. A lack of audit trail, due to a policy of not retaining overtime records for greater than 3 years, resulted in payments being estimated based on a sample size and agreed with the Police Federation as a full and final settlement of this historic debt.

   Significantly, such payments required the approval of the Police Authority, which was not sought. This lack of due process raised major governance issues with the Police Authority and led to independent audit reviews and legal advice to identify and hold the individuals responsible to account. Media reporting at the time clearly suggested that the councillors from the three Glamorgan councils (South, Mid, West) wished to attribute blame and discipline those responsible.

2. A second contributing factor was unplanned pension costs amounting to £0.8M as a result of a greater number of officers retiring than forecast. The police officer pension scheme is an unfunded scheme and at the time, the Home Office provided a pension grant based on estimated retirements within the police settlement. So the risk of higher levels of retirement (at the officer's discretion) remained with the force budgets.

3. Finally, there was a significant forecasting error in the 1993 year-end report to the Authority, which suggested that the South Wales Police would have a £2.0M underspend. The accurate position was that the force was heading for an overspend of around £0.5M. Based on this assessment the force approved purchase of additional computers and equipment, resulting in the three councils being left with a net year end

overspend that they would have to make-up. This increased political and media calls for retribution, as conveyed by a highly selective summary of newspaper headlines from the time, detailed in Table 5.2 below:

Table 5.2: Selected newspaper headlines

Date	Newspaper	Headline and abstract
18 February 1994	Western Mail	Cash Crisis Police look for a new Finance Director
02 September 1994	South Wales Echo	The Thin Blue Line Went into the Red
06 September 1994	South Wales Echo	Whose Head Is On The Block – Search for Police Bunglers
15 September 1994	South Wales Echo	QC Called in South Wales Police Cash Crisis
08 November 1994	South Wales Echo	Police Cut to Bone
08 November 1994	South Wales Echo	Chief Constable Warning Over Forces Future – Policing will Grind to a Halt
01 December 1994		Police Hit a New £3M Cash Crisis
03 December 1994	South Wales Echo	Thickening The Thin Blue Line. Millions of Pounds of Cuts Made to The Police Budget this Year May Be Reversed in April After £12.7M Extra Made Available

As it turned out, the final net overspend was not the £4.0M reporting suggested, but around £0.5M. However, the underlying financial difficulties were not resolved and the public dispute carried over impacting the budget settlements for the following 2 years with the Chief Constable being asked to deliver substantial further cuts. However, his room to manoeuvre was constrained. Police Officers are not employees but officers of the Crown, and therefore cannot be made redundant where police civilian post holders can. With a substantial salary budget and increase in pay awards (negotiated nationally) having to be factored in, some unpalatable options had to be put forward to try and balance the books, such as: a freeze in recruitment; reductions in transport costs including fuel and maintenance; station closures; cuts in consumables; and reductions in police overtime.

These matters were compounded by some uncertainty as to whether all the funding from Whitehall was finding its way to policing with arguments by the then Home Secretary that funding of £5M was being withheld by the County Councils. In the end, some of the underlying causes of the financial crises were resolved by a government shift in policy on police funding and the fact that South Wales Police were granted over £12M in additional funding through the direct grant, providing evidence that Chief Constable Lawrence's protestations to the Home Office that the force was underfunded were justified.

FUNDING REFORM

The funding challenges and tribulations seeded in South Wales during the 1990s were instrumental in inducing three significant reforms over the subsequent decade, that collectively transformed the police funding landscape across England and Wales:

1. Police Authorities were re-established in 1995/96 as independent public bodies to receive force funding direct from Whitehall, with powers to manage the budget and hold reserves, removing control of police finance from County Councils.
2. Police precept powers were introduced as part of the Police and Magistrates' Courts Act 1994, around the same time as the creation of council tax in Wales in 1993–94. April 1995 was a 'shadow Authority' year, with the independent police authorities starting fully in April 1996. In Wales, the amount of annual increase in the police precept was capped by the Secretary State for Wales and subsequently the Welsh Parliament.

3. Police pensions prior to 2006–07 were paid by police forces out of their general funding. After 2006–07, police force areas received ring-fenced pensions top-up grant funding for police pensions from outside of the agreed police settlement funding total. This funding was paid according to demand, taking into account a number of assumptions. This financing arrangement protected police forces from fluctuations in the number of retirees and therefore in pension expenditure.

The establishment of the independent police authority gave rise to a significant improvement in the management of police resources and provided further local flexibility to supplement the police grant with local funding through council tax. This additional flexibility was not unfettered, however, as the amount of precept had to be approved by the majority of the councillor members of the police authority.

Devolution in Wales added an additional layer of complexity. Whilst policing is not a devolved function, decisions on the amount of Council Tax are a matter for the Welsh Government who retained capping powers over and above the police authority approvals. This two-stage approval process has led to different decisions on police precept compared to other forces from 2002 onwards. With Council Tax in South Wales being significantly less than in the other Welsh police force areas, whilst the local authority proportion is on average higher, this resulted in a cumulative comparative underfunding of South Wales Police by 2019 of £187M. The gap on the police precept was gradually narrowed so that by 2019, the South Wales Police precept represented the average across Wales, instead of the lowest.

THE SECOND MAJOR FINANCIAL CRISIS - 2010

The consequence of the global financial crisis of 2008 was increased government borrowing, debt financing and a reduction in public spending that had a direct impact on central police funding, as illustrated in Figure 5.1.

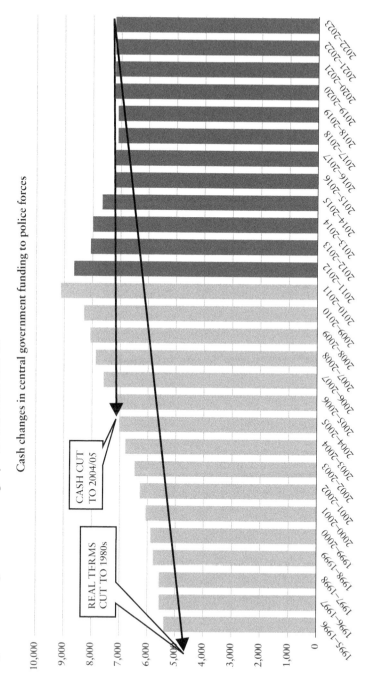

Figure 5.1: Central government funding to police forces since 1995-96

During 2009, the preparatory work for the 2010–11 South Wales Medium Term Financial Strategy anticipated a significant contraction in public expenditure was on the horizon, citing the Treasury's Summer Financial Statement and Budget Report (Red Book) which contained a stark indication of the future financial difficulties facing the public sector. Compared with the planning processes undertaken in some other police forces, the South Wales forecasting appeared relatively pessimistic, anticipating that the impacts would not present in the form of a 'short sharp shock', but would instead have a 'long tail' lasting several years. It was an analysis reflecting how the National Debt was expected to increase by around £800B by 2014 and the consequent debt servicing costs alone were expected to put a major strain on public finances, with inevitable public sector expenditure reductions regardless of political governance. The extent to which the police service would be affected was explicit, but ranged from a best-case scenario of cash freeze, to a cut in funding of around 10% as being reasonable parameters for planning purposes ahead of the next Comprehensive Spending Review.

At that time, for South Wales, a 10% reduction in funding equated to a budget cut of around £30M. This planning for a reasonable worst-case scenario proved to be prescient when the Chancellor of the Exchequer George Osborne set out the Government's spending plans for the next four years in the 2010 Comprehensive Spending Review. It heralded a prolonged period of financial contraction in public service finances, with central government police funding to be reduced by 20% in real terms by 2014/15. The Chancellor did add, however, that if police precepts were increased at the level forecast by the Office of Budget Responsibility, the overall reductions could be mitigated down to an average of 14% in real terms over the next four years.

The Home Office's departmental budget was to reduce by 33% in real terms over the same period, with reductions managed by focusing spending where government perceived it mattered most – protecting the public and ensuring the security of borders. Counter-terrorism specific policing was to be protected, with a smaller percentage cut of 10% in real terms and there were assurances that the right funding would be in place to deliver a safe and secure Olympic Games in 2012. Reforms were introduced claiming to be designed to make police forces more effective by driving out wasteful spending and increasing efficiency and productivity of the back office. Central targets and accompanying bureaucracy would cease, such as the Policing Pledge, accompanied by reduced reporting requirements for Stop and Search and the scrapping of the 'stop' form in its entirety. In addition, pay and conditions would be modernised. At the same time, the government announced its intention to replace Police Authorities with directly elected Police and Crime Commissioners.

The literally unprecedented level of cuts to police funding were forecast to have a major impact on the national level of police resources. The 43 forces in England and Wales anticipated a reduction in police officers of 14,253 (equivalent to all the officers in North Wales, Dyfed Powys, South Wales, Gwent, West Mercia, Gloucestershire and a large section of Avon and Somerset Police combined), as well as a reduction in police staff of 19,511 (the equivalent to removing all police staff jobs from 12 police forces covering the whole of Wales and much of South West and North West England).

Set against this backdrop, relations between police and politicians were adversarial, as captured in a newspaper headline from the time "'This crying wolf HAS to stop': Furious Home Secretary Theresa May attacks police officers for 'scaremongering' over budget cuts" (Drury 2015). A subsequent report by the National Audit Office (2018) reported that by March 2015, there had been a reduction of 16,542 officers and 20,250 police staff, even higher than initially projected, as summarised in Table 5.3 below.

The South Wales Police assessment of these cuts over the medium-term for the years 2011 to 2015 showed the budget gap increasing from £18.3M in 2011/12 to £47.8M by 2014/15. The real-world implications of which were reductions in the number of police officers by around 256 as well as 432 police staff. Equally important, however, was the fact that these kinds of budget reductions were not just directed at policing, but their public sector partners as well. As a consequence of which, there were compounding concerns about the potential for 'demand

Table 5.3: Summary of staffing reductions between 2010-18

Whole Time Equivalent	2010	2015	Losses by 2015	% loss	2018	Losses by 2018	% loss
Police Officers	143,734	127,192	16,542	12%	122,404	21,330	15%
Police Staff	96,514	76,264	20,250	21%	72,959	23,555	24%
Total	240,248	203,456	36,792	15%	195,363	44,885	19%

displacement' increasing the police's workload, as other providers struggled to cope with increases in requests for service, many of which if unmet would ultimately end up coming to police attention, given they are the emergency service of last resort.

South Wales Police faced the same financial challenges in terms of percentage reductions in the police grant formula funding as the 43 forces in England and Wales, and as an organisation it worked very hard to try and limit the 'downstream' impacts upon public facing services. But at the same time, internally, leaders were having to manage large numbers of officers and staff, with considerable experience and expertise, leaving the organisation, as part of a planned workforce contraction strategy. This consumed large amounts of energy and effort as they tried to ensure staff were able to leave with dignity.

An important consideration within the strategy was the pace of budget cuts required, given 81% concerned people. Re-playing a pattern already discussed in relation to previous decades, because police constables are officers of the Crown and redundancy is not a legal option, there were insufficient police staff posts to deliver the 30% cut in spending. That said, fairly extensive use was made of Regulation A19 of the Police Pension Regulations that enabled a police authority to require an officer with more than 30 years' service to retire in the 'general interests of efficiency'. But over and above this, a sophisticated and ambitious medium term financial strategy was devised that had a number of key strands:

1. Reductions in Police Officer posts;

2. Reductions in Police Staff posts;
3. Lean systems process analysis to improve business processes, whilst reducing waste;
4. Critical review of posts upon vacancy to determine if replacement should proceed.
5. Critical appraisal of consumption on goods and services, driven by a mantra that every pound saved means less pressure on jobs;
6. Investment in technology and information systems;
7. Investment in the estate to rationalise and bring about co-located functions to improve productivity;
8. Centralisation of budgets to reduce administration and improve use and prioritisation;
9. Extending collaboration between blue light services;
10. Responsible increases in police precept with a commitment to match every £1 increase in police precept with more than £1 reduction in police costs.

The strategy proved to be sound, and ended up being extended well beyond the initial CSR 2010 through to 2019 and beyond.

By 2018, police officer numbers in South Wales had been reduced by 383 and Police staff by 563. Figure 5.2, below, puts this into some long-term historical perspective with the thin line tracking changes in officer numbers for South Wales Police and the thicker black line for England and Wales. It clearly conveys how the strategy of trying to protect frontline services played out. The Graph also illustrates the implications of the 1990 financial crises and the sharp decline in officer numbers in that earlier decade.

Overall then, South Wales Police sought to manage the ramifications of public sector austerity by initiating their strategic reforms relatively early and by cutting quite hard in doing so, with the relentless aim of making key services either cheaper, faster or better. Critically, this enabled them to meet the central government-imposed budget reductions, whilst also creating sufficient financial headroom to invest significantly in a range of new technologies (as outlined in the preceding section) that would underpin further future efficiency and performance improvements. Over the long-term the investments made in new

Figure 5.2: Long term trends in police officer numbers

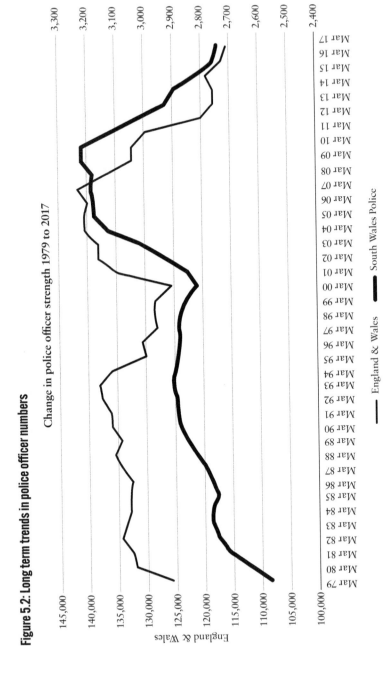

Change in police officer strength 1979 to 2017

technology stood them in good stead for the onset of the global health pandemic and the disruptions to working patterns and arrangements that it induced.

2020 VISION - OFFICER UPLIFT PROGRAMME AND A RECOGNITION OF CUTTING TOO DEEP

By 2019, after further and deeper cuts and a change in political leadership, the new government acknowledged the consequence of the reductions in policing and committed to increasing police officer numbers by 20,000 by the end of the financial year 2023. Whilst not quite restoring the losses and certainly not those losses of police staff, this programme if delivered will start to resolve the pressures on police resources arising from years of austerity. But it will take time to do so. For in the short-term, it will see a reduction in the overall experience levels of officers performing key response and neighbourhood policing roles. These impacts are further exacerbated by the fact that they are occurring following significant revisions to the ways in which police officers are trained. Implementation of the Police Education Qualifications Framework has extended the amount of up-front initial training officers are required to undergo, such that some estimates contend that in terms of workflow it takes 2 new recruits to deliver the same amount of activity as every fully experienced officer.

Equipped now with the detail and insight about how and why certain decisions were made and changes introduced in terms of the organisation of South Wales Police, we can return to interpret some of the data set out in the earlier Table 5.1 to construct a data-led comparison of how it has changed over its fifty-year history. One dimension of note is that whilst the total population only increased by less than 24,000, the calls for service for the whole of 1969 was equivalent to just 48 days of calls by 2019. This seismic shift and the changing nature and complexity of crime has clearly fed through in shifting the mix and level of police resources. Also evident in the data is how the gender mix and the greater diversity of specialist police staff roles have reshaped the makeup of the force.

Throughout the extended period of austerity, as an organisation South Wales Police did its utmost to protect and maintain a neighbourhood and community presence. It avoided shroud waving and focussed on its aspirational vision statement of 'being the best at understanding and responding to our communities' needs'. Intriguingly, there is a 'golden thread' here that connects back to precisely the same kinds of sentiment and public values articulated in Merthyr in 1969 that were used to open this chapter.

Despite the many financial challenges that were faced, some very significant improvements in performance were achieved and resulted in South Wales Police being recognised as one of the best performing forces in England and Wales. By 2019:

- There were significantly fewer crimes per 1,000 population when compared with the most similar forces year on year (HMICFRS 2022);
- South Wales was rated 1st in the country for positive outcome rate for violence with injury; 2nd for positive outcome rate for sexual offences; 3rd best for positive outcome rate for robbery; and 8th highest in the country for positive outcome rate for racially and religiously aggravated crimes (Ibid);
- 99.4% of 999 calls answered, within an average of 6 seconds;[2]
- And 90% of domestic abuse victims reported being satisfied with the service they receive.[3]

CONCLUSION

There are wider lessons for the future to be gleaned from South Wales Police's past experiences. Most notably, having experienced budgetary difficulties and the long-term ramifications they can have in the 1980s, facing up to a further period of austerity in the 2010s, a more strategic approach than just managing the cuts was adopted. This involved careful financial modelling designed to deliver cost savings that would support targeted investments in technology and thereby enable better, 'smarter', and more agile ways of working. It was about organisational transformation, whilst keeping the organisation's core vision and values front and centre.

Indeed, it is probably fair to say that, as an organisation, South Wales Police has radically transformed its relationship with technology, to establish itself as something of a 'path-finder' force. For a significant period, South Wales Police probably under-invested in their technological support structures, but this has been reversed over the last two decades. Most recently, this has been manifested in the leading role South Wales has taken globally in the development and adoption of Facial Recognition Technologies for policing. Whilst such innovations inevitably attract controversy, they signal an intent to explore new, and potentially more effective and efficient, methods for leveraging public safety.

For understandable reasons, much commentary and analysis on policing tends to focus on issues of strategy and service delivery, often as it pertains to particular roles and functions. For example, there is a recurring political trope about officer numbers as an indicator of the overall state of policing, that manifestly over-simplifies the issues and also obscures how some of the key threats and risks officers are being asked to manage have morphed and evolved. Set against this backdrop, the current chapter has sought to delve into the under-explored realm of the economics of policing, and how budgetary and financial decisions shape what front-line officers do and how they do it. The key 'take-home' message being that deeply engrained organisational values and commitments are important in terms of plotting how to navigate the blend of financial, technological and cultural influences and challenges, that come from both within and outside of the police organisation, and that act to shape both what is possible, and also desirable.

Notes

1. HC Deb 26 March 1969 vol 780 cc1725-561725 §8.31 p.m. §Mr. S. O. Davies (Merthyr Tydvil).
2. Internal South Wales Police data.
3. Internal South Wales Police annual victim survey data.

References

1965. Race Relations Act. *1965, c.73*. Available at: *https://www. parliament.uk/about/living-heritage/transformingsociety/private-lives/relationships/collections1/race-relations-act-1965/race-relations-act-1965*

1969. South Wales Police (Amalgamation) Order. *S.I. 1969 no. 484*.

1974. Health and Safety at Work etc Act. *1974, c.37*. Available at: *https:// www.hse.gov.uk/legislation/hswa.htm*

1975. Sex Discrimination Act. *1975, c65*. Available at: *https://www. legislation.gov.uk/ukpga/1975/65/enacted*

1976. Race Relations Act. *1976, c.74*. Available at: *https://www.parliament. uk/about/living-heritage/transformingsociety/private-lives/ relationships/collections1/race-relations-act-1965/race-relations-act-1965*

1994. Police and Magistrates Courts Act. *1994, c. 29*. Available at: *https://www.legislation.gov.uk/ukpga/1994/29/contents*

1997. Police (Health and Safety) Act. *1997, c.42*. Available at: *https:// www.legislation.gov.uk/ukpga/1997/42/contents*

2002. Police Reform Act. *2002, c. 30*.

Drury, I. 2015. '"This crying wolf HAS to stop": Furious Home Secretary Theresa May attacks police officers for "scaremongering" over budget cuts'. *Daily Mail* 20 May. Available at: *https://www.dailymail.co.uk/ news/article-3089363/This-crying-wolf-stop-Furious-Theresa-attacks-police-officers-scaremongering-budget-cuts.html*

HMICFRS. 2022. *Value for money dashboards*. Available at: *https:// www.justiceinspectorates.gov.uk/hmicfrs/our-work/article/value-for-money-inspections/value-for-money-profiles/value-for-money-dashboards*

National Audit Office. 2018. *Financial sustainability of police forces in England and Wales 2018*. Available at: *https://www.nao.org.uk/ report/financial-sustainability-of-police-forces-in-england-and-wales-2018/*

6

COMMUNITY POLICING IN SOUTH WALES

Catherine Larkman and Colin Rogers

INTRODUCTION

Writing in 1981, in his report to Parliament on the Brixton Disorders of April 1981, Lord Scarman stated 'community policing is too important a concept to be treated a slogan' (Scarman 1981, p. 140).

Succinctly summarising how the approach taken to policing communities should underpin the policing function throughout England and Wales, Lord Scarman's enquiry identified that lack of a focused and rigorous approach can lead to reduced legitimacy in the police for the people they serve. South Wales Police has, throughout its history, recognised the importance of the community and community policing has played a large part in their overall strategies since their creation in 1969. However, policing does not exist in a vacuum and is influenced by many factors and decisions made outside of its control, such as political, legal and other factors, including social opinion. These can have a major impact upon all aspects of policing but can impact upon and indeed damage carefully established relationships between the police and public if not adequately reflected in operational community policing activity. This chapter aims to chart the development of community policing throughout South Wales Police's history and the context of wider societal change during that time.

DEFINING COMMUNITY POLICING

Before considering the South Wales context it is important to define what is meant by Community Policing. Tilley (2008) refers to it as a decentralised function, involving strong two way communication between citizens and the police. Priorities are defined by the community, and they play an important part in determining and implementing locally relevant and acceptable solutions to their problems (Ibid, p. 40). In the US, the community policing movement has traditionally been much stronger than in Britain. In fact, it became so influential that Greene (2000) referred to it as becoming the national mantra for the American Police.

Whilst Community Policing is difficult to define, there are guiding parameters which are principles developed over several years in the US (Trojanowicz 1983; 1986). Notable principles worth highlighting here include:

- Community policing is a philosophy and a strategy. It allows police and community to work together. The philosophy rests on the belief that law abiding people in the community deserve input into the police process, in exchange for their participation and support.
- It requires implementation by all personnel. This means that everyone in the police, including sworn and unsworn officers must engage in the philosophy and seek ways to translate this into practice.
- It requires a different type of officer. This refers to the introduction of the Community Policing Officer, (CPO) who acts as the direct link between the police and the community. CPO's must be allowed to maintain direct, daily face to face contact with the people they serve.
- The CPO should work with volunteers. The CPO's role should work with people within communities to explore solutions to local concerns.
- It introduces a different relationship between officers and citizens. This relationship, based on trust, sees police acting as a catalyst, getting people to accept their share of responsibility for improving quality of life within their communities.

- It introduces proactive police work. Community policing broadens the police role by being proactive in making communities safer, rather than focussing on the traditional reactive role.
- It aims to protect the most vulnerable in society, such as young people, the elderly, minorities, the poor, disabled and the homeless. This is achieved by working closer with other agencies and communities themselves.
- It seeks to balance human skills with technological innovations. Community policing rests on the belief that nothing is better than humans talking to each other, working together to solve problems.
- It must be integrated and implemented force wide. This involves everyone in the force, with the CPOs as specialists, bridging the gap between the people and the police.
- It emphasises de-centralisation. Community Policing emphasises the fact that there should be de-centralised staff to work with the community. It supports the idea that communities should see the police as a resource they can use to help solve the problems within the community, rather than impose order.

What is common to these principles is accountability to both the police agency and community, decentralisation of authority and structure, shared decision making with the community and more empowerment of police officers (Michaelson et al. 1988). Having attempted to provide some understanding of just what community policing actually is, this chapter now turns to situating its development in a South Wales context.

COMMUNITY POLICING AND SOUTH WALES POLICE

In line with other forces at the time of its inception, South Wales Police initially undertook to introduce the concept of Unit Beat Policing (UBP). This introduced defined neighbourhood 'beats', worked by dedicated officers assisted by personal radios and the use of the 'panda car', in an attempt to improve efficiency and consequently police performance (Rogers 2004). By 1972, South Wales Police had 461 car beats and 206 area constables, as well as

468 town centre patrols (Jones 1996), but the UBP model did not appear to be particularly effective in terms of improved community engagement. Consequently, a decision was made to increase the number of area constables and in particular the number of constables walking the beat. Traditional methods involving beat patrols were reintroduced, as well as additional constables being deployed in both urban and rural areas. It would appear that the public appreciated these changes with a reportedly marked increase in public interaction with the police (Ibid).

In this less technological and digital age, police work relied more upon direct social interaction between the police and public. The need for local knowledge was essential, requiring police officers to integrate into communities where they both lived and worked, most notably in the detection of crime. The reliance on personal relationships between local police officers and members of the community meant information and intelligence was prized, and a good community officer with exceptional local knowledge was often the first port of call for investigations into serious criminal matters. Integration into communities, building trust, utilising discretion and being visible and approachable were all tools in the community police officer's armoury.

Officers were encouraged to live in police owned property in the neighbourhoods to which they were posted and become part of the local community there. They were commensurate with local schoolteachers, vicars, and the post office as being trusted community pillars to whom people could turn for help and assistance.

By 1981, 365 out of a total of 1,000 foot patrol officers in South Wales were designated as community police officers, all liaising with local representatives and institutions. The Chief Constable at the time, John Woodcock, stated that he thought community constables were as important in tackling crime as other officers on the front line, and that community policing such as that practised in South Wales could both inspire public confidence and lead to a reduction in crime (Jones 1996). In spite of the pressures upon them, South Wales Police has striven since those days to keep a balance between community policing, crime prevention and specialist crime tackling.

It was in the early 1980s however, that disorder in inner cities across England and Wales illustrated an apparent disconnect between police and public (Scarman 1981), a position exacerbated by a period of significant industrial unrest which was particularly felt in the South Wales Police area, with its preponderance of heavy industry such as coal mining and steel. The miners' strike of 1984 to 1985 posed great challenges for South Wales Police, given the great dependency of local people upon the industry. A polarisation occurred between mining communities in South Wales on the one hand, who feared the problems associated with the removal of the industry that bound communities together, and the police on the other hand, who were seen as mere puppets of government determined to enforce government policies.

Whilst democratic policing should support people's right to peacefully demonstrate, the scale of this dispute placed a strain on police resources, especially given mass picketing at the many coal mines in the South Wales area together with the steel works in Port Talbot. On several occasions up to 1,000 officers were deployed throughout the force area to police the dispute (South Wales Constabulary 1984–5).

Many community ties between the police and the community were fractured during this time, and community police officers recalled the distancing that appeared from within mining communities (Rogers 2007). It was many years before trust was re-established sufficiently to bolster community relations to a position where the close co-operation required to support local policing was possible. By the 1990s, a number of early community initiatives had helped in this regard. For example, the post coding of bicycles not only allowed for quicker recovery of stolen bicycles, but also brought individuals into direct contact with police officers in a crime prevention context, breaking down barriers to communication, and encouraging a joint approach to proactive community safety initiatives. More generalised engagement initiatives were also introduced to help re-establish and develop community relations. The 'Splash' programme, for example, aimed to promote healthy understanding between young people and the police by way of joint activities during the school summer holiday period, including free of charge activities or activities with substantially reduced costs (South Wales Constabulary 1990).

During 1991 South Wales Police introduced the Schools Liaison Officer scheme which promoted the attendance of police officers at local schools to assist in the delivery of curriculum topics around policing and crime prevention (South Wales Police 1991). Twenty-one constables were initially allocated the role full time, undergoing a two-week training course to equip them for the task. The concept involved making sure that pupils had a coherent and ongoing relationship with the police by:

· Informing schools and pupils about the role of the police;
· Informing about the law and the rights and duties of citizens;
· Making young people aware of potential dangers;
· Helping foster crime prevention activities.

(South Wales Constabulary 1990)

These later two initiatives introduced many young people to police officers in an effort to rebuild trust with a new generation. Simultaneously, accountability process which allowed for greater involvement of communities in policing activity developed during this period with the introduction in 1984 of the Police and Criminal Evidence Act (Home Office 1984), notably under Section 106 which outlines arrangements for conducting community consultation.

A signature feature of South Wales Police's approach to delivering Community Policing in the early 2000s, that also reflects the importance of partnership working to their operating concept, was the formal connection made to the Communities First programme. Communities First was designed by the Welsh Government as a place-based approach to delivering a range of public services in a targeted fashion towards areas of high deprivation in Wales. Each of the selected areas had a nominated co-ordinator with multi-agency teams from local agencies working with them.

A few months after the commencement of the programme the Chief Constable at the time, Tony Burden, took the decision to establish Communities First Policing Teams consisting of a sergeant and four constables, in each the seven communities in the South Wales Police area where the wider programme was being applied. Other roles and functions were brought alongside the teams, such as the Schools Liaison officers.

Via these and countless other community engagement initiatives, slowly but surely police and communities in South Wales began healing perceived rifts in the latter part of the twentieth century, forming a strong bedrock for the subsequent introduction nationally of the Neighbourhood Policing Model.

NEIGHBOURHOOD POLICING

During the early 2000s, central UK government made a commitment to invigorate and deliver effective community policing, rebranded as Neighbourhood Policing, to all communities across England and Wales. The aim was to 'make communities feel safe and secure by reducing crime and anti-social behaviour in their area' (Home Office 2006), through the work of visible and accessible Neighbourhood Policing Teams (NPTs) that were responsive to local priorities. The thematic report 'Open All Hours' compiled by Her Majesty's Inspectorate of Constabulary (HMIC) explored a disparity between success in crime reduction and the apparent lack of an equivalent impact on the public's confidence in the police and perceptions of crime, and identified a 'reassurance gap' (HMIC 2001). When asked what would improve their feelings of safety, satisfaction and confidence in the police, surveys consistently highlighted the public's desire for greater levels of foot patrol. Despite earlier commitments to 'beat' policing, an examination of how officers' time was spent (PA Consulting Group 2001) confirmed that most time outside the station had reverted to being spent responding to incidents and making investigative enquiries, and that most officer patrol was carried out in cars. In addition, many other activities were keeping police officers off the beat; making an arrest, for example, could keep an officer in the station for three and a half hours. There appeared to be a gap between the public desire for visible patrol and the ability of the police service to provide that function. Consequently, the issue of how to reassure the public was high on the agenda at this time.

In an attempt to better understand the issue, in 2003 the Home Office funded the pilot National Reassurance Policing Programme (NRPP). The NRPP aimed to examine the reassurance gap – a perception of rising crime whilst recorded crime rates were actually falling. The experimental design underpinning the programme was based on the theoretical construct of the Signal Crimes Perspective (Innes and Fielding 2002; Innes 2014), which suggested that different types of crime and importantly, neighbourhood incivilities such as anti-social behaviour, could have a direct and often disproportionate effect on how citizens think, feel or behave in relation to their security. The NRPP set out to explore whether, by carefully identifying and then targeting these specific issues in different neighbourhood contexts, police and partners could positively impact upon communities' fear of crime, improve confidence in policing and bridge the reassurance gap. As well as the importance of involving communities in identifying these priority problems, the NRPP model also relied upon working alongside other partner agencies and the community itself to co-produce solutions and on maintaining a visible, accessible and familiar policing presence to aid and sustain the process. The Home Office's own evaluation of the programme, conducted in 16 pilot sites across the UK, found positive improvements in public perceptions of crime, social and physical disorder, feelings of fear, safety and confidence in their local police (Tuffin et al. 2006), resulting in a significantly funded national roll out of a new Neighbourhood Policing Model centred around 10 key principles based on the core tenets of the NRPP (ACPO 2006). The successful implementation of the new model involved engaging the public and using local intelligence to target deployment of dedicated Neighbourhood Policing Teams (NPTs). Police Community Support Officers (PCSOs) were to have a key role to play in these local mixed teams that included officers, special constables, community wardens and others which constituted a new form of plural policing.

South Wales Police embraced the new model, creating dedicated NPTs for all ward level neighbourhoods across the force area. After further national evaluation suggested a robustness of implementation was key to the success of the model (Quinton and Morris 2008), the force invested in a significant programme of community engagement utilising Cardiff University's Intelligence-orientated Neighbourhood Security Interview methodology (I-NSI). Based on the Signal Crimes Perspective which had underpinned the NRPP, I-NSI combined one-to-one cognitive interviewing with state-of-the-art GIS (geospatial information system) mapping software, and its use in the SENSOR study (Innes et al. 2007) involved neighbourhood officers soliciting the views of some 746 members of the public across Cardiff to establish the key drivers of neighbourhood insecurity. The process enabled the force to expand their reach in terms of public engagement to better understand what really matters to people when constructing their sense of personal security within their surroundings, and where 'fear of crime' intersected with community intelligence pertaining to the 'what, where and who' of actual crime and disorder within the area. A further roll out of the same methodology across the entire force area followed, and findings enabled South Wales Police NPTs to fully implement the model by tuning into citizens' knowledge and perceptions to inform interventions to improve community wellbeing.

A detailed account of the design, development and delivery of Neighbourhood Policing across England and Wales is provided in Innes et al. (2020). This includes some of the key innovations trialled by South Wales Police, notably around the concept of using community intelligence feeds to steer and direct the organisation and conduct of Neighbourhood interventions in a systematic and structured fashion.

Police Community Support Officers

The introduction of the PCSO role in the Police Reform Act 2002 represented a fundamental shift in police resourcing. The Act extended the role of police staff (personnel employed by a police organisation who do not have the sworn status of a constable) to assist sworn police officers and carry out many front-line roles, giving authority to the chief officer of a police force to designate any person who is employed by the police authority as a

Community Support Officer and confer on that person any of a list of powers given in the Act (a list that has subsequently been expanded through the later legislation).

In order to assist with the introduction of PCSOs, Home Office funds were made available from 2002 onwards and implementation of the PCSO initiative was rapid. The work of PCSOs encouraged community social interaction with the hope of supporting social cohesion (Home Office 2006), thus reducing crime resistant communities. In 2004, 59 PCSOs were initially employed by South Wales Police which was 1.7% of the total PCSOs for England and Wales. By 2019, this figure stood at 374, or nearly 4% of the total for England and Wales (Home Office 2019).

PCSOs were particularly intended to provide a visible, uniformed patrolling presence and to tackle anti-social behaviour, thereby improving the community environment and providing general public 're-assurance'. In relation to improving perceptions of police effectiveness and feelings of safety, increased levels of foot patrols were found to be the most beneficial (Dalgleish and Myhill 2004). However, the introduction of PCSOs was challenging for some PCSO's themselves as well as for colleagues:

> My first supervisor was very anti-PCSO even though he himself was in a community policing team. He saw us as policing on the cheap, taking jobs away from the police officers and that we were 'Blunkett's Bobbies'.
> (PCSO who joined South Wales Police 2006)

Although the sentiments expressed in the quotation above have endured to a greater or lesser extent and persist in some areas to this day, PCSOs have developed a recognised role as the eyes and the ears of the police and are tasked with building relationships with communities. Whilst not universal across England and Wales, acceptance within South Wales Police and the communities they served has been largely achieved and the impact upon dealing with anti-social behaviour has been noticeable in many areas.

> There has been a massive change. People are more aware; most supervisors have to go through NPT

[Neighbourhood Policing Teams] for more involvement and they are now far more aware of what PCSOs do and the value that they add to the whole team.

(PCSO who joined South Wales Police in 2006)

By 2012, the role of the PCSO within Wales was so well established that, when public sector austerity began to bite across the country, the Welsh Government directly funded 500 additional officers to be deployed across each of the four Welsh Forces. Faced with a shrinking workforce as a result of cuts in central government funding, this additional funding allowed for a reconfiguration of South Wales Police's neighbourhood policing presence to ensure a local, visible policing capacity to underline its commitment to the values of community policing (Lowe et al. 2015).

Special constables

The Police Act 1964 is generally considered to be the Act that established the *modern* Special Constabulary.[1] Each force has its own Special Constabulary comprised of volunteers, who commit at least four hours per week to working with and supporting regular police officers. They wear similar uniforms and have the same powers as regular officers. 'Specials', as they are commonly referred to, are also subject to the same rules of conduct and disciplinary procedures as sworn officers. In the past, Specials have been subject to some abuse, being labelled as 'hobby-bobbies' for example (Berry et al. 1998), and experiencing problems surrounding integration and communication with the regular police. Nevertheless, they are representative of their community and have played a vital part in the Neighbourhood Policing approach within South Wales, working alongside NPTs on such activities as local, intelligence-based patrols and crime prevention initiatives, often targeted at specific problem areas. In 1995, there were 477 special constables volunteering in South Wales Police, which represented 40% of all special constables in Wales at this time. However, in line with the trend across England and Wales since that time, this number has declined such that by 2020, there were only 157 special constables in South Wales Police (32%).

Other volunteer schemes

The role of the volunteer in delivering community policing should not be underestimated. Indeed, one of the guiding principles of the Neighbourhood Policing Model is the co-production of solutions to neighbourhood problems between police, partners and the community themselves. Working with volunteers enables local concerns to be explored and solutions implemented, as well as a vehicle for building that trust between police and the communities they serve. South Wales Police since its creation has supported this idea not just through the use of special constables but also through implementation of the following schemes:

- *Police Support Volunteers*; These volunteers are citizen volunteers who complement and support roles in all aspect of police work. Some of the roles already utilised within South Wales Police involve being a victim contact volunteer, crime prevention volunteer, database maintenance volunteer and neighbourhood volunteers.
- *Police Youth Volunteers*; which is part of a nationally recognised scheme and encourages young people to engage in a range of activities. This is aimed at young people aged between 14–18 years, and who want to support their communities. At the time of writing South Wales Police has over 200 volunteers based across the force area.
- *Police Student Volunteers*; For a number of years students from local universities have become proactively involved in keeping their local campuses safe for the benefit of the community and the student population of the campus and student villages.

COMMUNITY REPRESENTATION IN LOCAL POLICING GOVERNANCE

Police authorities

As representatives of communities, police authorities were established by the Police Act 1964. Due to the amalgamation in 1969, the South Wales Police Authority was established by the amalgamation of the relevant authorities from the four forces, namely Glamorgan, Cardiff, Swansea and Merthyr Tydfil. As part of the tripartite agreement of police governance, it had responsibility for policing policy in its area, along with the chief constable and the Home Office (Jones 2008). It was composed of two thirds elected councillors and one third magistrates and whilst it gave local communities some input into the policing process in South Wales through elected officials, it was not until the Police and Criminal Evidence Act 1984 that the establishment of 'local consultative committees' occurred. These were designed to improve discussions between local police commanders and the people in their areas. This Act also allowed for the police to consult the public prior to setting of local policing objectives and to publish local policing plans. However, as time progressed, it was thought that these arrangements did not accord with the ideas of community involvement in the accountability processes for the police, and ultimately were dramatically changed by the Police Reform and Social Responsibility Act 2011.

The Police and Crime Commissioner

The Police Reform and Social Responsibility Act 2011 introduced wide ranging changes to the accountability process of the police by allowing for the introduction of elected Police and Crime Commissioners (PCCs) to replace police authorities outside of London (and for the Mayor's Office for Policing and Crime (MOPAC) to fulfil the PCC role within the Metropolitan Police area). The PCC's core functions are to secure the maintenance of an efficient and effective police force within their area, and to hold the Chief Constable to account for the delivery of a local police and crime plan, developed shortly after their election to office. That plan must include his or her objectives for policing their area, what resources will be provided to the Chief Constable in order to deliver on those objectives and how performance will be measured. To this end, PCCs are charged with holding the police fund (from which all policing of the area is financed) and raising the local policing precept, and are also responsible for the appointment, suspension and dismissal of the Chief Constable. Both the PCC and the Chief Constable must have regard to the police and crime plan in the exercise of their duties, and the PCC is required to produce an annual report for the public on progress in policing, a process involving much more consultation with communities that hitherto. In addition, and in contrast to the role of the previous police authorities, PCCs also have responsibilities which are broader than those relating specifically to policing and their local force, for example crime reduction and engagement with criminal justice agencies in the relevant police area. Given this, and the fact that PCC is an elected office, community consultation and public involvement in policing objectives have become increasingly more significant features in everyday policing across England and Wales over the last decade.

REFLECTING THE COMMUNITY

When considering just what makes a community, there is a tendency to think of 'the community' as one entity, homogeneous and containing people who all think and act alike. However, this is often seen as a contested concept (Cohen 1985) and in reality there are many 'communities' making up the wider citizenry in areas such as South Wales. Many police officers in South Wales Police identify with their 'Welshness', drawing upon perceived cultural characteristics as friendliness and openness, which may explain to some extent, the relationship between police and community in South Wales (Harrison 2020).

As part of the democratic model of policing, a police service should reflect the makeup of the community it represents, and there are several areas within South Wales Police that reflect serious attempts by them to achieve this aim. However, this aspect of policing has always been problematic, as there needs to be a detailed understanding of the communities themselves. Put another way; 'does the service understand if it gets it right on the inside, it may get it right with the outside?' (officer from an ethnic minority group who joined South Wales Police 1982).

At the time of writing, the South Wales Police website[2] describes its approach to establishing a representative workforce as:

> We have a strong commitment to equality and diversity both within the organisation and in the service

we provide. Our aim is to attract, recruit, support and promote talented individuals who represent the diverse communities we serve across South Wales. To value difference we must be inclusive: we recognise that people with a variety of skills, attitudes and experiences, from diverse backgrounds and cultures, bring fresh ideas and perspectives. Encouraging and harnessing these differences can only enhance South Wales Police and we are committed to achieving a workforce that is representative of the communities we serve.

In support of this aim, the force has adopted an approach known as REFLECT,[3] an acronym which stands for:

R   Reflective of the community they serve
E   Expertise and skills from a diverse workforce
F   Future, using the Policing Vision 2025 to promote a more representative workforce
L   Legitimate in how they police their communities
E   Engaged workforce
C   Complex crimes – different policing skills and knowledge in specific communities
T   Trust and confidence in communities will increase

Reflecting the community, part of the community policing idea, means a concerted effort needs to be made to engage with different sections of that community. The history of South Wales Police contains concerted efforts to achieve that engagement.

Ethnic minority groups

Over recent decades, South Wales Police, like many other police forces in England and Wales, has come to realise the disparity in representativeness of members of ethnic minority communities. The murder of Stephen Lawrence in 1993 (Macpherson 1999) highlighted not just this disparity, but also identified a lack of training and education for police officers in terms of diversity, a situation that had been in place for generations. In the 1990s, the then Chief Constable of South Wales Police, Tony Burden, instituted within the training department a unit responsible for diversity training and education for all its officers. Chief Constable Burden was chair of the diversity portfolio for the Association of Chief Police Officers (ACPO), and consequently the Diversity Training Unit was recognised as being one of the best in the country at the time, drawing visitors from many other forces.

In spite of all of these initiatives the reality of working in South Wales Police and their communities for some officers was illuminating.

> It (South Wales Police) didn't know how to deal with the issues of race. How do you engage with communities if you don't know them? It was a big thing, but we didn't know what our communities looked like. We did things which we thought the community wanted.
>
> (Officer who joined South Wales Police in 1982)

However, despite all of the efforts of the force, recruitment of individuals from ethnic minority backgrounds remained a problem. In 2015, South Wales Police was at its lowest representation for this generation and the Office of the Police and Crime Commissioner undertook a thematic review to understand why this was the case. Consequently in 2015, the representative workforce team was established in order to attract, support, recruit and retain staff from a diversity of backgrounds and has had some success, increasing the proportion of the workforce with a minority ethnic background from 3.48 to 3.9% by 2019 (South Wales Police 2020).

In a wider context reflecting the position of the communities in Wales as a whole, the Welsh Language Act 1993 led to an increased profile of the language, including for South Wales Police the signage of buildings, livery on vehicles and a plethora of official forms etc.

Gender balance

From its inception in 1969, the then South Wales Constabulary, in line with other forces in England and Wales, operated with a separate 'policewomen's' department. This reflected many other occupations where women were regarded as being somewhat different to men undertaking the same work, where occupational segregation was legal. Female officers then had a separate rank structure, were often located in separate buildings, and dealt mainly with incidents involving women and children. However, the Equal Pay Act 1970, which came into effect on 29 December 1975 (superseded by the Equality Act 2010) and the Sex Discrimination Act 1975, meant female officers became integrated with their male counterparts in shift work, roles and of course equal pay. The Sex Discrimination Act of 1975 was responsible for the removal of the policewomen's department and shaping a significant amount of what is taken for granted today in the police service. For example, the Act influenced the removal of the 'W' prefix in WPC. For some male officers, equality in terms of doing the job was difficult but they were, nevertheless, perceived in a positive way.

> I have to say that my experiences with male officers were on the whole very positive. Certainly in the early days. The only negatives were the limitations as to what you were allowed to do. There was one female per shift, but if you went to an incident with male colleagues, especially the older colleagues, they would say things like 'stay there, you don't want to get involved in this' or 'you don't want to see this'. I think they thought that a woman shouldn't be in this type of position and were trying to be protective.
>
> (Female South Wales Police officer who joined in 1982)

South Wales Police has continued to improve significantly with regards to the representation of women since those times. In 1989, the first female officer was appointed to the South Wales Police dog section, with female officers being appointed regularly to the CID before that. In 2004, Barbara Wilding was appointed as the first female Chief Constable of South Wales Police. At the time Miss Wilding was co-director for the Police National Assessment Centre for Senior Command, and also oversaw a national mentoring scheme for female superintendents.

In the most recent data from 2020 (Home Office 2020) women make up 32% of the work force, compared to 1985 when the percentage of women in South Wales Police was just 5%, and this increase has been steady and incremental. Whilst this figure falls short of reflecting the latest Census data (2011), which indicates that 51% of the population are female, it is a marked improvement on the data from as recently as 2004/5 which showed just 21% of officers were female. Today female police officers and staff take an active part in every aspect of police life from walking the beat to managing human resources, collaboration with other forces and leading international affairs. South Wales Police has continually recognised their value and contribution, attempting to ensure the force reflects the makeup of the community they police.

Identifying that the community comprises many different individuals and that the police should reflect those differences, South Wales Police has instituted a policy to support those individuals who identify as part of the LGBT community. The policy provides support to any member of South Wales Police who make known they wish to transition from their birth gender to the opposite gender during their employment with South Wales Police.

IMPROVING PERFORMANCE

Whilst South Wales Police has made significant efforts to continually improve its community policing profile it has not always achieved what it set out to in terms of involvement of communities in policing delivery. The 2006 HMIC report on South Wales Policing baseline data (HMIC 2006), for example, highlighted this as an area for improvement with a view of providing a more personal/local function. In addition, the report recommended an increase in feedback to communities at a local level, and that the then current arrangements for reaching hard to hear groups were not necessarily successful. Since that time great strides have been made to recognise these shortcomings with Her Majesty's Inspectorate of Constabulary's Police Effectiveness, Efficiency and Legitimacy (PEEL) report for 2019 stating:

The force recognises the importance of working closely with communities. Officers and staff understand the importance of treating people with fairness and respect. The force has a strong understanding of the threats facing its communities. It is good at protecting the public from harm. (HMICFRS 2019)

Working in the field of community policing is clearly a challenging one, and one that requires constant attention. Police officers are now trained in the process of Problem Oriented Policing (Goldstein 1990), utilising the SARA approach (Scanning, Analysis, Responding and Assessing) to solving a particular problem. This approach has, in some instances, developed into the OSARA approach with the idea being to identify the Objective and then apply the SARA model to solving the problem. The underlying approach relies upon close cooperation between police and community, along with other agencies to solve community problems. However, community involvement in policing, listening to community concerns, representing the community in terms of diversity etc., as well as being clearly held accountable for their actions has been a thread throughout the South Wales Police organisation since its creation in 1969. Changes in society have obviously impacted upon previous attempts to conduct community policing and the future contains many more challenges that could impact upon the community policing approach.

CHALLENGES FOR THE FUTURE

Predicting the future is fraught with danger. The unexpected can suddenly impact upon any environmental planning but there are some areas of the future which can clearly be considered to be more influential than others. Community policing will undoubtedly be influenced by these challenges.

Technology
The impact of social media through innovative use of technology will impact upon perceived ideas concerning interaction between police and communities. Increases in social media use could

mean less direct personal interaction, which could influence the perceived legitimacy of the police in the eyes of the community. The visual icon of the 'Bobby on the Beat', which for many years was seen as a sign of reassurance, may need to be replaced by different approaches to reassurance of communities. Technology provides opportunities for greater engagement with a wider community, but the police organisation itself needs to understand the full impact of its increased use upon their dealings with the public.

Economic pressure

There are, and will be no doubt, increased calls for service for the police in the future. Public finances are not finite, so with the recent mantra of 'doing the same with less' for public services following austerity may be a significant pointer for the future. Sworn officers may be directed to more 'core' valued functions, such as online crime etc. This may mean fewer officers available for community policing functions. However, an opportunity arises for South Wales Police to have greater involvement of volunteers and opening up of police functions hitherto restricted for volunteers, within the framework of the UK Government's policy of increased recruitment of police officers.

Continued diversity of community

Communities continue to diversify with greater movement of people due to economic and social reasons. Increased travel opportunities and travel infrastructures encourage resettlements and people movement. This means South Wales Police will have to ensure they have strategies in place to engage with diverse communities, and also to ensure they have representatives from different groups working for them.

Environmental

Changes in the environment may introduce different demands upon police resources for other pressing matters. However, an increase in partnership work, including engagement with different volunteer groups, may assist in maintaining close working relationships with communities.

Changing nature of demand

As social media rises, different forms of criminality will occur which will mean a possible refocusing of scarce resources. In particular, serious organised crime, the perpetual threat of terrorism and increased cross border crime such as 'county lines' means that resources may be needed to be redirected towards those activities, including an increase in the number of officers allocated to central services. This may mean difficult choices have to be made concerning the use and numbers of community role officers.

The unexpected

This is probably the most difficult challenge to prepare for. For example, the current Covid-19 pandemic, and responses to such, was unexpected, despite the warnings of this potentially happening (Cabinet Office 2017), and has meant great changes to police activities. Stronger environmental scanning at local, national and international level may be required, and a realisation that events at a global level can impact upon the local level. However, a strong community link will make tackling these kinds of issues easier, especially if there are strong partnership links to other agencies.

CONCLUSION

Community policing in South Wales has been part of the overall strategy for delivery of policing services to the community. Since its creation, South Wales Police has prided itself on its local links, its ability to work and live amongst its communities, and be accepted as an integral part of the social structure. In its early days this was achieved through more informal means, dependent upon local knowledge, good use of discretion and its officers living amongst the communities themselves. Whilst structures existed for community initiatives such as bike stamping etc., at a local level, it was only later that more structured attempts at initiatives such as Splash were organised at a force level. The force is now far better organised in community engagement, consultation and accountability. Changes over time in organisational structures and demands placed upon the police, coupled with demographic and other variations, have seen the introduction of many modifications to the delivery of policing. Despite that there has been a growth in community engagement, trust in the use of volunteers, and brave attempts to ensure that a diverse community is well represented amongst the officers and staff of South Wales Police. However, it is vital for South Wales Police that they are able to identify and represent the many forms of communities that exist. The future will bring many challenges for police organisations in terms of community policing. However, the history of South Wales Police suggests that tackling these challenges can be made easier by working with and through communities and by being supportive of its community policing function.

Notes

1. The idea of special police is much older than the Police Act of 1964, and this historical context is worthy of note in order to understand the reasons behind the importance of the volunteer police officer's role.
2. *https://www.south-wales.police.uk/police-forces/south-wales-police/areas/careers/careers/working-towards-a-representative-workforce/* (accessed 26 May 2022).
3. South Wales Police (2020), The Reflect Initiative, internal South Wales Police data.

References

1964. Police Act. *1964, c48.* Available at: *https://www.legislation.gov.uk/ukpga/1964/48/contents*

1970. Equal Pay Act. *1970, c. 41.* Available at: *https://www.legislation.gov.uk/ukpga/1970/41/enacted*

1975. Sex Discrimination Act. *1975, c65.* Available at: *https://www.legislation.gov.uk/ukpga/1975/65/enacted*

1984. The Police and Criminal Evidence Act. *1984, c60.* Available at: *https://www.legislation.gov.uk/ukpga/1984/60/contents*

1993. Welsh Language Act. *1993, c38.* Available at: *https://law.gov.wales/culture/welsh-language/welsh-language-act-1993*

2011. The Police Reform and Social Responsibility Act. *2011, c. 13.* Available at: *https://www.legislation.gov.uk/ukpga/2011/13/contents/enacted*

Association of Chief Police Officers (ACPO). 2006. *Practice advice on professionalising the business of neighbourhood policing.* Wyboston: Centrex. Available at: *library.college.police.uk/docs/acpo/ Professionalising-NeighbourhoodPolicing.pdf*

Berry, G., Izat, J., Mawby, R., Walley, L. and Wright, A. 1998. *Practical police management.* London: Police Review Publishing Co.

Cabinet Office. 2017. *National Risk Register 2017.* Available at: *https:// www.gov.uk/government/publications/national-risk-register-of-civil-emergencies-2017-edition* (accessed 5 October 2020).

Cohen, S. 1985. *Visions of social control.* Oxford: Blackwells.

Dalgleish, D. and Myhill, A. 2004. *Reassuring the public: a review of international policing interventions.* London: Available at: *http:// citeseerx.ist.psu.edu/viewdoc/download?doi=10.1.1.604.1940&rep =rep1&type=pdf*

Goldstein, H. 1990. *Problem-oriented policing.* New York: McGraw-Hill.

Greene, J. 2000. 'Community policing in America: changing the nature, structure and function of the police'. In: Horney, J. ed. *Criminal Justice 2000: policies, processes, and decisions of the criminal justice system.* Washington D.C.: U.S. Department of Justice.

Harrison, M. 2020. *A case study analysis of how public order policing is interpreted and practised in South Wales.* University of South Wales.

HMIC. 2001. *Open all hours: a thematic inspection report on the role of police visibility and accessibility in public reassurance.* London: Her Majesty's Chief Inspector of Constabulary.

HMIC. 2006. *South Wales Police: baseline assessment.* Her Majesty's Chief Inspector of Constabulary. Available at: *https://www. justiceinspectorates.gov.uk/hmicfrs/media/south-wales-baseline-assessment-20060929.pdf*

HMICFRS. 2019. *PEEL: Police effectiveness, efficiency and legitimacy 2018/19: An inspection of South Wales Police.* Available at: *https://www. justiceinspectorates.gov.uk/hmicfrs/wp-content/uploads/peel-assessment-2018-19-south-wales.pdf* (accessed 28 July 2023).

Home Office. 1984. *Joint departmental circular on crime prevention.* Home Office, Department of Education and Science, Department of Health and Social Security and Department of the Environment. Available at: *https://depositedpapers.parliament.uk/ depositedpaper/2201265/details*

Home Office. 2006. *Crime and cohesive communities: research, development and statistics*. London: The Stationery Office. Available at: *http://citeseerx.ist.psu.edu/viewdoc/download?doi=10.1.1.510.6857 &rep=rep1&type=pdf*

Home Office. 2019. *Police workforce, England and Wales*. Available at: *https://assets.publishing.service.gov.uk/government/uploads/system/ uploads/attachment_data/file/831726/police-workforce-mar19- hosb1119.pdf* (accessed 5 October 2020).

Home Office. 2020. *Police workforce, England and Wales*. Available at: *https://assets.publishing.service.gov.uk/government/uploads/system/ uploads/attachment_data/file/955182/police-workforce-mar20- hosb2020.pdf* (accessed 8 July 2022).

Innes, M. 2014. *Signal crimes: social reactions to crime, disorder and control*. Oxford: Oxford University Press.

Innes, M., Abbott, L., Lowe, T., Roberts, C. and Weston, N. 2007. *Signal events, neighbourhood security, order and reassurance in Cardiff*. Cardiff: Cardiff University.

Innes, M., Roberts, C., Lowe, T. and Innes, H. 2020. *Neighbourhood policing: the rise and fall of a policing model*. Oxford: Oxford University Press.

Innes, M. and Fielding, N. 2002. 'From community to communicative police: "Signal crimes" and the problem of public reassurance'. *Sociological Research Online* 7(2). Available at: *http://www. socresonline.org.uk/7/2/Innes.html*

Jones, D. J. V. 1996. *Crime and policing in the twentieth century: the South Wales experience*. Cardiff: University of Wales Press.

Jones, T. 2008. *Handbook of policing*. Cullompton: Willan.

Lord Scarman. 1981. *The Scarman report*. Harmondsworth: Penguin.

Lowe, T., Innes, H., Innes, M. and Grinnell, D. 2015. *The work of Welsh Government funded Community Support Officers*. Cardiff: Welsh Government. Available at: *https://orca.cardiff.ac.uk/id/eprint/88880/ 1/150226-wg-funded-community-support-officers-en.pdf*

Macpherson, W. 1999. *The Stephen Lawrence Inquiry*. London: Stationery Office.

Michaelson, S., Kelling, G. and Wasserman, R. 1988. *Toward a working definition of community policing*. Cambridge, MA: John F Kennedy School of Government.

PA Consulting Group. 2001. *Diary of a police officer, Home Office research report*. London: Home Office.

Quinton, P. and Morris, J. 2008. *Neighbourhood policing: the impact of piloting and early national implementation*. London: Home Office. Available at: *https://www.bl.uk/collection-items/neighbourhood-policing-the-impact-of-piloting-and-early-national-implementation*

Rogers, C. 2004. 'From Dixon to Z Cars – the introduction of unit beat policing in England and Wales'. *Police History Journal* (19), pp. 10–14.

Rogers, C. 2007. *Policing the miners' strike. The crime of our lives*. BBC Radio 4.

South Wales Constabulary. 1984–5. *Annual Report of the Chief Constable 1984 and Annual Report of the Chief Constable 1985*. Glamorgan Archives. Available at: *http://calmview.cardiff.gov.uk/TreeBrowse.aspx?src=CalmView.Catalog&field=RefNo&key=DSWP%2f16*

South Wales Constabulary. 1990. *Splash 90, programme of events*. Bridgend: South Wales Police.

South Wales Police. 1991. *Communicating with youth: schools liaison officers*. Bridgend: South Wales Police.

South Wales Police. 2020. *Working towards a representative workforce*. Available at: *https://www.South-Wales.police.uk/en/join-us/working-towards-a-representative-workforce/* (accessed 28 July 2020).

Tilley, N. 2008. 'Community policing'. In: Newburn, T. and Neyroud, P. eds. *Dictionary of policing*. Cullompton: Willan.

Trojanowicz, R. C. 1983. 'An evaluation of a neighbourhood foot patrol programme'. *Journal of Police Science and Administration* 11(4), pp. 410–19.

Trojanowicz, R. C. 1986. 'Evaluating a neighbourhood foot patrol programme: The Flint Michigan Project'. In: Rosenbaum, D.P. ed. *Community crime prevention*. Beverly Hills: Sage, pp. 157–78.

Tuffin, R., Morris, J. and Poole, A. 2006. *An evaluation of the impact of the National Reassurance Policing Programme*. London: Home Office. Available at: *http://doc.ukdataservice.ac.uk/doc/7450/mrdoc/pdf/7450_hors296.pdf*

7

HOMICIDE AND MAJOR CRIME INVESTIGATIONS

Cheryl Allsop and Mark O'Shea

Criminal homicide, as the archetypal major crime, exerts a peculiar and particular pull on the public, political and police 'imaginations'. For police, responding to and investigating homicides is central to their organisational self-identities, and the stories they tell themselves about themselves. As Peter Manning (1997), amongst several other learned commentators on policing, have pointed out, murder investigation is freighted with a particular symbolic load, that feeds back into the resource and normative investments police organisations make in investigating fatal violence. In part this is because of how where much police work involves 'negotiating order' in terms of dealing with frequently 'messy', ambiguous and contingent disputes between citizens, criminal homicide has a certain degree of clarity. Someone is dead, the causes need to be identified, and persons held responsible and accountable for their actions.

That this is so, links to the importance that major crime assumes in the politics of policing. Everyone connected to policing is aware that although there are clear patterns to fatal violence, in that most cases involve persons known to each other rather than strangers, almost every case has the potential to function as a 'signal crime'. That is an incident that changes how people, individually, collectively and institutionally think about risks to their sense of safety and security (Innes 2014). Indeed, the politics of policing and the criminal justice system very often pivots around major crime cases. This can be in the sense that when cases involving especially egregious harms are 'solved' by police this can deliver significant public reassurance. But equally, in the small minority of cases where a prime suspect is not identified, or mis-identified, this can have a negative impact on public legitimacy.

This 'signal crime' status also shapes and influences how and why media reporting about police work very often pivots around homicide cases. Successive generations of studies on press and broadcast media have documented how reportage about murder and manslaughter consumes a disproportionate amount of journalistic attention. The combination of danger, harm and drama resulting from the police pursuit of individuals who have clearly infringed society's moral code, are the ideal ingredients for journalists to tell stories that they know will interest the majority of their readers. Equally however, these are also the staple ingredients for much crime fiction, wherein both written and broadcast accounts of the work of the police overwhelmingly pivot around their role in answering the essential question of such genres of 'whodunnit'.

There is then something of a mismatch between the amount of cultural attention directed to criminal homicides and their investigation, and the frequency with which such things happen 'in real life'. The nature of which is highlighted by examining some data relating to South Wales. Figures released by the Office for National Statistics suggest that on average South Wales has a slightly higher rate of homicides than is the case for Wales, and England and Wales more generally. Based upon data for the year April 2019–March 2020 there were 14.2 homicides per million in South Wales, this compares with a figure of 12.4 for Wales as a whole, and a high in the Gwent police force area of 19.2 (and low in North Wales of 5.4). The same figure for England and Wales was 11.7.

Such figures, however, tend to mask the fact that, as is the case nationally, homicide remains a rare occurrence. With a generally low base number, even small increases in the number of cases can give the impression of dramatic shifts. This is conveyed if we look at the data in Table 7.1 below, that sets out the number of incidents recorded as homicide in the South Wales Police force area for the past eight years (Office for National Statistics 2022).

Table 7.1: Crimes recorded as homicide in South Wales by year (from April-March)

Year	2012–13	2013–14	2014–15	2015–16	2016–17	2017–18	2018–19	2019–20
Number	12	5	9	17	15	10	10	19

What is striking about such data is the overall low numbers of cases that we are talking about and the fluctuations that can occur year-on-year. Layered on top of which, is the well evidenced empirical finding (rehearsed above) that stranger homicides are rare. This combination of factors feeds into the overall 'demand profile' for homicides that South Wales Police deal with, in terms of their Major Crime Unit. Most such cases conform to the pattern of what Innes (2003) labelled as 'self-solving' investigations, where the identity of the prime suspect is fairly evident at an early stage. As such, the principal focus of the investigators' work in such cases is ensuring the construction of a case that proves beyond 'reasonable doubt' that the individual identified, should be held legally responsible for the acts that they are accused of. Consequently, what Innes (2003) labels 'whodunnit' investigations comprise only a minority of major crime incidents that South Wales Police process each year.

This notwithstanding, whilst the majority of South Wales's major crime investigations result in a suspect being apprehended and convicted, on occasions things do, and have, gone wrong. This can be in terms of being able to identify a suspect, or secure sufficient evidence to obtain a conviction, or most troublingly, prosecuting and/or convicting the wrong individuals. As South Wales Police has experienced across its history, when such issues do arise, they can have an 'outsized' impact upon organizational reputation. This chapter investigates all of these issues.

THE ESSENTIALS

In 2008, Her Majesty's Inspectorate of Constabulary defined a 'major crime' as any incident where the policing response requires the appointment of a Senior Investigating Officer (SIO) and the deployment of specialist resources (HMIC 2008). Thus, 'major crime' in its broadest official definition, encompasses the most serious crimes of violence and death, sexual violence, kidnapping and arson. It is the role of the SIO to lead the investigation, set the strategic direction the investigation must take, and make strategic decisions. In what follows, we principally focus the discussion around the investigation of homicide.

Homicide investigations are structured and organised differently to most other types of crime enquiries, as is the volume of resources deployed. It is very much a 'team' effort, as opposed to the more individualistic nature of much detective work. Day-to-day management of a major crime investigation may be delegated to a Deputy SIO, or Office Manager dependent on the size and complexity of the investigation. The Officer in Charge (OIC) is usually designated to prepare the case file. These roles are defined within the Major Incident Room Standardised Administrative Procedures (MIRSAP), which are the standardised governance arrangements used in England and Wales to manage major crime enquiries.

The Major Incident Room (MIR) is the hub of the investigation where information coming into the investigation is received, reviewed, and processed with the Outside Enquiries Team progressing specific 'actions' allocated, including for example, conducting house to house enquiries (Innes 2007). Specialist resources deployed will depend on the particular circumstances and complexities of the crime, but often include crime scene managers, forensic investigators, media support and, increasingly, digital technology experts.

Comparatively little has been written by academics about these most serious of crimes and especially how they are investigated. That which is known suggests that investigations are information work (Ericson 1982, 1993; Manning 1997, Innes 2003), bureaucratic endeavours (Ericson 1993) investigated by detectives drawing on entrepreneurial skills (Ericson 1993;

Manning 1997; Innes 2003), albeit, as Fox (2014) contends, stifled by bureaucracy and endless guidance. Achieving procedural success is seen as important as the case outcome, in homicide investigations (Brookman and Innes 2013). Innes (2003) and Brookman et al. (2020) consider how detectives and forensic experts construct and adjust narratives of the homicide event to make sense of the information in an investigation.

Investigations have also been considered both an 'art' and a 'craft', with detectives drawing on intuition borne of experience (Repetto 1978). This can be contrasted with rhetorics accenting 'the science' of investigations, both in terms of using forensic science techniques, and technologies to identify and connect suspects to the crimes and in following defined processes and procedures (Innes 2003; Tong et al. 2009; James 2013; O'Neill 2018). Many though have found that forensic science does not solve most crimes (McCartney 2006; Brodeur 2010; Brown and Keppel 2012). Conversely, Roycroft (2007) and Brookman et al. (2018) found science and technology to be vital to the success of homicide investigations. This is especially so in cold case homicide and stranger rape investigations (Allsop 2017; 2018).

Smith and Flanaghan (2000) document 'twenty-two skills' required to be an effective detective SIO, which can be grouped into investigative abilities, knowledge skills and management skills. Stelfox (2009) notes that whilst there have been many technological, legal, and procedural changes to the investigation of major crime, it is still the inherent skills of individuals who will solve these crimes, making training important. In their aforementioned 2008 examination of Major Crime Capability, the HMIC stated: 'The development of skilled investigators remains fundamental to ensuring an effective response on major crime' (HMIC 2008, p. 13).

Coherent with which, South Wales Police have invested heavily in detective training and are at the forefront of SIO training, regularly running Senior Investigating Officer (SIO) courses, and very early on investing in Hydra[1] with all training now done on it. Indeed, South Wales Police has successfully 'detected' all of the confirmed murders in its area over the last twenty years; despite the complexities of many of them. This, in large measure is due to a long-term investment in detective development programmes as a result of national initiatives and a determination by South Wales Police to learn lessons from errors which have occurred in some cases in the past.

If the period since the formation of the force in 1969 is considered, South Wales Police have investigated over 700 homicides and, in line with the detection rate for police forces in the rest of England and Wales, have solved around 90% of them, although, as will be seen, some investigations have not been without controversy.

What such performance statistics cannot capture however, is what has been going on 'behind the scenes'. Notably, modern murder investigations have become far more complex, not least because of the expansion of technology and the ever-growing interconnectivity of people's lives; developments that routinely pose challenges for detectives to unravel. Yet despite these more complex and challenging investigations more homicides, in particular, are being solved, by learning from what has gone before and through maximising developments in forensic science.

However, this trajectory of increasing complexity is not just attributable to technology. For there have been equally important 'social drivers' of change in terms of how major crimes are investigated. One especially important development in this regard has been increasing recognition of the impact which crimes, especially those involving death, have on victims and those close to them (Rock 2004). Inflected by wider and deeper shifts in the recognition of victims' rights, police investigators have become increasingly aware of the need to establish an empathetic relationship with those directly affected by a crime, whilst at the same time maintaining the necessary levels of independence and objectivity. It is against this backdrop that new roles such as Family Liaison Officers have been introduced into Major Investigation teams. These are officers trained with specialist practical and administrative skills to assist in dealing with those suffering the consequences of the most harmful crimes. It has been found that such roles can be helpful to those suffering the pains of the crime, but can also, more pragmatically, improve the quality of information that flows into the investigation from those close to the victims. Not dissimilar considerations and pressures have been involved in the development of Independent Advisory Groups (IAG). But whereas the Family Liaison Officer role is primarily concerned with gathering evidence and information to help the SIO with the investigation and helping to manage the impacts on individuals directly affected, the focus of IAGs is more strategic and directed more to managing 'collective' community-level impacts. This can be especially important where there are issues of community concern or tension, resulting either from the nature of the crime or from the police investigation itself. Operating at a strategic level, IAGs can advise an SIO in these very particular cases, with an independent PIP 4 SIO[2] being the strategic interface between the SIO in charge of the investigation and the Gold Command group.

To understand how and why these 'social' and more technologically driven reforms came to be, in the next section, we examine the history of major crime investigations in South Wales. This in turn, sets up an exploration of some of the more problematic cases that have been encountered, and the learning and reforms that have resulted.

HISTORICAL LEGACIES

During the 1970s, detectives had very limited investigative options available to them compared to the techniques and technologies available now, and that have been outlined above. There was no HOLMES – the Home Office Large Major Enquiry System – used to store and process information in homicide investigations today. Investigations were managed using index cards and paper systems, so it is little wonder information was lost[3] (Allsop 2018). The investigative doctrines outlined in the Murder Investigation Manual had yet to be codified and there were no major incident room standardised administration procedures (MIRSAP) to follow.

That said, South Wales Police was able to record as 'solved' the vast majority of its murder cases and it is apparent in looking back at these, that whilst investigators didn't have the benefit of so many of the techniques which are now available, they were able to follow processes which, in their own way, sought to achieve the same ethical, successful outcomes. One thing which has not, however, changed is the pressure to obtain results and the risk that this gives rise to flawed investigations and potentially miscarriages of justice.

Maintaining an archive of historic cases gives South Wales Police a unique research ability and the chance to review these crimes years later. What is also evident is the absence of much of what is relied upon in today's investigations. Technologies including CCTV, now often used to prove or disprove alibis when CCTV cameras put the victim and offender together, and Automatic Number Plate Recognition (ANPR), which provides the means, among other things, to plot the journeys of suspect vehicles, had not yet been introduced. Nor had mobile phones, which are now routinely used by detectives to pinpoint the location of the phone, and by extension the phone holder, as well as contacts and communications between potential suspects. In addition, there were no computer systems to manage investigations. Detective training was also limited, often to 'just learning on the job' (Allsop and Pike 2019). Investigations were then focused on identifying suspects and witnesses and questioning them until either the suspect confessed, or sufficient information was provided to prove guilt. Little wonder then that cases were difficult to solve and that miscarriages of justice could occur.

Forensic science capabilities were also limited, largely constrained to fingerprints and blood grouping, which could eliminate suspects, but could not necessarily implicate them, given how common some blood groups are. Yet, though extremely limited, we will see how, years later as forensic science and DNA profiling techniques have improved, many crimes have been detected because investigators collected and retained samples from crime scenes. Two murders from 1973 are a case in point. The murders of Geraldine Hughes and Pauline Floyd, two young women who were murdered after a night out in Swansea, remained undetected for almost 30 years until 2001 when Joseph Kappen was identified through Familial DNA searching.[4] DNA profiling was not available at the time of the murders but years later, following advances in profiling techniques, a DNA profile from biological material collected from the crime scenes at the time, was obtained. While the offender was not on the National DNA Database (NDNAD), he was identified when his son's DNA profile, which was on the database as a result of a conviction for a minor offence, was found to be closely similar to the crime scene profile. Kappen had by then died but his body was exhumed and he was later confirmed as the killer.

1980-99 OPPORTUNITIES AND CHALLENGES

The development of DNA profiling for forensic purposes, has been a major development in criminal investigations, and began in the latter part of the 1980s. Detectives in Leicester investigating the murder of Lynda Mann in 1983 and Dawn Ashworth in 1986 contacted Alec Jeffreys, a scientist based at Leicester University, who was working on a new technique known as DNA finger-printing for paternity testing, to understand whether it could be used in their investigation. A local man Richard Buckland had confessed to one of the murders and detectives wanted to know if this new DNA fingerprinting could identify him as the offender. Jeffreys produced a profile that confirmed that the same man had murdered both girls, but that man was not Richard Buckland. Mass voluntary DNA swabbing also failed to identify the offender. It was not until a man was overheard saying that he had given a swab for Colin Pitchfork, that the offender was finally identified, when detectives contacted Pitchfork to obtain a voluntary swab from him. His DNA profile matched the profiles from the crime scene and in 1987 Pitchfork was convicted of the two murders. Since then, forensic science techniques and technologies have expanded exponentially.

The murder of Karen Price demonstrates the value of these scientific advances and how South Wales Police embraced the opportunities available to them, particularly to detect previously unsolved crimes. Karen was fifteen years of age when she went missing from a residential children's home in Pontypridd in July 1981. Her skeletal remains, wrapped in a carpet, were found by workmen buried at the rear of a house in Cardiff in December 1989.

Despite being a child when she went missing, her details were inadvertently removed from the missing persons database, meaning her disappearance was not fully investigated. Today no-one is removed from the database until they are confirmed to be found. Karen was ultimately identified, and a conviction secured for her murder, after South Wales Police drew upon several forms of expertise, including forensic analysis of insect larvae found in the carpet and facial reconstruction of Karen which was used in media appeals. This led to Karen being recognized and her identity could then be confirmed through DNA which matched DNA taken from her parents.

Alongside noting such success it is important to recall that the 1980s saw three cases of miscarriage of justice, which posed considerable challenges to the reputation of South Wales Police. They provided a catalyst for changes which are referred to later.

The first case was that of the murder of sex shop manageress Sandra Phillips in Swansea in 1985. A major police investigation followed as a result of which two brothers, Wayne and Paul Darvell, were later convicted of the murder. Subsequently, amid concerns about the safety of the convictions, Devon and Cornwall Police undertook a full review of it on behalf of South Wales Police. This resulted in the Home Secretary referring it to the Court of Appeal, and the convictions were set aside as being unsafe due, amongst other things, to improperly obtained confession evidence. Three South Wales Police officers were tried and acquitted of criminal offences in respect of the investigation. It is important to note that the case was a hybrid one in relation to the Police and Criminal Evidence Act 1984. The Act, designed to provide safeguards for the arrest and detention of suspects, was not in force when the investigation took place, but was when the Court of Appeal considered the safety of the convictions.

The second case concerned the murder of newsagent Phillip Saunders in Cardiff in 1987. Three men, Michael O'Brien, Ellis Sherwood and Darren Hall, were later convicted of the murder. Again, there emerged concerns as to the safety of the convictions because of the unreliability of confession evidence amongst other matters. In this case, Thames Valley Police undertook a review that resulted in a referral to the Court of Appeal which quashed the convictions largely on the basis of breaches of the Police and Criminal Evidence Act. In later years, there were a number of subsequent legal challenges to the way in which the case had been investigated and prosecuted, including claims for damages by O'Brien and Sherwood, which were settled by South Wales Police.

The third case is the most complex, protracted and infamous of the three.

Lynette White was a sex worker in Cardiff who was murdered on 14 February 1988. Five men – John Actie, Ronnie Actie, Stephen Miller, Tony Paris and Yusef Abdullahi – were charged with the murder and stood trial. The Acties were acquitted, whilst the other three were convicted.

Concerns were raised as to the safety of the convictions and, on referral to the Court of Appeal in 1992, they were quashed, largely because of breaches of the Police and Criminal Evidence Act. In a landmark judgement, the Court found that the confession of Miller was inadmissible due to oppressive interviewing by police officers over a lengthy period of time. In doing so, the Court benefitted from the tape recording of interviews, which had been introduced shortly before the investigation, and listened to key parts of the interviews with Miller.

The quashing of the convictions was merely the beginning of many years of scrutiny, challenge, reviews, investigations and legal actions. Whilst space does not permit a detailed examination of all of these matters, they include: the re-investigation of the murder and the conviction of Jeffrey Gafoor for it; the settlement by South Wales Police of claims for damages by the Acties, Miller, Paris and Abdullahi; the prosecution and conviction of key witnesses who gave perjured evidence at the original trial; the prosecution, and acquittal, of police officers involved in the original investigation; and a review of the collapse of the latter prosecution.

The impact of these cases cannot be overstated. As has been mentioned, they were the driving force behind initiatives by South Wales Police to establish structured systems of case reviews, and of investigative training.

CHANGES TO THE LEGAL LANDSCAPE

What is especially significant about the Saunders and White cases is that, as mentioned, they occurred after the Police and Criminal Evidence Act 1984 (PACE) came into force in 1986. PACE was designed to prevent miscarriages of justice by balancing police powers with suspects rights, including limiting the length of time suspects can be questioned and detained, and for vulnerable suspects to have access to an appropriate adult.

The Act, and the Codes of Practice made under it, replaced the wholly inadequate and widely criticised Judges' Rules on police questioning of suspects. It's likely that in the early days of PACE, detectives who had been used to the latitude of the previous regime found difficulty in implementing the comprehensive checks and balances of the new system. That said, it could be argued that the Saunders and White cases were signal examples of the Act's effectiveness, albeit at the point of appeal.

Another legal development that had a considerable effect on the police was the creation of the Crown Prosecution Service, also in 1986. The conduct of criminal prosecutions by an independent body, rather than the police themselves, marked a fundamental change to the criminal justice system.

Allied to this there is little doubt that over the years the judiciary became far more interventionist in criminal proceedings, by, for example, upholding challenges to alleged improprieties in the obtaining of evidence and holding the prosecution to account in relation to the disclosure of evidence.

Legal and procedural changes continued into the 1990s with the passing of the Criminal Procedure and Investigations Act 1996 (CPIA). It is designed to further improve investigative practices and places a legal duty on investigators to disclose all relevant material gathered, and to explore all reasonable lines of enquiry. The Human Rights Act also came into force in 1998.

LEARNING FROM THE PAST

In 1999, in light of the challenges to major crime investigation which had arisen, notably from those cases referred to above, the then Chief Constable, Sir Anthony Burden, made the decision to establish a Major Crime Review Unit (MCRU) with a brief to examine, in particular, all unsolved cases. In addition, external reviewers, often retired police officers from other forces, were used to undertake reviews as happened in the Lynette White case.

Sir Anthony's leadership on reviewing past cases and improving the selection and training of detectives was supplemented by the key role played by Assistant Chief Constable Tony Rogers, who chaired the Association of Chief Police Officers Homicide Working Group and led on the development of its Murder Investigation Manual.

Whilst it was necessary for firm and decisive action to be taken to meet the criticisms of South Wales Police made by the judiciary, elected representatives, the media and those wrongly convicted, it must be borne in mind that the problems which had arisen were not unique to South Wales. The miscarriages of justice in relation to the Birmingham Six and Guildford Four, in addition to the activities of the West Midlands Serious Crime Squad, also played a part in a gradual re-appraisal of police investigative techniques and the ethical standards required for investigations and prosecutions.

Of the cases mentioned in South Wales it is the Lynette White case which had the biggest impact. As has been referred to earlier, officers involved in the original investigation were, in due course, prosecuted for offences such as perverting the course of justice. Those prosecutions in the case known as *R v Mouncher*, collapsed at trial in 2011, due mainly to failures in the process of disclosure of documents to the defence. There were calls for a public inquiry into the failure of the prosecution, but the Home Office resisted them and instead appointed Richard Horwell QC, a leading criminal barrister, to examine the case. He made a number of recommendations in his report in 2017, particularly regarding the handling of unused material.

COLD CASE REVIEWS - MAKING USE OF SCIENTIFIC ADVANCES

Establishing the MCRU demonstrates how South Wales Police have reflected on and learned from the past. With the introduction of DNA profiling and subsequent advances in profiling techniques and technologies, especially the introduction of the National DNA Database (NDNAD) in 1995, which now enables crime scene and offender profiles to be databased and new DNA profiles compared against those on the database, South Wales

Police MCRU have been able to detect six out of thirteen unsolved murders. These successes include finally catching the killer of Lynette White. Despite the controversy of the investigation, it was a cold case review of the investigation in 2002 that resulted in the offender, Jeffrey Gafoor, finally being convicted of Lynette's murder. In so doing, reinforcing the value of having in place a robust and well-resourced review process, including a dedicated review team, learning from the past and being open to having unsuccessful investigations looked at again.

In 2000, South Wales Police were at the forefront of cold case review work when Operation Moscow was established, in this instance to detect unsolved stranger rapes through advances in DNA profiling techniques (Police Standards Unit 2005). Operation Moscow resulted in twelve detections, eleven arrests and three convictions, two of which were serial offenders. In addition, thirty-seven DNA profiles were added to the NDNAD such that, if these offenders offend again, the match to the earlier crime scenes will provide new investigative opportunities (Lloyd-Evans and Bethell 2009). DNA profiles added to the NDNAD from historic crime scenes following reviews will enable previously undetected rapes to be solved years later, and shows the investment South Wales Police have placed in detecting serious crimes. Today stranger rapes are still being detected because of the investment made in Operation Moscow – in 2019, Anthony Carling was convicted for a rape he committed in 1991 in Cardiff.

Until it was closed down in 2012, the Forensic Science Service (FSS) was also pivotal to the success of many of the cold cases that were reviewed. The FSS had retained the crime scene samples pertaining to the crimes and as new forensic techniques were developed, they were able to work closely with the review team to identify cases to be progressed. While many items have been retained in the forensic archives, the knowledge these scientists had of the cases has been lost and the continued success now relies on building and retaining strong working relationships with private forensic science providers.

On the back of the many cold case successes South Wales Police had achieved, and in recognition of the value of learning from past cases, and from other detectives doing similar work, the

Head of the Major Crime Review Unit set up the Major Crime Review Network. This enables review officers and detectives to learn from each other through the regional review network and the national review conference. South Wales Police has proudly hosted a national review officers conference for fifteen years. A gathering of over one hundred senior detectives from across UK and European law enforcement agencies, along with forensic specialists, share best practice and professional learning in the field of cold case investigations.

CONCLUSION: LOOKING TO THE FUTURE

When investigating major crimes, to both capture and make sense of the complexity of interlocking sources of information and intelligence, South Wales Police relies upon the HOLMES system supported by Niche RMS. Looking to the future, these data storage and management platforms will require continued investment to grow in capability and respond to future challenges. It is envisaged that artificial intelligence software will supplement investigative systems and aid detectives in filtering and prioritising large data sets. The ability to adapt to this changing landscape will be as important going forward as it has been to learn from the past.

In recent years, the major crime department has already learnt to adapt to the changing crime patterns when challenged to investigate hitherto unseen homicide types. For example, murders motivated by criminal vendetta often come with complex intelligence pictures stretching across multiple policing jurisdictions. These sorts of investigations pose new challenges for South Wales Police, in common with many colleagues across the UK. The movement of urban street gangs from big metropolitan areas into smaller towns and cities to exploit untapped drug markets, brings new threats to South Wales. The recent murders of Lynford Brewster, Fahad Nur and Harry Baker all have their origins in the 'county lines' crime problem, where young men are exploited into dealing drugs by criminal gangs, getting caught in the crossfire of drugs warfare.

Most SIOs recognise that investigating a murder is often part investigative science and part police 'craft'. The 'human aspects' of investigating homicides has always been, and will continue to be, the most important element of any incident room. South Wales Police has learnt in the past 50 years the real benefit of having well trained and motivated detectives, led by experienced SIOs in its major crime department.

Having trained and experienced senior detectives leading murder enquiries brings focus and rigour to an incident room. Equally important, is the understanding that the 'room' must also contain trained and experienced detectives who are able to further the 'human aspects' of policing a major enquiry. A 'coppers instinct' learnt during a career of observing and interacting with a myriad of differing individuals, often affords an almost 'instinctive' sense that something or someone is 'not right'.

This police 'craft' is learnt from thousands of human interactions that most major crime detectives have before they are entrusted with a role within an incident room. The investigative 'craft' in being able to elicit information from reluctant or intimidated witnesses, has all too often, made the difference in a murder case. For example, the murder of Christine James saw the case breaking event arising from a traditional house-to-house enquiry and the instinct of one officer that the occupier seemed suspicious. This experiential learning is balanced by the formal training of detectives in the principles outlined in the Core Investigative Doctrine and the Murder Manual.

The future success of South Wales Police's major crime department requires them to learn the lessons of the past whilst continuing to scan horizons for future investigative opportunities and emergent challenges. South Wales Police has learnt that investing in detective training and continued professional development programmes allows them to grow a cadre of detectives that have the capability to take on the most complex of crimes. Keeping those officers and police staff 'well' whilst undertaking those duties requires focus on their mental and physical health. Dealing with the killing of another human being is often an exposure to the most depraved and undesirable aspects of humankind. For detectives exposed to trauma and tragedy on a frequent basis the investment that South Wales Police makes in their wellbeing will ensure the maintenance of an effective detective cadre.

The interconnectivity of people's lives continues to open new avenues for investigators to follow. The SIOs of the next two decades will have to make sense of large data sets obtained from the connected devices that people will carry with them every day. Smart devices that communicate with each other throughout the day, will provide rich seams of evidence for the detectives of tomorrow. There is a continuing challenge to making sense of 'big data' and compartmentalising different data sets in such a way that juries can understand and digest. The investigative challenge of ethically assessing and disclosing unused material in a digital age adhering to the principles set out in the Criminal Procedure and Investigations Act (1996) requires continued focus and investment.

Continuing advances in forensic sciences means techniques for the recovery of DNA are becoming far more sensitive and discriminatory in nature. The importance of maintaining the integrity of a crime scene from cross contamination has never been more important. The 'chain of evidence' from a crime scene to a laboratory and into a courtroom is subject of intense scrutiny, particularly in homicide cases. Defence advocates pay particular attention to the audit and handling of key exhibits. The sensitivities of the next generation in DNA sequencing will identify hitherto undetectable evidence, whilst bringing new complexity to the role of crime scene manager. The retesting of exhibits in as yet undetected cases remains a focus for South Wales Police and the professional practice that has grown from the Major Crime Review Unit has led to numerous cold case successes. Looking back at cold cases brings renewed opportunities to learn from previous investigations (Orde 2006). It is one of the strengths of the major crime capability of South Wales Police.

Within South Wales, the nature of the murders that the force investigates continue to change as crime patterns alter. The communities that South Wales Police serve have become more complex and diverse with far greater global reach. The two cities in the South Wales Police area, Cardiff and Swansea, have large and growing student communities as well as growing resident populations. This has and will continue to attract criminal enterprises seeking to exploit new markets. The rise in homicide and other serious violence in recent years often associated with control of these markets by criminal gangs (Morgan et al. 2020) means it is likely that the major crime capability of South Wales Police will have to continue to develop and adapt to respond to more complex incidents.

Notes

1. The Hydra suite is a training simulation suite that enables delegates to work together on real world crime simulations.

2. PIP is the Professionalising Investigations Programme, of which there are 4 levels designed to ensure that officers are trained, skilled and accredited to conduct high quality investigations at each level. A PIP 4 strategic investigator provides independent advice, support and review for high profile, complex and serious and organised crimes.

3. HOLMES was introduced in 1986 following the Byford inquiry into the investigation of the murders committed by Peter Sutcliffe, the so-called Yorkshire Ripper, which identified a lack of an adequate system of communication as one of the failings in the investigation. HOLMES 2 was developed in 1999. There have been several upgrades since then and there is continuous national investment in this sophisticated police IT network.

4. Familial DNA searching is used to identify an offender when their DNA profile is not stored on the National DNA Database, but the profile of a close relative is, and this profile closely matches DNA obtained from the crime scene.

References

1984. The Police and Criminal Evidence Act. *1984, c60*. Available at: *https://www.legislation.gov.uk/ukpga/1984/60/contents*

1996. Criminal Procedure and Investigations Act *1996, c. 25*. Available at: *https://www.legislation.gov.uk/ukpga/1996/25/contents*

Allsop, C. 2017. 'Cold case homicide reviews'. In: Brookman, F., Maguire, E.R. and Maguire, M. eds. *The handbook of homicide*. Chichester: Wiley Blackwell.

Allsop, C. 2018. *Cold case reviews DNA, detective work and unsolved major crimes* Oxford: Oxford University Press.

Allsop, C. and Pike, S. 2019. 'Investigating homicide: back to the future'. *Journal of Criminological Research, Policy and Practice 5*, pp. 229–39. *https://doi.org/10.1108/JCRPP-03-2019-0021*

Brodeur, J. P. 2010. *The policing web*. Oxford: Oxford University Press.

Brookman, F. and Innes, M. 2013. 'The problem of success: What is a "good" homicide investigation?' *Policing and Society* 23(3), pp. 292–310. *https://doi.org/10.1080/10439463.2013.771538*

Brookman, F., Jones, H., Williams, R. and Fraser, J. 2020. 'Crafting credible homicide narratives: forensic technoscience in contemporary criminal investigations'. *Deviant Behavior* 43(3), pp. 340–66. *https://doi.org/10.1080/01639625.2020.1837692*

Brookman, F., Maguire, E. and Maguire, M. 2018. 'What factors influence whether homicide cases are solved? Insights from qualitative research with detectives in Great Britain and the United States'. *Homicide Studies* 23, p. 108876791879367. *https://doi.org/10.1177/1088767918793678*

Brown, K. M. and Keppel, R. D. 2012. 'Child abduction murder: the impact of forensic evidence on solvability'. *Journal of Forensic Sciences* 57(2), pp. 353–63. *https://doi.org/10.1111/j.1556-4029.2011.01970.x*

Ericson, R. V. 1982. *Reproducing order: study of police patrol work*. Toronto: University of Toronto Press.

Ericson, R. V. 1993. *Making crime: a study of detective work* Toronto: University of Toronto Press.

Fox, J. 2014. 'Is there room for flair in a police major crime investigation?'. *The Journal of Homicide and Major Crime Investigation* 19(1), pp. 2–19.

HMIC. 2008. *The thematic inspection of major crime*. London: Her Majesty's Chief Inspector of Constabulary. Available at: *https://www.justice inspectorates.gov.uk/hmicfrs/media/major-challenge-20090630.pdf*

Innes, M. 2003. *Investigating murder. Detective work and the police response to criminal homicide*. London: Oxford University Press.

Innes, M. 2007. 'Investigation order and major crime investigations'. In: Newburn, T., Williamson, T. and Wright, A. eds. *Handbook of criminal investigations*. Cullompton: Willan Publishing.

Innes, M. 2014. *Signal crime: social reactions to crime, disorder and control*. Oxford: Oxford University Press.

James, A. 2013. *Examining intelligence-led policing: developments in research, policy and practice*. Hampshire: Palgrave Macmillan.

Lloyd-Evans, M. and Bethell, P. 2009. 'Review of undetected serious historic crime: why bother?'. *Journal of Homicide and Major Incident Investigation* 5(2), pp. 3–16.

Manning, P. 1997. *Police work: the social organisation of policing.* 2 ed. Prospect Heights, Illinois: Waveland Press, Inc.

McCartney, C. 2006. 'The DNA Expansion Programme and criminal investigation'. *British Journal of Criminology* 46(2), pp. 175–92. *https://doi.org/10.1093/BJC/AZI094*

Morgan, N. et al. 2020. *Trends and drivers of homicide main findings* London: Home Office. Available at: *https://assets.publishing.service. gov.uk/government/uploads/system/uploads/attachment_data/ file/870188/trends-and-drivers-of-homicide-main-findings-horr113. pdf*

O'Neill, M. 2018. *Key challenges in criminal investigation.* Bristol: Policy Press.

Office for National Statistics. 2022. Appendix tables: homicide in England and Wales. Available at: *https://www.ons.gov.uk/peoplepopulation andcommunity/crimeandjustice/datasets/appendixtableshomicidein englandandwales*

Orde, H. 2006. 'Policing the past to police the future'. *International review of law, computers & technology* 20(1–2), pp. 37–48. *https:// doi.org/10.1080/13600860600699445*

Police Standards Unit. 2005. *Good practice guide – cold case reviews of rape and serious sexual assault.* London: Police Standards Unit.

Repetto, T. 1978. 'The detective task – state of the art, science, craft?', *Police Studies* 1(3), pp. 5–10. Available at: *https://www.ojp.gov/ ncjrs/virtual-library/abstracts/detective-task-state-art-science-craft* (accessed 13 September 2023).

Rock, P. 2004. *Constructing victims' rights: the Home Office, New Labour, and victims.* Oxford: Oxford University Press.

Roycroft, M. 2007. 'What solves hard to solve murders? Identifying the solving factors for Category A and Category B murders. Does the SIO's decision making make a difference?', *The Journal of Homicide and Major Incident Investigation* 3(1), pp. 93–107.

Smith, N. and Flanaghan, C. 2000. *The effective detective: identifying the skills of an effective SIO.* London: Home Office.

Stelfox, P. 2009. *Criminal investigation: an introduction to principles and practice.* Devon: Willan Publishing.

Tong, S., Bryant, R. P. and Horvath, M. A. H. 2009. *Understanding criminal investigation.* Chichester: John Wiley and Sons Ltd.

8

VIOLENCE AND THE CARDIFF MODEL FOR VIOLENCE PREVENTION

Jonathan Shepherd, Jonathan Drake and Wendy Gunney

This chapter tells the story of the conception, development and maturation of the Cardiff Model for Violence Prevention, the ways it fed into the development of the Violence Prevention Unit for Wales, and how South Wales Police and their partners have sought to understand and respond to the challenges associated with violent crime. Perhaps more so than some of the other contributions to this book, it is thus a story of 'policing' and not just *the* police, in South Wales and beyond. It accents the partnerships, collaborations and co-productions through which a range of actors and agencies, in South Wales and further afield, have engaged in activities intended to control and constrain violence.

Most police forces and urban managers understand the importance of managing and mitigating the impacts of violence. Not just for the harm and misery it involves for those directly impacted by it, but also because of the public fear it can elicit, and the reputational damage it can do to an area over an extended period. Moreover, it has been estimated that violence costs the NHS in Wales over £45M in direct costs annually. Such consequences notwithstanding, the work of violence prevention sometimes struggles to command the attention it warrants, getting over-looked amongst the ongoing series of emergencies and calls for service that constitute the workload of modern police organisations.

The Cardiff Model thus provides an especially useful instrument for telling this story, for in addition to playing an influential role in tactical and practical local responses to violence, it also illuminates some deeper and wider facets of modern policing. These include how effective policing, especially preventive actions, often requires looking beyond the police, to consider the enabling and supportive contributions made by diverse public service and civil society partners. Also significant are the insights the Cardiff Model affords the conduct of evidence-led policing. These include recognition that not everything 'works' and some innovations fail, and even those components that are effective have to be able to flex and respond to changes in the prevailing, social, economic and political conditions. Robust and rigorous evaluation, data, and evidence are important, but so too are the people who ultimately operationalise any model; sustaining their commitment and involvement is vital.

It has become quite fashionable in policing recently to talk about adopting 'public health approaches to crime reduction'. Sometimes initiatives adopting this rhetoric do not make it clear what this means in practice, nor how it differs from what they would do anyway. Setting such quibbles aside however, the Cardiff Model does have a legitimate claim to be the original prototype of how a 'public health' lens can afford a particular methodology for engaging with often complex and 'knotty' challenges. It is not especially surprising, therefore, that many of the very pragmatic and practical techniques that were originated by the Cardiff Model have been an explicit influence upon the recently implemented Violence Prevention Units in England and Wales, and the violence reduction work conducted in Scotland as well.

Framed in this way, the chapter starts by mapping out the 'pre-history' of what developed into the Cardiff Model's perspective on violence prevention. The next section of the chapter provides a 'deeper dive' into some of the Model's key features and innovations. This is then followed with a discussion about how the Cardiff Model has been exported 'from Wales to the World', having been adopted and adapted by a range of violence reduction practitioners globally. The closing sections consider how the work performed over many years has informed the more recent roll-out of Violence Prevention Units in Wales and England.

ON THE ORIGINS OF THE CARDIFF MODEL

The roots of what developed into the Cardiff Model lie in the clinical work of one of the authors, Jonathan Shepherd, and his informal observation that there was an association between the number of assault patients (people injured in violence), and particular places and events. In effect, constructing violence not just as a problem for the justice system, but a public health problem also. On moving to Bristol University as a senior lecturer and NHS consultant in the Bristol and Weston Health Authority this became the subject of his PhD research (1988). One chapter compared Bristol Royal Infirmary emergency department (ED) records of treatment of people injured in violence with Avon and Somerset Police records of violent offences which took place in the same area of the city over the same period. The findings, replicated later in Cardiff and Swansea, were astonishing: only 23% of the incidents recorded in the ED appeared in police records (Shepherd et al. 1989; Sutherland et al. 2002). This raised the obvious question why this might be. Funding from the Economic and Social Research Council supported a study that followed consecutive people injured during violent assaults from the ED where they were treated through the justice system. It revealed that police knowledge of violence depends almost entirely on injured people reporting these offences, and, crucially, that many choose not to report. This was because they were afraid of reprisals, they did not want their own conduct scrutinised, and they often could not identify their assailant and therefore could not see what the police could do to respond (Clarkson et al. 1994; Cretney et al. 1994).

The overall implications of these findings were that ED records might provide unique new information about violence, which could make prevention of violence more effective, and also provide the basis for a new local and national measure of violence.

Following appointment as a professor in 1991 at the University of Wales College of Medicine (from 2004 part of Cardiff

University), Shepherd established the Violence Research Group (see below). Then, to explore multi-agency violence prevention in the County of Cardiff, he invited South Wales Police, Cardiff County Council, the local district health authority and the third sector organisation, Victim Support, to send representatives to a meeting. It was proposed at this meeting that violence prevention should be based not only on police intelligence – incomplete because so much serious violence is not reported – but also on information collected and shared by the University Hospital of Wales ED, in Cardiff.

THE FIRST VIOLENCE REDUCTION UNIT

This first meeting of what became the Cardiff Violence Prevention Board – the prototype Violence Reduction Unit – took place on 25 July 1997. This group continues to this day to be central to the Cardiff Model for Violence Prevention, using combined police-ED data to prevent violence by turning surveillance data into action (Mercer Kollar and Sumner 2018).[1] Made up of executives with the authority to deploy prevention resources it works through its constituent agencies, predominantly South Wales Police, Cardiff County Council and the Cardiff and Vale NHS Health Board, it exemplifies a public health approach to violence prevention.

Informed by these pioneering innovations located in South Wales, this public health approach influenced the 1998 Crime and Disorder Act and its creation of 373 Crime and Disorder Reduction Partnerships (Community Safety Partnerships in Wales and subsequently elsewhere) across Great Britain, notably by including the NHS as a formal partner. The Cardiff Model was highlighted in guidance to the Act as an example of good practice.

Developing this approach initially in Cardiff involved several important and consequential steps. First, setting up a sustainable flow of useful, high quality information from the emergency department of the University Hospital of Wales was crucial. To do this, the ED software was adjusted to include a facility to record precise violence locations, times, dates, weapons used, numbers of assailants, and the relationship between the injured and those who reportedly caused injury. A research trial showed digital recording of this information by ED receptionists worked far better than paper recording by clinicians who, in any event, were too busy with their clinical duties for this extra task (Warburton and Shepherd 2004). Anonymisation and sharing of these data became a routine, weekly task for the Health Board IT unit.

A substantial grant secured from the Home Office funded establishment of a 'Tackling Alcohol Related Street Crime' (TASC) team. This included a full-time analyst who analysed the combined data, identified violence hotspots in the county from these, and summarised findings and other key information for the decision-making violence prevention board (Maguire et al. 2001). In 2001, this work was mainstreamed by Cardiff's Community Safety Partnership. Along the way, NHS ethics committee and Information Commissioner approval were obtained, facilitated by a key feature of the Model, that all information collected in the ED is anonymised before it is shared with analysts and other partners. This new strategy was not and is not about bringing more offenders to justice or increasing the numbers of police investigations; it is about using specific information collected by emergency health services to better target prevention (Shepherd 2005).

PRACTICAL VIOLENCE PREVENTION

A key feature of the data analysis was how it was used to drive action and innovation. For example, working through South Wales Police, patrol routes were adjusted weekly to include hotspots identified by the combined data. Police officers were redeployed from largely crime-free suburbs into the city centre at night, as part of the 'Cardiff After Dark' approach, which has been con-tinued and refined to the present day (see below). Working from the data and through the local authority and South Wales Police, the board also instituted changes in alcohol licensing. Opening hours were restricted, a few premises including Bar Risa in the new Millennium Plaza adjacent to the Millennium Stadium lost their licences, and a licensing condition was introduced on major event days (international rugby match days, for example), to the effect that premises could only sell drinks in toughened glass, and, subsequently, only in non-glass drinking vessels. In 2000, the board published a 'top ten' list of Cardiff licensed premises, based upon numbers of violent incidents reported to the ED and South Wales Police. This naming and shaming strategy has been used by the board from time to time since, including to highlight premises where selling alcohol to intoxicated customers appeared to be taking place according to reports of drunk patients in the ED. This approach has subsequently been replicated in Australia (Miller et al. 2019) (see below).

An additional full time ED nurse was funded by the Home Office. This role was established to scrutinise records of those injured in violence in domestic settings, principally but not exclusively women, and then supporting and helping protect them from repeat harm through multi-agency risk assessment conferences (MARACs), in accessing refuge accommodation where necessary, and in other ways.

Many specific operations were prompted by the combined data. These included joint South Wales Police, local authority parks department work to cut down shrubs in Cardiff's Gorsedd Gardens and Castle Grounds to increase natural surveillance; this cut homophobic and other serious violence in these locations almost to zero. A park in the Fairwater neighbourhood was identified as the location of youth violence and successfully targeted. St Mary's Street, the centre of Cardiff's entertainment district, was pedestrianised when it was apparent that restricting hundreds, sometimes thousands, of intoxicated, hungry people to narrow pavements, especially when they were seeking transport home, triggered violence. Street lighting was installed in a previously poorly lit pedestrianised side street where a late-night opening nightclub was situated.

PARTNERSHIP WITH CARDIFF UNIVERSITY'S VIOLENCE RESEARCH GROUP

Throughout its existence, the Violence Prevention Board has worked closely with Cardiff University's Violence Research Group, founded in 1996 – now part of the University's Crime and

Security Research Institute. Both the board and the group were chaired for two decades by the clinical academic who convened them. This close relationship has afforded a number of benefits, including: rigorous evaluation of the Cardiff Model; evaluation of new interventions suggested by the prevention board; rapid transfer of effective new approaches into prevention practice; and termination of interventions which proved not to work.

In this last category, free, confidential phone lines installed in the ED waiting area, together with 'Silence Hurts Too' advice leaflets, were given to patients, and posters encouraging injured people to report to South Wales Police and to seek help from the third sector organisation Victim Support, were not effective and were discontinued (Whitzman 2008). Victim Support clinics designed in various ways were also introduced in the ED, but uptake was minimal, and these were not continued. It was thought that probation and judiciary representation on the violence prevention board would increase its effectiveness, but this turned out not to be the case. A glass cashback scheme designed to reduce the availability of glasses and bottles which could be used as weapons was initiated in the city, but a lack of any legislative framework, or funding support, meant it could not be implemented.

But many interventions initiated by the board did work (see evaluation findings below). It was found, for example, that rather than displacing violence, targeted police activity creates 'a halo of prevention' around the targeted locations (Weisburd et al. 2006; Braga et al. 2014). Effective interventions flowing from violence research group knowledge, observations and evaluations, also included CCTV camera installations to cover previously hidden violence hotspots, for example outside a row of shops in the Cardiff Bay area (Sivarajasingam et al. 2004). South Wales Police operations targeted fast-food outlets and night clubs identified as violence locations and included deployment of drug detection dogs among queues of people seeking nightclub access. This last strategy was prompted by the research finding that antisocial lifestyles comprise not only violence but also drug misuse, truanting, car crime and a range of other risky behaviours harmful to health (Shepherd et al. 1995; 2002; 2004).

HELPFUL AND UNHELPFUL INFLUENCES

Over its first two decades, the Cardiff Violence Prevention Board has experienced pressures to deviate from data and evidence driven approaches. Examples include pressure from organisations wanting the principal focus to be women and girls at risk rather than men and boys too, who, as the available data continues to show in Cardiff and elsewhere, are most at risk of harm, at least from violence in public places. A further pressure, as in tackling the Covid-19 epidemic, has been to copy non-evidence-based interventions, often loudly and persistently advocated, being tried elsewhere. Unbridled enthusiasm and curiosity can get in the way too, for example, when the collection of further information is suggested when such information has not been shown to be useful for violence prevention. An important lesson was learnt here; ED receptionists can record a limited volume of new data items, such as those essential to the Cardiff Model, but add too many items and the whole data recording enterprise becomes too burdensome in a busy ED.

A multi-agency violence prevention board and the professionals associated with it constantly come up with new ideas. All these need to prompt the question, are they evidence based? In other words, have they been tried, tested and found to be effective in at least one controlled trial? If not, they are put into the research and development category where the research partner – Cardiff University's Violence Research Group – can evaluate them.

Learning from the Model also shows multi-agency groups need to develop and sustain strong links with partner organisations, not least so that proposals to disinvest in posts key to multi-agency work can be forestalled. Cuts in local authority funding in Cardiff after the 2008 economic downturn led to more than one proposal to disinvest in a crucial data analyst post; retaining this was achieved through the Local Service Board. Just as damaging, without reference to the Violence Prevention Board, the University Hospital dispensed with the nurse post responsible for identifying and supporting people injured in violence in domestic settings. This gap in provision was eventually filled with an Independent Domestic Violence Advisor, funded by the South Wales Police and Crime Commissioner.

Key to successful implementation of the Cardiff Model continues to be an effective board made up of motivated professionals with the right prevention and communication skills and enough authority in their respective agencies to bring about change – such as redeploying police resource. The data supply chain needs to be strong; if ED receptionists, or the NHS IT officer who anonymises and shares ED data, or the data analyst lose motivation or are not replaced, this breaks down. Sustained senior leadership is important; chairing such a board is not a job for a trainee, however senior. The key agencies represented around the table can be kept engaged if the board meets in their various headquarters in turn – in County Hall, the Central Police Station and the University Hospital where the ED is located, for example.

Flexibility is needed to reflect the need to prevent violence affecting all age groups, and the emergence of new agencies and new research findings. For example, in response to an audit of Health Board safeguarding responses to children reporting violent injury, preventive work expanded into the education sector (Shepherd et al. 2010). The unit also recruited the manager of Cardiff's street pastor scheme with its 50–60 church-based volunteers – 'capable guardians' in criminology (Cohen and Felson 1979) – out on city centre streets at weekends assisting and protecting vulnerable people. The addition of a representative of the Police and Crime Commissioner's team was helpful when the Commissioner implemented the Model across the South Wales force area in 2012. Implementation of the Model in other settings – see below – also requires variation in the Model to fit country and local circumstances.

EVALUATION OF THE CARDIFF MODEL; IS IT EFFECTIVE AND COST BENEFICIAL?

Funded by grants mainly from the Wales Office of Research and Development (the then NHS Research and Development scheme in Wales), evaluations showed that the approach was effective. For example, when the NHS was involved in targeting, violence levels in licensed premises were significantly reduced compared to when the NHS was not involved (Warburton and Shepherd 2006). Home Office iQuanta 'woundings' data, which the violence prevention board uses to monitor progress, showed Cardiff becoming steadily safer in its family of fifteen Home Office designated 'most similar' cities in England and Wales. In 2007, Cardiff became the safest city in its family according to this measure.

Based upon health service records of hospital admissions related to violence, and police records of woundings and less serious assaults in Cardiff and other cities after adjustment for potential national confounders, it was found that in the intervention city (Cardiff) hospital admission rates fell from seven to five a month per 100,000 population compared with an increase from five to eight in comparison cities (adjusted incidence rate ratio 0.58, 95% confidence interval 0.49 to 0.69). The average rate of woundings recorded by police changed from 54 to 82 a month per 100,000 population in Cardiff, compared with an increase from 54 to 114 in comparison cities (adjusted incidence rate ratio 0.68, 0.61 to 0.75). There was a significant increase in less serious assaults recorded by the police, from 15 to 20 a month per 100,000 population in Cardiff compared with a decrease from 42 to 33 in comparison cities (adjusted incidence rate ratio 1.38, 1.13 to 1.70). This led to the conclusion that an information sharing partnership between health services, police, and local government in Cardiff, altered policing and other strategies to prevent violence, based on information collected from patients treated in emergency departments after injury sustained in violence. This was associated with an increase in police recording of minor assaults in Cardiff compared with similar cities in England and Wales where this intervention was not implemented.

Most convincingly, a systematic review by public health academics at Deakin University, Australia, (Droste et al. 2014) and a meta-analysis led by public health academics at the University of Cape Town, South Africa (Jabar et al. 2019), of evaluations of the Model provided robust evidence of effectiveness. The Deakin University review of nine evaluations concluded that:

All studies attempting to measure intervention effectiveness reported substantial reductions of assaults and ED attendances post-intervention, with one reporting no change. Negative logistic feasibility concerns were minimal, with general consensus among authors being that data-sharing protocols and partnerships could be easily implemented into modern ED triage systems, with minimal cost, staff workload burden, impact to patient safety, service and anonymity, or risk of harm displacement, or increase to length of patient stay.

The University of Cape Town led meta-analysis of evaluations of the model (which the authors termed 'injury surveillance systems (ISSs) that address violence prevention') concluded: '... the introduction of ISS showed significant results in reducing assault (Incidence rate ratio=0.80; 95% CI 0.71 to 0.91)'.

A cost benefit analysis estimated that the approach reduced the economic and social costs of violence by £6.9 million in 2007 compared with the costs the intervention city (Cardiff) would have experienced in the absence of the programme. This includes a gross cost reduction of £1.25 million to the health service and £1.62 million to the criminal justice system in 2007. By contrast, the investments associated with the programme were modest: setup costs of software modifications and prevention strategies were £107,769, while the annual operating costs of the system were estimated as £210,433 (2003 UK pound). The cumulative social benefit-cost ratio of the programme from 2003 to 2007 was £82 in benefits for each pound spent on the programme, including a benefit-cost ratio of 14.80 for the health service and 19.1 for the criminal justice system (Shepherd et al. 2010).

Further evidence of effectiveness came from homicide data collected independently by Manuel Eisner, Professor of Criminology at Cambridge University. The graph below shows that during the period when the Cardiff Model was implemented in Cardiff, homicide levels fell whereas in Birmingham, London, Leeds and Edinburgh, homicide levels rose (Eisner 2016).

Figure 8.1: Homicide rates in major UK cities

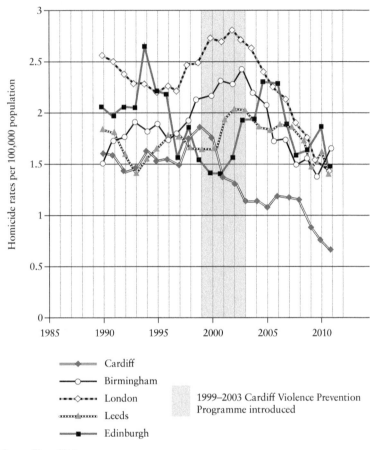

Source: Eisner 2015

IMPLEMENTATION OF THE CARDIFF MODEL IN THE UK

From its inception in the late 1990s, police forces, cities and regions elsewhere in the UK showed interest in the Cardiff Model. Early adopters included the Wirral/Merseyside Police, Glasgow/Strathclyde Police, Cambridge/Cambridgeshire Constabulary, and the then Government Office for the Southeast, which implemented it in the early 2000s. National government also showed interest, first in 1996/7. Home Secretaries Jack Straw, Charles

Clarke and Alan Johnson visited the Cardiff Violence Prevention Board, and The Board chair contributed to Prime Ministerial summits on Youth Violence (2000) and Serious Violence (2019). In 2007, the Cardiff Model was included in the UK government's updated Alcohol Strategy, 'Safe Sensible Social' (Department of Health and Home Office 2008).

Implementation of the Model across the UK was included in the Liberal-Democrat manifesto prior to the 2010 General Election. As a result of which, the new Conservative-Liberal Democrat coalition included it in its programme for government. This prompted the establishment of: a new cross-government information sharing group based in the then Department of Health; a new Information Sharing to Tackle Violence (ISTV) information standard (ISB 1594) published by NHS Digital which codified Cardiff Model data items; mandatory data collection by NHS Hospital Trusts in England; and two England and Wales audits of implementation (Department of Health and Social Care 2014; NHS Digital 2014). The second of these audits showed that by 2013, 60% of community safety partnerships had implemented the Model, at least to some extent (Social Care, Local Government and Care Partnerships Directorate Analytical Unit 2015).

However, the economic downturn from 2008 onwards and subsequent local authority and police service cost saving programmes reduced the capacity for multi-agency violence prevention. In Cardiff, and elsewhere, the community safety partnership was disbanded leaving little except its name; CSP staff were redeployed or laid off. Perhaps this was not that surprising as successive annual Crime Surveys of England and Wales were showing year on year falls in violent offending – evidence corroborated by the Violence Research Group's annual surveys of violence related ED attendances (Sivarajasingam et al. 2016). However, the upturn in homicides and knife violence in the mid-2010s showed that reinvestment was urgently needed.

THE CARDIFF MODEL IN LONDON AND INTERNATIONALLY

By 2019, all 29 London EDs were collecting and sharing Cardiff Model (Mayor of London 2019). These successes were not without their challenges though. For example, in 2018 at St George's Hospital (the major NHS trauma centre serving Southwest London), concerns were raised whether data sharing might breach the new General Data Protection Regulations (GDPR), and data sharing was suddenly halted. However, because the Information Commissioner had already approved such arrangements for the prevention of crime, these concerns were overcome and data sharing was quickly re-established (Davenport 2019).

Across London, these ED data have revealed many violence hotspots which would otherwise be invisible. Violence hotspot maps of Tower Hamlets looked very different when they were made using data from EDs compared with those generated from Metropolitan Police Service intelligence. Here, ED data showed concentrations of violence around the Royal London Hospital, Stepney Green Park and immediately to the west of Bethnal Green Technology College, whereas, from police intelligence, the only obvious hotspot was at the junction of Whitechapel and Mile End Roads (Shepherd et al. 2016). Cardiff Model data also showed that hotspot locations vary by day of the week. Most strikingly perhaps, these data 'discovered' crack houses, for example, immediately south of the Homerton Hospital in North London and east of Heathrow Airport in West London.

Implementation of the Model in London identified that injury at the hands of more than one assailant was a potential signal of gang violence (Cardiff Model data include numbers of assailants involved in each incident). This enabled the Metropolitan Police to identify gang violence more often, even if injured people involved seek treatment in an ED far from the scene of this violence. The Integrated Hackney Gang Unit uses these data to identify and target gang activity across the metropolis (Wright 2018).

The World Health Organization first highlighted the Model as an example of good practice in its 2004 report (2016). International interest in implementing the model came in 2011 from the city of Milwaukee in the United States where a professor of emergency medicine, Stephen Hargarten, convened a series of workshops with city authorities. A key outcome of these meetings was that Cardiff Model data collection began in Froedtert Hospital, one of two Level I adult trauma centres in the state of

Wisconsin, and in the Children's Hospital of Wisconsin (Bureau of Justice Assistance 2016). Discoveries from these data included a school and parks in the West Allis suburb of the Milwaukee metropolitan area which were hotspots of violence in which children were injured; these were not apparent from law enforcement data. Following on from which, in 2020 a national US network was established that, at the time of writing, includes more than a dozen cities that have either implemented, or are planning to introduce the Cardiff Model.

In 2012, Amsterdam decided to replicate the Model and the Mayor convened a round table conference. Invitees included the chief executives of all the Amsterdam hospitals with EDs, the chief executive of the biggest health insurance provider in the Netherlands, and leaders of other key agencies. A pilot was launched funded, in part, by the justice department, followed by a second pilot in Tilbourg (Draisma et al. 2016).

Encouraged by WHO endorsement, interest, pilot projects and implementation in other countries followed, including in: Colombia in South America, Nova Scotia in Canada; the Western Cape province of South Africa; and, as part of Jamaica's 2018–30 National Plan of Action for an Integrated Response to Children and Violence (Violence Prevention Alliance 2019). In 2021, the South African Local Government Association together with the Joe Slovo Foundation, decided to implement the Model throughout South Africa.

In Australia, led by public health academics at Deakin University, the Cardiff Model has been implemented in Sydney, Melbourne, Canberra, Geelong and Warrnambool. A randomised trial called 'Driving change' has been used to test how emergency department data can be used to reduce alcohol-related injury and violence. Public health interventions include information sharing with licensed premises, with police and other community agencies, and public release, as has been carried out in Cardiff (see above) of 'Top 5' premises lists. Logistic and feasibility concerns are documented, together with clinical impacts of implementing this systems-change model in an Australian context. Economic impact and return on investment are being evaluated in a formal economic cost–benefit analysis (Miller et al. 2019).

TACKLING VIOLENCE TODAY

One of the key learning points that can be distilled from the long-term implementation of the Cardiff Model in South Wales is how the type, prevalence and distribution of violence can evolve and adapt. Displacement of drug related violence in response to deliberate interventions introduced by police and their partners was observed. Other times though, such shifts can be driven by changes in the prevailing social, political and economic conditions. Such considerations are very much 'front-of-mind' at the time of writing, where in the wake of the Covid-19 global health pandemic, public services of all kinds are having to think carefully about the volume and make-up of the various risks and threats they will need to manage. For the measures taken to try and limit the spread of coronavirus have delivered a 'shock' to the social, political and economic system that is unprecedented. This has included decreases in violence outside the home during Covid lockdowns and closure of on licence premises, and quite significant impacts upon the supply of social support services to young people and those living in economically struggling areas.

In common with a number of other cities and regions nationally, particular concern in South Wales has recently alighted upon indicators of a possible rise in serious violence, which may or may not be related to the pandemic. These gang-related incidents often have catastrophic immediate and long-term consequences for the individuals and families involved, as has been tragically exemplified by a series of high-profile fatal stabbings in Cardiff that have taken place between 2019 and 2021.

Because of their lifestyle, gang members are very likely to be injured in violence and to need emergency treatment. But they are most unlikely to report this to police (see section on the Cardiff Model in London). Consequently, the kinds of ED based data collection advocated under the auspices of the Cardiff Model, has particular value. To strengthen responses to knife and gang violence, two new nurse posts have been created in the University Hospital of Wales ED. This facilitates prompt identification and reports to police of violent penetrating injury – particularly useful when the injured live outside the force area and have little footprint on local police systems. These roles, working in partnership with others such as the Independent Domestic Violence Advisors funded by the Police and Crime Commissioner, also play an important part in safeguarding and supporting people injured in domestic violence.

OPERATION SCEPTRE AND THE VIOLENCE PREVENTION UNIT

The establishment of the Wales Violence Prevention Unit[2] followed the Home Office allocation of £51 million to police forces in April 2019, to strengthen their response to serious violence, especially knife violence (Home Office 2019; National Crime Agency 2019). This 'surge funding' enabled forces most affected to increase patrols and weapon sweeps, equipment for officers and overtime. The £1.2 million awarded to South Wales Police funded its Operation Sceptre teams that target street, gang and drug related serious violence. Police Officers work mainly in plain clothes, with a particular focus on policing hotspots for knife crime in Cardiff and Swansea.

Stop and search has been an important tactic employed by the Sceptre Teams. For example, in the first six months of 2020, the team conducted over 600 stop searches and arrested 115 people in Cardiff alone. Stop and search has become a highly emotive and controversial topic in discussions of policing, in part, because of how it has become connected to the over-policing of black and minority communities in London and other urban centres (Delsol and Shiner 2015). There is certainly research evidence that if deployed in an indiscriminate and untargeted way, stop and search can have detrimental consequences, such as undermining public perceptions of police legitimacy. That said, there is, according to Tiratelli, Quinton and Bradford (2018) some research evidence for a weak association between stop and search and a suppressant effect on drug crime. Overall, then, the organisation and conduct of stop and search by police displays the traits of what Joan McCord described in her seminal paper 'Cures that Harm' (2003). She argued that with reference to criminal justice treatments, there is a need to try and foster a more nuanced and sophisticated conversation around some of the practical and moral dilemmas that surround issues like violence reduction and prevention, where there can be both benefits and disbenefits.

Operational police officers argue that, appropriately conducted, stop and search is an important tool for combatting serious crime. Criminological evidence indicates that violence often tends to cluster in space and time, with one incident acting as a trigger for others, in the form of retaliation and reaction (Collins 2008). As such, when there is a series of stabbings in an area, where citizens are causing life-changing and life-threatening injuries to one another, targeted stop and search by the police provides a way to 'grip' the situation, so that the effectiveness of more sustainable, longer-term, preventive interventions can work their way through. The key issue here, then, is one of precision policing. What Cardiff Model data supplied by the NHS emergency departments, blended with other sources can provide, if they are subject to rigorous analysis, is a targeting mechanism that ensures that tools like stop and search are directed towards those people, places and problems where they are most needed, and in ways that seek to limit any potential 'spillover' effects.

This is, then, a highly practical and very focused conception of violence prevention and reduction. In this regard, it is rather different in its orientation from the turn towards 'early intervention', which is also part of the remit of the Violence Prevention Unit (VPU). Stimulated in part, by the kinds of logics and perspectives adopted in public health, this strand of activity is about trying to get 'upstream' of the onset of violent behaviour, to reduce individual and population level exposure to risks known to be associated with violence. The latter are sometimes labelled 'Adverse Childhood Experiences' or 'ACEs'. In South Wales, as in other police forces, many victims and perpetrators of violent offences are already known to the police, and often have multiple 'flags' and 'markers' linked to their name for drugs problems and prior histories of violence (Newbury 2020). In South Wales, research confirmed the long-established finding that harmful behaviour was significantly more prevalent in individuals who reported adversity during their childhood , including those who had been exposed to violence (Bellis et al. 2016; Ford et al. 2018). In the twelve months preceding them being surveyed, a significantly higher proportion of respondents with four or more ACEs had been a victim of violence (27%) or perpetrated violence

(21%) than respondents without ACEs (3% and 2% respectively). Similarly, incarceration was significantly more prevalent in those with four or more ACEs (36%) than those without ACEs (4%) (Newbury 2020).

Developing the implications of such insights and translating them into practical measures has been placed at the centre of the work of the Wales VPU. It is reflected in its mission 'to prevent violence across Wales through the implementation of a public health approach'. South Wales was one of 18 Police force areas to receive funds (£880k pa) from the Home Office to establish a VPU.[3] Although its initial work prioritised serious violence in South Wales, reflecting how levels of crime in the region account for a large proportion of what happens in Wales as a whole, the unit now has an all-Wales remit.

As rehearsed above, whilst the VPU aims to prevent all forms of violence, its principal focus is on knife crime and public space violence linked to drugs and gangs. These are priorities consistent with the UK government's 2018 Serious Violence Strategy. Operationally, the unit has evolved to base its service delivery on what is known as the '4 As':

1) Aware – One of the roles that the VPU is seeking to develop and perform is to maintain an up-to-date awareness of the current national and international knowledge base and best practices in the field of violence prevention and reduction, and to be a conduit for channelling this to potential users across the public, private and civil society sectors. A clear example concerns the public value demonstrated in relation to media-led concern about a possible increase in drink 'spiking' in pubs, clubs and bars. The VPU team identified research that had been conducted in Australia, and sought to rapidly distil the lessons associated with this work that could be applied in Wales.

2) Advocate – The VPU seeks to provide a strong and authoritative voice that can influence the behaviour of other bodies and organisations in Wales, to maximise the opportunities to prevent and reduce the harms stemming

from violence. For example, an assessment of the impact of the COVID 19 pandemic on Children and Young People was used to advocate for effective practice to prevent all forms of violence impacting on children during and following this period.

3) Assist – Assistance is given by the VPU to a range of violence prevention activities, to enhance cross-sector capacity and capability. For instance, VPU analysts are engaged in the provision of analytic products integrating data from a range of partners, to afford an up-to-date picture of the prevalence and distribution of different forms of violence in Wales.

4) Adopt – An important strand of the unit's work is in mobilising innovations to prevent violence and reduce vulnerability, by getting them into practice quickly, such as happened with the introduction of Nurse Violence Advocates at the Emergency Department of the University Hospital of Wales, Cardiff. By engaging with victims of serious violence at the point of treatment, opportunities have been identified to prevent further harm.

Membership of the Wales VPU has grown, to now include over forty members. Staff from public and third sector organisations are able to work with the team on a part-time unfunded basis, and over £1.2M worth of staff time has been provided to the VPU in this way. This is a clear indicator of the strong buy in of partners in Wales to preventing violence. Any benefits which may flow from this can be attributed, at least in part, to fostering a more joined-up, inter-agency approach.

Through its membership and the partners represented on its board, the Wales VPU seeks to take account of the policing, social care, health, housing and other needs of vulnerable children and young people recognised in the 'Early Action Together' strategy in Wales (Krug et al. 2002). The implementation of this strategy involves police forces and Police and Crime Commissioners, Barnardo's and other third sector organisations, and national public health, prison, probation and youth justice agencies. In effect, the VPU is seeking to enable a 'whole system approach' in which collaboration, co-production strategies, cooperation in data sharing and community consensus are foundation principles. This stretches from early intervention measures, to mitigating the mental health and other effects of incidents that cannot be prevented. This latter function reflects the public health strategy of tertiary prevention.

It is striking how a strong partnership ethos was generated by both the Cardiff Model and the VPU for the specific purpose of violence prevention. A plausible explanation for this is that the building of relationships between people and the organisations they represent, creates an informal mode of accountability that helps to get things done and changes made when this needs to happen.

THE FUTURE

As the suddenness of the Covid-19 outbreak demonstrated so clearly, the future is difficult to forecast, even in the short-term. But as far as the management and mitigation of violence in South Wales is concerned the direction of travel has now been set (Krug et al. 2002). To provide guiderails for these ongoing developments, there are some key lessons that have been learnt in the last fifty years which should not be forgotten. Taking the elements of the public health approach in turn, these are: police and NHS surveillance needs to be continuous; every ED in Wales should be sharing Cardiff Model data; analysts are just as important as front-line staff – how can violence be pinpointed or monitored otherwise?; interventions work better when they are fitted to local contexts and situations, with robust analysis augmented by high resolution local knowledge; violence prevention interventions known to work and to be cost beneficial need to be identified, targeted and implemented with fidelity to their original design; interventions which do not stand up to rigorous testing should be discontinued.

At its core, the Cardiff Model and its approach to violence prevention and reduction demonstrate the power of 'policing' defined in its broadest sense. That is, as an activity drawing in a range of capacities and capabilities, not just those possessed by the police as an organisation. Getting it to work depends on negotiating a range of influences including: city, regional and national trends in violence, public concern; and commitment to evidence based, data driven strategies, and prevention, for example. All multi-agency work has its challenges, especially in difficult economic times, which is likely to be an apposite descriptor for the post-pandemic world.[4]

Notes

1. See also this briefing by Cardiff University's Crime and Security Research Institute: *https://www.cardiff.ac.uk/crime-security-research-institute/publications/research-briefings/the-cardiff-model*
2. Initially called the South Wales Violence Prevention Unit, the Wales Violence Prevention Unit subsequently broadened its geographical remit to cover all Wales.
3. In England, the preferred terminology is 'Violence Reduction Units'.
4. The authors would like to acknowledge the support of the large number of South Wales Police officers and staff who have made significant individual and collective contributions to the development and implementation of the Cardiff Model for Violence Prevention.

References

1998. Crime and Disorder Act. *1998, c. 37*. Available at: *https://www.legislation.gov.uk/ukpga/1998/37/contents*

Bellis, M., Ashton, K., Hughes, K., Ford, K., Bishop, J. and Paranjothy, S. 2016. *Adverse Childhood Experiences and their impact on health-harming behaviours in the Welsh adult population*. Cardiff: Public Health Wales NHS Trust. Available at: *https://www.ljmu.ac.uk/~/media/phi-reports/pdf/2016_01_adverse_childhood_experiences_and_their_impact_on_health_harming_behaviours_in_the.pdf*

Braga, A. A., Papachristos, A. V. and Hureau, D. M. 2014. 'The effects of hot spots policing on crime: an updated systematic review and meta-analysis'. *Justice Quarterly* 31(4), pp. 633–63. *https://doi.org/10.1080/07418825.2012.673632*

Bureau of Justice Assistance. 2016. *The Cardiff Model: strengthening community capacity to reduce violence*. U.S. Department of Justice. Available at: *https://bja.ojp.gov/funding/awards/2016-aj-bx-k042*

Clarkson, C. M. V., Cretney, A., Davis, G. and Shepherd, J. P. 1994. 'Assaults: the relationship between seriousness, criminalisation and punishment'. *Criminal Law Review*, pp. 4–20.

Cohen, L. E. and Felson, M. 1979. 'Social change and crime rate trends: a routine activity approach'. *American Sociological Review* 44(4), pp. 588–608. *https://doi.org/10.2307/2094589*

Collins, R. 2008. *Violence: a micro-sociological theory*. Princeton, NJ; Oxford: Princeton University Press.

Cretney, A., Clarkson, C. M. V., Davis, G. and Shepherd, J. P. 1994. 'Criminalising assault: the failure of the 'offence against society' model'. *British Journal of Criminology* 34, pp. 15–26.

Davenport, J. 2019. 'London hospitals "risk lives" by not sharing anti-violence data'. *Evening Standard* 4 February. Available at: *https://www.standard.co.uk/news/health/london-hospitals-risk-lives-by-not-sharing-antiviolence-data-a4056681.html*

Delsol, R. and Shiner, M. 2015. *Stop and search: the anatomy of a police power*. Basingstoke: Palgrave Macmillan.

Department of Health and Home Office. 2008. *Safe. Sensible. Social.* London: Home Office. Available at: *https://ranzetta.typepad.com/files/sss-toolkit.pdf*

Department of Health and Social Care. 2014. *A&Es and police will share information to help tackle violence*. London: DHSC. Available at: *https://www.gov.uk/government/news/aes-and-police-to-share-information-to-help-tackle-violence*

Draisma, C., Stam, C., Toet, H. and Blatter, B. 2016. *Pilot 'Preventieve aanpak geweld' Amsterdam-Amstelland*. Amsterdam: VeiligheidNL.

Droste, N., Miller, P. and Baker, T. 2014. 'Review article: Emergency department data sharing to reduce alcohol-related violence: A systematic review of the feasibility and effectiveness of community-level interventions'. *Emergency Medicine Australasia* 26(4), pp. 326–35. *https://doi.org/10.1111/1742-6723.12247*

Eisner, M. 2016. 'Homicide rates in major UK cities'. In: Shepherd, J.P., Avery, V. and Rahman, S. eds. *Targeted policing*. Police Professional, pp. 14–16.

Ford, K., Barton, E. R., Newbury, A., Hughes, K., Bezeczky, Z., Roderick, J. and Bellis, M. A. 2018. *Understanding the prevalence of adverse childhood experiences (ACEs) in a male offender population in Wales: The Prisoner ACE Survey*. Available at: *https://phw.nhs.wales/files/aces/the-prisoner-ace-survey/*

Home Office. 2019. 'Home Office allocates £51 million to police forces for increased action on knife crime ahead of Easter weekend'. Available at: *https://www.gov.uk/government/news/home-office-allocates-51-million-to-police-forces-for-increased-action-on-knife-crime-ahead-of-easter-weekend*

Jabar, A., Fong, F., Chavira, M., Cerqueira, M. T., Barth, D., Matzopoulos, R. and Engel, M. E. 2019. 'Is the introduction of violence and injury observatories associated with a reduction in violence-related injury in adult populations? A systematic review and meta-analysis'. *BMJ Open* 9(7), p. e027977. *https://doi.org/10.1136/bmjopen-2018-027977*

Krug, E. G., Mercy, J. A., Dahlberg, L. L. and Zwi, A. B. 2002. 'The world report on violence and health'. *Lancet* 360(9339), pp. 1083–8. *https://doi.org/10.1016/s0140-6736(02)11133-0*

Maguire, M., Morgan, R. and Nettleton, H. 2001. *Early lessons from the crime reduction programme: tackling alcohol related street crime in Cardiff (TASC Project)*. Available at: *https://citeseerx.ist.psu.edu/viewdoc/download?doi=10.1.1.499.1819&rep=rep1&type=pdf*

Mayor of London. 2019. *ISTV – History of Information Sharing to Tackle Violence*. Available at: *https://data.london.gov.uk/information-sharing-to-tackle-violence/istv-history-of-information-sharing-to-tackle-violence/* (accessed 29 July 2023).

McCord, J. 2003. 'Cures that harm: unanticipated outcomes of crime prevention programs'. *The ANNALS of the American Academy of Political and Social Science* 587(1), pp. 16–30. *https://doi.org/10.1177/0002716202250781*

Mercer Kollar, L. M. and Sumner, S. A. 2018. *Cardiff Model Toolkit: community guidance for violence prevention*. Atlanta, GA: Centers for Disease Control and Prevention. Available at: *www.cdc.gov/violenceprevention/publichealthissue/fundedprograms/cardiffmodel/toolkit.html*

Miller, P. et al. 2019. 'Driving change: a partnership study protocol using shared emergency department data to reduce alcohol-related harm'. *Emergency Medicine Australasia* 31(6), pp. 942–7. *https://doi.org/10.1111/1742-6723.13266*

National Crime Agency. 2019. *County lines*. London: NCA. Available at: *https://www.nationalcrimeagency.gov.uk/what-we-do/crime-threats/drug-trafficking/county-lines* (accessed 28 July 2023).

Newbury, A. 2020. *Serious youth violence in South Wales: strategic needs assessment*. Cardiff: Violence Prevention Unit. Available at:

https://www.violencepreventionwales.co.uk/cms-assets/research/FINAL_Strategic-needs-assessment-highlight-report-compressed.pdf

NHS Digital. 2014. *Information sharing to tackle violence minimum dataset.* NHS Digital. Available at: *https://digital.nhs.uk/data-and-information/information-standards/information-standards-and-data-collections-including-extractions/publications-and-notifications/standards-and-collections/isb1594-information-sharing-to-tackle-violence-minimum-dataset*

Shepherd, J. P. 2005. 'Victim services in the National Health Service (NHS): combining treatment with violence prevention'. *Criminal Behaviour and Mental Health* 15(2), pp. 75–81. *https://doi.org/10.1002/cbm.38*

Shepherd, J. P., Avery, V. and Rahman, S. 2016. *Targeted policing.* Police Professional.

Shepherd, J. P., Farrington, D. and Potts, J. 2002. 'Relations between offending, injury and illness'. *Journal of the Royal Society of Medicine* 95(11), pp. 539–44. *https://doi.org/10.1258/jrsm.95.11.539*

Shepherd, J. P., Farrington, D. and Potts, J. 2004. 'Impact of antisocial lifestyle on health'. *Journal of Public Health (Oxford)* 26(4), pp. 347–52. *https://doi.org/10.1093/pubmed/fdh169*

Shepherd, J. P., Peak, J. D., Haria, S. and Sleeman, F. 1995. 'Characteristic illness behaviour in assault patients: DATES syndrome'. *Journal of the Royal Society of Medicine* 88(2), pp. 85–7.

Shepherd, J. P., Shapland, M. and Scully, C. 1989. 'Recording by the police of violent offences; an Accident and Emergency Department perspective'. *Medicine, Science and the Law* 29(3), pp. 251–7. *https://doi.org/10.1177/002580248902900311*

Shepherd, J. P., Tuthill, D., Parry, B. and Dowd, H. 2010. 'An audit of emergency medicine responses to children injured in violence'. *Emergency Medical Journal* 27(2), pp. 125–7. *https://doi.org/10.1136/emj.2008.069526*

Sivarajasingam, V., Page, N., Wells, J., Morgan, P., Matthews, K., Moore, S. and Shepherd, J. P. 2016. 'Trends in violence in England and Wales 2010–2014'. *Journal of Epidemiol Community Health* 70(6), pp. 616–21. *https://doi.org/10.1136/jech-2015-206598*

Sivarajasingam, V., Shepherd, J. P. and Matthews, K. 2004. 'Effect of urban closed circuit television on assault injury and violence detection'. *Injury prevention: Journal of the International Society for*

Child and Adolescent Injury Prevention 9, pp. 312–16. *https://doi. org/10.1136/ip.9.4.312*

Social Care, Local Government and Care Partnerships Directorate Analytical Unit. 2015. *Information sharing to tackle violence: audit of progress*. London: Department of Health. Available at: *https://assets. publishing.service.gov.uk/government/uploads/system/uploads/ attachment_data/file/478613/Information_sharing_audit.pdf*

Sutherland, I., Sivarajasingam, V. and Shepherd, J. P. 2002. 'Recording of community violence by medical and police services'. *Injury prevention: Journal of the International Society for Child and Adolescent Injury Prevention* 8, pp. 246–7. *https://doi.org/10.1136/ip.8.3.246*

Tiratelli, M., Quinton, P. and Bradford, B. 2018. 'Does stop and search deter crime? Evidence from ten years of London-wide data'. *The British Journal of Criminology* 58(5), pp. 1212–31. *https://doi.org/ 10.1093/bjc/azx085*

Violence Prevention Alliance. 2019. National Plan of Action officially launched. *The Peace Guardian*; 3: October–December.

Warburton, A. and Shepherd, J. P. 2004. 'Development, utilisation, and importance of accident and emergency department derived assault data in violence management'. *Emergency Medicine Journal* 21, pp. 473–7. *https://doi.org/10.1136/emj.2003.004978*

Warburton, A. L. and Shepherd, J. P. 2006. 'Tackling alcohol related violence in city centres: effect of emergency medicine and police intervention'. *Emergency Medicine Journal* 23(1), pp. 12–17. *https://doi. org/10.1136/emj.2004.023028*

Weisburd, D., Wyckoff, L. A., Ready, J., Eck, J. E., Hinkle, J. C. and Gajewski, F. 2006. 'Does crime just move around the corner? A controlled study of spatial displacement and diffusion of crime control benefits'. *Criminology* 44, pp. 549–92. *https://doi.org/10.1111/ J.1745-9125.2006.00057.X*

Whitzman, C. 2008. *Handbook of community safety, gender and violence prevention*. London: Routledge.

World Health Organization. 2016. *INSPIRE: seven strategies for ending violence against children*. Geneva: World Health Organization. Available at: *https://apps.who.int/iris/handle/10665/78176*

Wright, R. 2018. 'On the frontline of London's surge in fatal gang violence: Hackney Integrated Gangs Unit is tackling violence by treating it as a public health issue'. *Financial Times* 10 May. Available at: *https://www.ft.com/content/661e8750-4f01-11e8-a7a9-37318e776bab*

9

PUBLIC PROTECTION IN THE SOUTH WALES POLICE

Amanda L. Robinson, Lorraine Davies and Kath Pritchard

The evolution of public protection in policing holds a mirror up to society and how societal concerns, norms and expectations themselves have evolved and adapted. The journey of the South Wales Police is particularly instructive, as there is a general recognition within policing circles that the Force has been something of a thought-leader in respect of public protection issues, especially with regards to violence against women and girls (VAWG). This is evident through the development and application of novel approaches in South Wales that have become standard practice throughout the UK as well as influential further afield (e.g. in Europe, Australia and Canada). The aim of this chapter is to document some of the key innovations that have been developed in this arena, how and why they were implemented, and the wider influence they have had on policing in other jurisdictions. The chapter is organised into three sections to provide a chronological account of how South Wales Police responded to public protection issues from its amalgamation in 1969 until the present day. Discussion includes the key issues, challenges and achievements in each of those periods, as understood by those directly involved. Recurring themes include: the police organisation as a site for socially constructed gendered action; the gendered division of labour within police work; and the gendered values underpinning traditional policing styles, as well as innovative reform strategies.

These personal reflections are illustrative of the wider policy and practice issues documented in the extant literature.

First, a brief note on terminology. This chapter is about the concept of 'public protection' and how it has informed the organisation of police work, including its integration into dedicated Public Protection Units. But we are concerned with charting the influence of the concept within South Wales Police, rather than providing a detailed focus on the work of particular operational units.

Second, a brief note on the approach taken to compile the information discussed in this chapter. During 2020 interviews were conducted with: serving and retired frontline officers and staff from South Wales Police; strategic leaders in policing, including Basic Command Unit (BCU) Senior Management Teams, Heads of Public Protection and Specialist Crime; the Office of the Police and Crime Commissioner; and Operational and Strategic partners within the National Society for the Prevention of Cruelty to Children (NSPCC), Probation, Sexual Assault Referral Centres (SARCS) and Women's Aid. These interviews were conducted online due to the Covid-19 pandemic and lockdown. Most were interviews of a single individual by at least two of the authors, from which notes were taken and then reviewed for accuracy. Direct quotations are used throughout to illustrate the findings drawn, but are not attributed to individuals in order to preserve their anonymity. Additionally, we accessed South Wales Police information systems to obtain policy and other relevant documents from these time periods. This information was used to triangulate the interview material, as well as for the creation of the timeline contained in the Appendix.

BEFORE PUBLIC PROTECTION: POLICING SEEMINGLY PRIVATE MATTERS

It might seem like stating the obvious to say that all police organisations, including the South Wales Police, are profoundly shaped by the societal context in which they are situated. Of course, police officers themselves are members of society and they will have been taught certain social norms and values like any anyone else. For example, ideals in terms of how family life should be organised, the division of gender roles, the desirability of women's participation in the labour market, and acceptable child-rearing practices, will all be derived rather than distinct from those views and values generally held at the time. Peoples' employment within a police organisation does not fundamentally change this. Thus, it is important to acknowledge that police officers' beliefs about personal or 'private matters' will have some bearing on how they understand their professional role and responsibilities. Indeed, the extent to which police, as well as ordinary citizens, perceive that police powers should legitimately extend into the private sphere of domestic life is the pertinent point for this section. Today, it is clear that societal expectations for police intervention in cases of child abuse, domestic and sexual violence have dramatically changed, but this was certainly not the case prior to the 1980s. At that time, it was more acceptable than not to 'turn a blind eye', because these were seen to be 'private matters', rather than matters for public servants such as the police to deal with. In fact, police were explicitly advised against taking action when responding to domestic incidents on the grounds that doing so would compromise the sanctity of the family unit.[1] Our various interviewees recalled:

Society was different. Domestic abuse was deemed a private matter in society and not just by the police. That equally applied to other areas of public protection in particular child abuse, missing persons and mental health.

As a uniform officer in the 1980s I attended domestic abuse incidents, missing persons, mental health issues and child protection matters. However looking back at that time calls to such incidents certainly were not as prevalent as today ... I do not believe the reason for less calls would be lower volume, quite the contrary. I suspect the main reason lay in society's approach to domestic abuse and its almost acceptability ... reinforcing it was a private matter between a man and a woman.

This was not a systemic failure in the police to consciously not intervene this was systemic in the society we all lived in, police and public alike. It may appear abhorrent to us now but domestic arguments, threats and violence were a way of life for many women.

Traditional gender norms underpinned public and police perceptions alike, leading these issues to be seen as mostly marginal to the proper role of police. Although not completely invisible to police and police work, prior to the 1980s 'women's issues' such as VAWG and tasks pertaining to children (looking after lost children or dealing with those caught up in their parents' offending) occupied a niche position, both in terms of the level of police activity and also who was tasked to undertake it. Female officers represented a very small proportion of the overall total, leading them to be perceived as tokens within police organisations at the time:

> My subdivision was a vast geographical area with a significant population, yet when I joined there was only one policewoman per shift. This was by design and not accident, and was replicated in other subdivisions across South Wales Police. The one policewoman on the shift was only replaced if an individual left and many did.

> It is fair to say that the Constabulary was predominantly male in my early career and the detective world even more so. At times you felt like the 'token female' on a shift parading 25–30 officers and your female role models were far and few between and more often than not working out of other stations.

> On a personal level as a probationer and young police officer I received considerable support and advice from my team. That was not always the case however and there were many male officers, peers and those of rank that openly discriminated against you based on your gender. Bullying in the workplace wasn't a phrase that existed in those days. You certainly had to be resilient and determined to carve out a career in policing as a woman in the 1980s.

If there was animosity and on occasions hostility towards us female officers on shifts you can imagine the response from some members of the community we were dealing with.

It is instructive that those officers who were (at best) unsupported and marginalised, and (at worst) subjected to workplace bullying and harassment, were given those policing tasks also generally considered to be marginal and/or unimportant. Reflecting the world outside, there was a pronounced division of labour along gender lines inside of the police organisation. There remain gender orders and regimes that place men in a dominant position at both macro levels of society and in specific locations like the workplace and the family (Connell 2009). As Miller (1998) points out, policing emphasizes gendered divisions of labour and the construction of different police images for male and female officers, a view reflected by our interviewees:

As a policewoman in the early days you could only wear police issue trousers on night shifts and had to carry your police issue handbag with you at all times!

As rare as female police officers were, female officers that were also mothers juggling childcare and work were even more rare. Even so, I recall as a female Detective who was also a mother being called out in the middle of the night to babysit a Scenes of Crime Officer's child as he was required at a scene and his wife was away …

In the 1980s as a probation officer the perspective was very different. SWP had an entrenched social culture. The police worked and socialised together in the gym and the clubs and it was seen by partners as a 'closed shop'.

Both female officers and their work were often relegated to a less prominent position and certainly one that was not prioritised or afforded much esteem or recognition, revealing policing as one of many sites for socially constructed gendered action. This is consistent with prior scholarship, which has demonstrated how the masculine ethos of policing can promote the trivialisation of 'private matters', as opposed to street crime and public order offences (Edwards 1989).

> As the policewoman you took the witness statement but you were never involved in the suspect interviews. You were predominantly the only support for the victim ... you would deal with the victim only and male colleagues would deal with the suspect.

> In those early days ... I quickly became a 'go to' female officer for my male colleagues who would ask me to make contact with female complainants of rape and serious sexual offences.

> I was the only female in the Department replacing the previous female DC who had transferred to another area. The vast majority of my caseload would be interviewing children who had been sexually abused.

> It was irrelevant if you had no children yourself or any experience with children you were just deemed to be the most appropriate resource to deal with a child purely because you were a woman.

Police officers, whether male or female, were operating in an organisational context which did not equip or support them to take a skilled, interventionist approach to policing 'private matters'. As late as 1989, the official police training guidance referred to domestic disputes as 'a breakdown in day-to-day domestic family relationships' often involving 'no criminal offences', with the stated aim of police attendance being to 'restore the peace' (Bourlet 1990, p. 17):

> I do not recollect the guidance we had if any in the training centre but out on the street we dealt with incidents by the seat of our pants. Common Sense was the usual

yardstick. Public Protection was not a phrase I heard being used. There was no specific department to deal with or follow up at that time.

Training at this stage was mainly classroom based and concentrated on definitions and the law itself. Public protection as a concept did not exist and training at this stage from a public protection perspective centred mainly on sexual offences. Its focus was on identifying criminal offences and bringing offenders to justice. I do not recall any input on prevention, early intervention or working with partners.

In contrast to training provided now it was limited to the tasks you were required to carry out as the officer dealing with a report of a sexual offence e.g. obtaining a full and detailed witness statement, obtaining evidential medical samples but did not include raising awareness or understanding of the complainant's perspective or offender behaviour traits.

Not only hindered by limited training, those policing 'private matters' at the time were also having to work with rudimentary procedures, such as intelligence kept on index cards in a filing cabinet. Additionally, the absence of any specialist or purpose-built facilities meant that interviews of sexually abused children routinely took place at home, school or NSPCC offices.

'Public protection' was a term that I had never heard of or used in those early days. Rather, it was the embryonic safeguarding of a minority few at best.

In essence we were not equipped to provide victims/survivors with the service they deserved. We did the best we could with what was available to us at the time but it was not good enough.

Echoing scholarship on how female officers have 'feminised' police work (Miller 1998), it is notable that it was those officers working within this particular organisational and temporal 'space' who were instrumental in bringing forth both a recognition of the unsuitability of the current approach, as well as directions for improvement. It is to those changes we now turn.

CRIME FIGHTING AND THE EMERGENCE OF PUBLIC PROTECTION

In this section, we document the transition of VAWG from being seen as private matters and largely absent from policing, to criminal offences visible and present on the policing agenda as such. The inception of second wave feminist activism in the 1970s and 1980s drew attention to the scale of domestic violence and the need for agencies to take action. Feminist attention to domestic violence was initially directed at criminalisation and the unlocking of the potential of the criminal justice system on behalf of victims. This was achieved via a reframing of violence within the family from a private matter to a criminal activity, which made criminal justice responses a possible resource. The first priorities for action were raising awareness and addressing the attitudes, behaviours and policies of the police in particular, as likely first responders to these crimes and the 'gatekeepers' to the criminal justice system.

A significant national policy change took place in 1990, when the Home Office officially reversed the non-interventionist position by issuing circular 60/90 that called for a more interventionist approach based on the presumption of arrest when an offence had been committed. Subsequently, across police forces in England and Wales, there was widespread adoption of policies that mandated arrest or other forms of 'positive action' following police attendance, as one way to try to counteract what was perceived to be an indefensible culture of negligence by police.

This was hugely significant for both the police and victims of domestic abuse. It took discretion out of the equation, took control from the offender and removed the responsibility/ onus and subsequently perceived blame from the victim. It made the police service far more accountable for their actions and most importantly non-action.

The most significant drawback with this approach, however, was that the impact on the victim was not necessarily considered.

During this era, more formalised structures were implemented within South Wales Police to improve the police response. With the Temporary Chief Constable's approval, in 1990 the first specialised unit opened in Whitchurch in Cardiff. At that stage it was called the Juvenile Abuse Unit, but subsequently became the Family Support Unit (FSU). This unit operated for three months or more as a trial and then units were rolled out across the Force area. South Wales Police were very much at the forefront with this model, which involved the creation of bespoke settings away from working police stations that included child friendly interview rooms, monitoring rooms and medical suites. Very few forces had specialised units and South Wales Police was the only force to have specialised in victim-only units. One example of the commitment to this approach was that in Treforest, near Cardiff, where two police officers and their families were moved from their adjoining police houses as it was felt this was the best location for the new unit in that area.

FSUs represented a key site for bringing together and fostering expertise in relation to investigating the types of crimes now considered public protection issues – child abuse, domestic abuse and sexual violence. The creation of specialised units affords officers higher status and satisfaction (Jolin and Moose 1997). The establishment of these units was seen to be progressive reform that had a significant impact on the operational and strategic approach to VAWG within South Wales.

The officers within the FSUs were predominantly drawn from uniform resources but were specialist trained officers. Their primary role was to interview children who had been subject to familial abuse. At this time they did not interview the suspect. They would prepare an evidential package including the interview of the child victim and any witness statements and this would be allocated to the Divisional CID officer to progress the investigation and arrest the suspect. The FSU officer worked closely with the CID officer providing support to the victim and their family and liaising with partners.

The FSU was a real game changer and formed the foundation stone of the Public Protection Departments we have today ...

However, one challenge noted with the initial set-up of the FSUs were that they dealt with half of the case, and the Criminal Investigation Department (CID) the rest. This investigative split occurred along gendered lines – FSUs handled victims (women and children) and CID dealt with offenders (men). A gendered division of labour existed both in terms of the units' remit, as well as their staffing.

A significant drawback at this time was that the unit only dealt with the victim and was reliant on the CID officer arresting the offender and expediting the investigation. This proved difficult for a number of reasons including: competing CID priorities; some individual CID officers' reluctance to deal with such cases; and a performance culture and demands of murder investigations that abstracted CID staff from their normal duties sometimes for months on end.

In 1992, I 'aided' with the FSU based at Skewen, near Neath. At that time we dealt only with the children; meeting them with our partner social worker, interviewing them via video at the Family Support Suite and then compiling an investigative package to forward to the relevant CID office for the area where the offence took place. As an FSU detective, you had no say in which CID officer was allocated to progress the suspect element of the investigation. This process, owing to other demands and often the skillset of the officer assigned, led to investigative delays which I found so frustrating and must have no doubt led to further distress of the child who had bravely shared the most personal of information. Thankfully, by 2000, when I deployed full-time to the FSU in Cockett, Swansea, the detectives there were assigned to investigate the crime in its entirety.

FSUs represented change, but not a complete overhaul of the gendered order within the police organisation. Both those working in the units as well as their business portfolio were still viewed by some as occupying the bottom rung of the police hierarchy in terms of status and recognition.

Significantly also the unit was now resourced by both male and female officers. As mentioned this was definitely a step in the right direction, however they were seen by some CID colleagues as 'joking detectives' and in the early days did not receive the recognition they so rightly deserved. Many of their peers just did not recognise that these officers were working with the most vulnerable in our communities who had suffered the most harrowing ordeals at the hands of their own family members. That every day they came to work they dealt with offences that were abhorrent to most in society and they had to soak up the emotional and mental impact that these matters had on the victims, their supportive family members and themselves.

Despite such challenges, these units provided the initial organisational infrastructure necessary to facilitate partnership working with other agencies; for example, with the newly established Women's Safety Unit (WSU) in Cardiff. From 2001, the WSU provided a central point of access for VAWG victims in the Cardiff area. The overriding aim of the WSU was to help victims gain safety, through the provision of advice, advocacy, specialist counselling services, legal services, housing services, refuge provision, and target hardening (Robinson 2003). Victims were provided with an effective, immediate and consistent range of support services at one referral point. Through the provision of these services, the WSU aimed to restore women's faith in the criminal justice system in order to improve reporting rates and to reduce the level of attrition of these types of cases by facilitating inter-agency co-operation. To that end, the WSU developed protocols with South Wales Police (including the secondment and co-location of a South Wales Police officer directly into the WSU) and the Crown Prosecution Service to provide more effective and sensitive treatment of victims.

> The Women's Safety Unit offered services for women in domestic violence relationships. In 2000 women were dying in such relationships and what was being experienced is that perpetrators were not eligible for MAPPA [Multi-Agency Public Protection Arrangements: see next section] as they often had no previous convictions. Prior to the WSU, there was no true sharing of information with partners 'keeping secrets'. There was no systematic response other than the offer of refuge. There was no provision for children per se.

The development and implementation of FSUs and accompanying increased partnership working is both a cause and a consequence of the changing position of women in policing and gendered divisions of police work. Women in senior leadership positions (South Wales Police as well as other agencies) were instrumental in instigating and achieving these changes. For example, in Autumn 2001, the Cardiff Domestic Violence Forum, chaired by Julie Morgan, MP, secured a £300,000 grant during the second wave of funding from the Home Office under the 'Violence Against Women Initiative' of the Crime Reduction Programme. Projects funded under the first wave were almost entirely related to England; therefore, the WSU represented the sole Welsh project funded under this initiative.

> Much progress depended on individuals and their motivation and drive to make the strategic vision of governments and chief officers a reality. Such individuals, often women, were a driving force in making the FSUs a success. In addition, and speaking as a CID officer at this

time, the staff within these units never failed to impress me. They were committed passionate individuals who wanted to do the very best they could for the children they dealt with.

Individual personalities amongst our partners were key to making things happen. Senior positions were held by driven and passionate women who were instrumental in founding Sexual Assault Referral Centres (SARCs) in the South Wales Police area and who had to overcome negativity and obstruction to ensure survivors were provided with the best service possible. This approach continues with women-led teams in the Merthyr, Swansea and Cardiff SARCs.

The early relationship between Welsh Women's Aid and South Wales Police was very much driven by individuals. There did not appear to be a strategic driver instead the desire to make something happen came down to individuals.

Reflecting the changing view of VAWG from private matters to criminal offences, the primary focus at this time was on improving 'crime-fighting' capabilities through better investigative tactics. This was in order to reduce the attrition of cases moving through the criminal justice process, as this was considered the key measure of success at the time:

In these days the police appeared very process driven. It was very much you need to do A, B and C but did not seem to consider the impact on the individual. Police wanted to apprehend the perpetrator to 'sort it out' and were less keen to join our work up. This would often create a disconnect and tension.

Criminal justice outcomes such as arrest, charge and conviction were usually assumed to equate with success from a victim's point of view. As Sherman (1992) noted, 'the effectiveness of the criminal sanction may depend upon the strength of the social fabric in which it is used' (p. 248). A purely crime-fighting approach neglects this fact. The idea of reducing harm through effective risk management and safeguarding (only one component of which might be a pursuing a criminal case) in order to improve victim safety, as the primary aim of police action, had not yet taken hold. We explore the transition to this mode of public protection policing in the next section.

RISK AND THE ASCENDENCE OF PUBLIC PROTECTION

In this section, we chart the initial development and continuing expansion of risk-led approaches to public protection issues. The innovations instigated in South Wales Police during the early 2000s had a significant influence both 'up and out' (in terms of national policy and practice), as well as 'across and within' (the force itself). During this time, several high-profile cases solidified public concern about crime and heightened feelings of fear about the risk posed to members of the public – particularly children – from violent sexual offenders (e.g. the murders of Sarah Payne in 2000, and Holly Wells and Jessica Chapman in 2002). Public concern about crime led to risk management being the chosen route to demonstrate agency effectiveness and to provide reassurance to the public, who felt 'at risk', that 'something was being done' (Nash and Williams 2010).

> These cases created a perfect storm I suppose in terms of changes in society and demands for changes in policing and the police being more accountable. Along with ramifications from the Yorkshire Ripper case, these murders certainly influenced training within South Wales Police and were catalysts for identifying Threat Risk and Harm in large scale voluminous information/intelligence enquiries.

The concept of 'risk' has come to imbue much of the everyday work of criminal justice and partner agencies, perhaps most notably when dealing with domestic abuse. A wealth of research in North America and, increasingly, Europe, is both a cause and a consequence of this shift towards risk-based approaches (Cattaneo and Goodman 2005). The widespread use of risk assessment tools and procedures has been partly due to the need to manage volume in the context of trends towards criminalisation and the introduction of statutory requirements to identify and manage high-risk offenders. The Criminal Justice Act 2003 established Multi-Agency Public Protection Arrangements (MAPPA) in each of the 42 criminal justice areas of England and Wales. These arrangements are designed to protect the public, including victims of crime, from serious harm by sexual or violent and other dangerous offenders. MAPPA requires criminal justice agencies and other bodies to work together in partnership with these offenders, and formalized risk assessment is a key part of this process (Kemshall and Wood 2007).

Risk assessment is also seen as a means to improve more tailored responses to victims. The police, along with a number of partner agencies, have changed their practices in an attempt to take account of the differing levels of risk, danger and harm they face. A multi-staged risk-led approach to responding and investigating domestic abuse has been acknowledged in guidance on policing for a number of years (ACPO 2005; NPIA 2008). Briefly, these are: (1) risk identification, involving the use of a checklist to help police officers identify whether certain risk factors are present for the victim; (2) risk assessment, where the information obtained is translated into a risk level or grade (e.g. standard, medium or high risk) which is designated to the victim, and (3) risk management, where police and other agencies take actions informed by risk assessment to try and prevent further violence and abuse. Since 2009, the Domestic Abuse, Stalking, and Honour-Based Violence (DASH) has been the recommended tool for use by UK police (Robinson 2010). It was developed by a multi-agency expert panel during 2008, building on the development of existing tools by South Wales Police (the FSU9, see Robinson 2004) and the London Metropolitan Police Service (SPECSS, see Richards 2003).

It has been a huge shift for officers to expect them to dynamically assess the situation with victims, to use their 'peripheral vision', listening to what is not said as well as what is said to help 'join the dots' with perpetrators. This was the beginning of an ongoing journey to improve our response to victims as well as to become more perpetrator focussed with our interventions (e.g. the WISDOM project – Wales Integrated Serious and Dangerous Offender Management – which seeks to reduce reoffending through a multi-agency approach).

The key intervention for the third stage of the risk-led approach is the Multi-Agency Risk Assessment Conference (MARAC). First developed in Cardiff in 2003, MARACs put in place plans and responsibilities for monitoring and protecting a proportion of victims deemed to be at high risk, and are attended by a range of agencies including police, probation, specialist domestic abuse services, housing, health and social services (Robinson 2004). Recognising the ability of MARACs to deliver improved safety to victims, the Home Office announced nearly £2 million in funding in March 2007 to support the national implementation of MARACs. Since then, MARACs have become a mainstream intervention, with more than 290 currently in operation across the UK, responding to approximately 110,000 victims and an associated 137,000 children annually (SafeLives 2021).

> The inception of the MARAC in Cardiff really invited good information sharing and collation of data between partners to safeguard victims of domestic abuse.

> There was no consistency force-wide or Wales-wide prior to MARAC. The Home Office model was developed and interest was generated culminating in a number of roadshows. Programme integrity was essential.

Unquestionably, initiatives instigated within South Wales Police prompted a step-change in the scale and coordination of partnership work in response to Domestic Violence and Abuse across the UK, and also have been influential in Europe (e.g. they are prominent within a recently prepared evidence-based guide circulated to police in all EU member states, EIGE 2019), Australia (Commonwealth of Australia 2015; McCulloch et al. 2016) and Canada (Contini and Wilson 2019). By providing a prototype that successfully demonstrated how a multi-agency process for managing risk and reducing harm can be both established and embedded, they shifted public protection work from the margins to the centre.

> There was now a much greater understanding of Threat, Risk and Harm amongst officers working outside of public protection units and that public protection was everyone's business.

> By 2009 tasking and intelligence became much more proactive. Daily tasking across all areas of police business would look at Threat, Risk and Harm. Public protection was fast becoming front and centre of policing.

The South Wales Police Public Protection review in 2011 provided a 'corporate model' for public protection whilst recognising the importance of allowing some flexibility within BCUs to adapt to local needs. Chief Officers made a commitment despite the austerity measures of the time to invest in public protection and increase staffing levels. This led to the employment of specialist domestic abuse risk assessors that then allowed domestic abuse police officers to be more proactive. Subsequent reviews saw continued investment of resources in this area of work.

> Public Protection had arrived on the stage of policing in South Wales. The saying 'what gets measured gets done' saw some of the difficult to measure areas of public protection start to feature in Force Performance. Force Compstat as it was called previously focused on numbers and detection rates of traditional crime types (e.g. Dwelling Burglary, Robbery, Grievous Bodily Harm, Rape etc.). This era saw a shift to include and put on an equal footing focus on threat/risk/harm (e.g. initially top 10 domestic abuse repeat victims, offenders, top 10

missing persons). Developed then to include: SARC referrals, RASSO [Rape and Serious Sexual Offences] attrition rates at court, MOSOVO [Management of Sexual or Violent Offenders] officer caseloads, referrals to victim support, section 136 Mental Health Act, risk assessment and referral of Public Protection Notices (PPNs), etc.

Chief Officers championed public protection, giving kudos and recognition through Force awards and embedding knowledge and understanding of safeguarding and public protection in Promotion Boards. Simultaneously, we were seeing staff that had come through the Public Protection Units rising to senior ranks in policing and with their previous knowledge and skills at grass roots level being able to make a difference strategically.

This was a time in which there was a notable rise in women police officers occupying senior leadership positions. Following Barbara Wilding's appointment as the first woman Chief Constable of South Wales Police in 2004, there was growing female representation across all ranks as well as the appointment of the first female Deputy Chief Constable, BCU Commanders, Head of Criminal Justice, and Head of Specialist Crime. In 2011, the first woman Head of Public Protection was appointed with the first all-female Command Team, all of whom were experienced detectives. There were women leaders within the PCCs Office in addition to those holding national positions within ACPO and the National Police Chiefs Council for the first time.

> In 2004, Chief Constable Barbara Wilding was appointed to South Wales Police and her drive and commitment to the domestic abuse agenda drove performance.

> Public protection was no longer seen as a desk job and this change was reflected in the appointments of senior police officers where it was certainly advantageous to have public protection experience within the officer's portfolio.

Yet even such significant and positive changes cannot provide immunity against poorly skilled responses at the frontline and investigative levels. Around this time the high-profile case involving the Lostprophets band member Ian Watkins came to light. The evidence obtained in the Independent Police Complaints Commission (IPCC) investigation into this case indicated that South Wales Police received multiple reports about his behaviour over an extended period of time, yet in some instances did not carry out even rudimentary investigation, consequently missing opportunities to bring a predatory paedophile to justice earlier than he ultimately was. The Ian Watkins case was perceived to be instrumental in terms of convincing all parties of the necessity to expand the public protection task and accompanying organisational infrastructure even further in order to effectively safeguard the community.

> Intelligence sharing was identified as a failing within the case and although work was already well underway to develop a MASH this case may well have been a catalyst in overcoming obstacles and bringing everyone to the table to make it happen.

Multi-Agency Safeguarding Hubs (MASH) were first introduced in South Wales in May 2015. There were a number of key individuals within South Wales Police and partner agencies with the drive to ensure this model was adopted. MASH are single locations where police and partners are co-located, providing an environment where police officers and staff from many different agencies are able to work together, in effect sharing information in 'real time'. This development further reinforces the need for 'synchrony' between agencies in terms of understanding and communicating about risk and harm (Nash and Williams, 2008, p. 109).

> This real-time information-sharing in MASH enables early identification as well as the right interventions at the earliest opportunity. In South Wales, there is a core team within the hub with specialist services brought in

when need arises to tackle specific concerns – such as practitioners working with victims or perpetrators of domestic abuse. Having this flexibility and an ability to draw on experts means that the hub is able to support complex cases where more than one concern is identified. For example, in families where domestic abuse exists and there are also mental health, drug and/or alcohol problems. In these cases information is gathered from multiple sources and systems and analysed by expert practitioners. This information supports risk assessments and underpins the decision-making process – this then determines what tactics are deployed – and what support is to be provided. By having a range of options from many different partners we are able to tailor the most appropriate intervention. It is truly victim focused.

The expectations for police at all levels towards safeguarding the most vulnerable have been clearly evident in South Wales Police and operational protocols for some time now. Since 2016, the stated definition of vulnerability reads as follows:

> 'A person is vulnerable if as a result of their situation or circumstances, they are unable to take care of or protect themselves from harm or exploitation'. It goes on to advise that 'a situation or circumstances may include, but is not limited to: personal circumstances and characteristics, health and disability, economic circumstances'.

This shift from public protection operationalised as protecting the public from criminal offenders, to one involving a much wider remit concerned with protecting the public from harm, is significant. Obviously, victimisation from crime can be a major source of harm, but so too can harm arise from other (non-criminal) circumstances such as poor mental health, adverse childhood experiences, alcohol and substance misuse. Additional focus and investment of resource into the 'vulnerability agenda' has promoted the growth of both the size and complexity of the public protection task. For example, following an analysis of demand showing a significant increase over time in the number of mental health-related calls received by South Wales Police (e.g. from approximately 10,000 in 2012 to 33,000 in 2016) the South Wales Police increased its 'protecting vulnerable people' (PVP) capacity designated to mental health over and above the one strategic mental health lead member of staff in existence. Four additional roles (Mental Health Liaison Officers) were created and deployed to each of the 4 BCUs. Another example is the establishment of the Missing Persons Critical Incident Group to influence strategic partners to adopt a better approach to children missing from Local Authority care. This involved the provision of two new specialist 'Misper Coordinators' within the control room to risk assess any report of a missing child (e.g. for risk of sexual exploitation). As the pilot was deemed successful in terms of both reducing demand and also focussing more resources according to vulnerability, the specialist control room staff have been substantially increased. A further example is the evolution of the DASH risk checklist into the PPN to include assessment of a range of vulnerabilities alongside domestic abuse. Indeed, the public protection portfolio is now so extensive that it cannot be seen purely as a 'women's issue' for women police to handle.

> Maybe the success is that this is no longer a gender issue but that the right individual with the right skills and experience is appointed to the role. Evidence of the journey for South Wales Police is that protecting vulnerable people is not about one person or one department but that it is a collective responsibility and approach to protecting our communities.

Commenting more than a decade ago on the expansion of public protection, Nash and Williams warned that, 'The police service finds itself with a growing workload in an area which has not been its traditional focus' (2008, p. 256). By the time the Covid-19 pandemic emerged in 2020, South Wales Police was working with a public protection portfolio that included 14 different named areas of vulnerability (Child Exploitation and Online Protection, Child Abuse, Child Sexual Exploitation,

Domestic Abuse, Female Genital Mutilation, Forced Marriage, Honour Based Abuse, MASH, Missing Persons, Mental Health, RASSO/SARCs, MOSOVO/MAPPA/WISDOM, Stalking and Harassment, Vulnerable Adults), each of which needed to be re-evaluated in terms of tactical approaches in the context of the lockdown and accompanying strain on services. As our interviewees noted at the time:

> Covid has created the need to re-evaluate how we reach victims and perpetrators using both back to basics-leaflet drop and more sophisticated approaches to problems, such as Recency, Frequency, Gravity plus algorithms.

> Recognising many children might be in lockdown with their abusers and expecting an increase in reports of child abuse hidden during the pandemic South Wales Police have utilised a local You Tuber with over a million followers to promote support options available to children.

CONCLUSION

In this chapter, we have charted the emergence and continuing social construction of 'public protection' over the past fifty years – as a concept, strategic aim, escalating priority and organising principle for the delivery of operational policing within the South Wales Police.

The social construction of public protection is evident from the shift over time in how child abuse, domestic abuse and sexual offending have been viewed: first as private matters between individuals; then as crimes perpetrated by offenders; and most recently, to harms which are undisputed matters of public concern. These are not mutually exclusive conceptualisations, but are nevertheless useful for explaining why operational responses have changed from predominantly peacekeeping and order maintenance, to law enforcement, and then most recently, to multi-agency working on risk-based harm reduction.

The prominence or otherwise on the policing agenda of these gendered crimes, which disproportionately affect women and girls, is also markedly different across time. So too is the visibility and influence of women in policing during the past fifty years: first as often marginalised tokens; then a minority few exerting some leadership; and then as established insiders at all levels able to instigate strategic changes. Thus, there is a parallel progression in the gender roles and expectations for women in society generally, as well as within police organisations specifically. Today, public protection is not articulated and responded to solely as a 'women's issue', but rather it is 'everyone's business', and starting to be judged accordingly.

Despite the progressive account conveyed within this chapter, we choose to end with a cautionary note. As demonstrated, the definitional boundaries of public protection policing are dynamic, ambiguous and contested. They appear to be constantly revisited, mostly in the direction of expansion and escalation of this portfolio, which is now all encompassing. On the one hand, due recognition and attention to vulnerability and the importance of harm reduction as cross-cutting issues affecting all areas of police work can be seen as a positive development. Historically, the harms associated with VAWG and other public protection issues were underacknowledged if not entirely overlooked as a policing responsibility. Now, clearly the case is different. Indeed, the changing police response to VAWG has been a catalyst for more proactive recognition and responses to other forms of 'hidden' harms such as child exploitation, female genital mutilation and modern slavery, amongst others. However, looking ahead, we have sympathy for the concern raised by Nash and Williams (2008) that public protection has become a 'runaway bandwagon', with the concomitant production of an ever-growing 'basket of worry' that is shouldered mostly by frontline staff. The Covid-19 pandemic provides the police, in South Wales and beyond, the opportunity to re-evaluate approaches to the policing of public protection and, in so doing, reaffirm its priorities for harm reduction within an increasingly pressurised context of limited and stretched resources.

Note

1. As commented by the House of Commons Select Committee on Violence in Marriage (1975).

References

ACPO (Association of Chief Police Officers). 2005. *Identifying, assessing and managing risk in the context of policing domestic violence.* London: Association of Chief Police Officers.

Bourlet, A. 1990. *Police intervention in marital violence.* Milton Keynes, UK: Open University Press.

Cattaneo, L. B. and Goodman, L. A. 2005. 'Risk factors for reabuse in intimate partner violence: a cross-disciplinary critical review'. *Trauma, Violence, & Abuse* 6(2), pp. 141–75. *https://doi.org/10.1177/1524838005275088*

Commonwealth of Australia. 2015. *Domestic violence in Australia.* Finance and Public Administration References Committee. Available at: *https://www.aph.gov.au/parliamentary_business/committees/senate/finance_and_public_administration/domestic_violence/report*

Connell, R. 2009. *Gender.* Cambridge: Polity Press.

Contini, M. and Wilson, B. 2019. *Canadian Multi-Agency Risk Assessment Committee (MARAC) Model Program.* Guelph, Ontario: University of Guelph. Available at: *http://hdl.handle.net/10214/17415*

Edwards, S. 1989. *Policing 'domestic' violence: women, the law and the state.* London: Sage.

EIGE (European Institute for Gender Equality). 2019. *A guide to risk assessment and risk management of intimate partner violence against women for police.* Luxembourg: Publications Office of the European. Available at: *https://eige.europa.eu/gender-based-violence/risk-assessment-risk-management*

Jolin, A. and Moose, C. A. 1997. 'Evaluating a domestic violence program in a community policing environment: research implementation issues'. *Crime & Delinquency* 43(3), pp. 279–97. *https://doi.org/10.1177/0011128797043003003*

Kemshall, H. and Wood, J. 2007. 'Beyond public protection: an examination of community protection and public health approaches to high-risk offenders'. *Criminology & Criminal Justice* 7(3), pp. 203–22. *https://doi.org/10.1177/1748895807078860*

McCulloch, J., Maher, J., Fitz-Gibbon, K., Segrave, M. and Roffee, J. 2016. *Review of the Family Violence Risk Assessment and Risk Management Framework (CRAF).* Melbourne: Monash University.

Miller, S. L. 1998. 'Rocking the rank and file: gender issues and community policing'. *Journal of Contemporary Criminal Justice* 14(2), pp. 156–72. *https://doi.org/10.1177/1043986298014002004*

Nash, M. and Williams, A. 2008. *The anatomy of serious further offending*. Oxford: Oxford University Press.

Nash, M. and Williams, A. 2010. *Handbook of public protection*. Abingdon: Willan Publishing.

NPIA. 2008. *Guidance on investigating domestic abuse*. London: National Policing Improvement Agency.

Richards, L. 2003. *MPS domestic violence risk assessment model*. London: Metropolitan Police Service.

Robinson, A. L. 2003. *The Cardiff Women's Safety Unit: a multi-agency approach to domestic violence*. School of Social Sciences: Cardiff University. Available at: *https://www.researchgate.net/publication/251416613_The_Cardiff_Women's_Safety_Unit_A_Multi-Agency_Approach_to_Domestic_Violence* (accessed 29 July 2023).

Robinson A. L. 2004. *Domestic violence MARACs (Multi-Agency Risk Assessment Conferences) for very high-risk victims in Cardiff: a process and outcome evaluation*. School of Social Sciences: Cardiff University. Available at: *https://www.researchgate.net/publication/237442284_Domestic_Violence_MARACs_Multi-Agency_Risk_Assessment_Conferences_for_Very_High-Risk_Victims_in_Cardiff_Wales_A_Process_and_Outcome_Evaluation* (accessed 29 July 2023).

Robinson, A. L. 2010. 'Risk and intimate partner violence'. In: Kemshall, H. and Wilkinson, B. eds. *Good practice in risk assessment and risk management* 3 ed. London: Jessica Kingsley Publishers, pp. 119–38.

SafeLives. 2021. *Latest UK Marac data*. Available at: *https://safelives.org.uk/practice-support/resources-marac-meetings/latest-marac-data* (accessed 29 July 2023).

Sherman, L. W. 1992. *Policing domestic violence: experiments and dilemmas*. New York: The Free Press.

APPENDIX

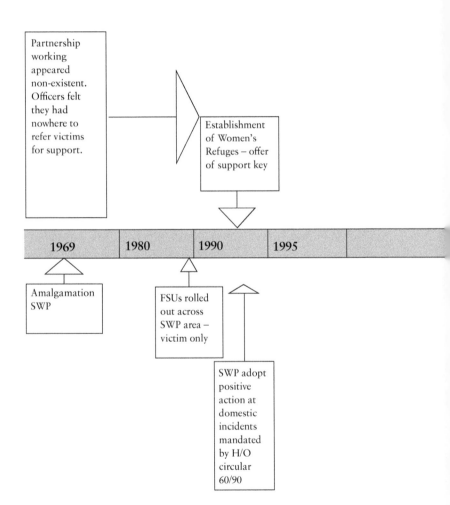

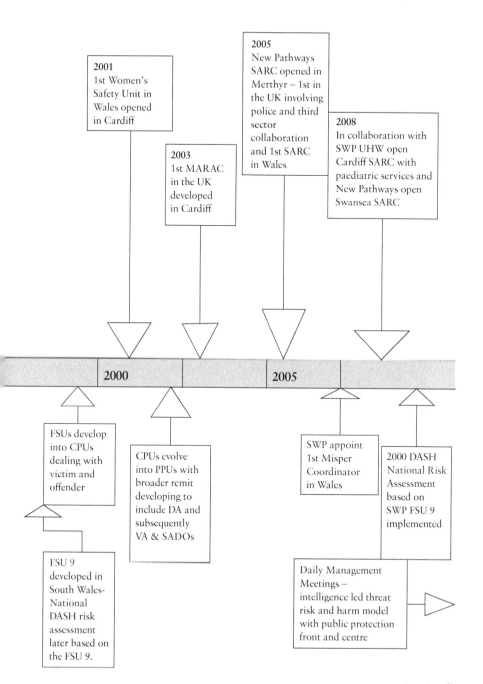

2001
1st Women's
Safety Unit in
Wales opened
in Cardiff

2005
New Pathways
SARC opened in
Merthyr – 1st in
the UK involving
police and third
sector
collaboration
and 1st SARC
in Wales

2008
In collaboration with
SWP UHW open
Cardiff SARC with
paediatric services and
New Pathways open
Swansea SARC

2003
1st MARAC
in the UK
developed
in Cardiff

2000

2005

FSUs develop
into CPUs
dealing with
victim and
offender

CPUs evolve
into PPUs with
broader remit
developing to
include DA and
subsequently
VA & SADOs

SWP appoint
1st Misper
Coordinator
in Wales

2000 DASH
National Risk
Assessment
based on
SWP FSU 9
implemented

FSU 9
developed in
South Wales-
National
DASH risk
assessment
later based on
the FSU 9.

Daily Management
Meetings –
intelligence led threat
risk and harm model
with public protection
front and centre

(continued)

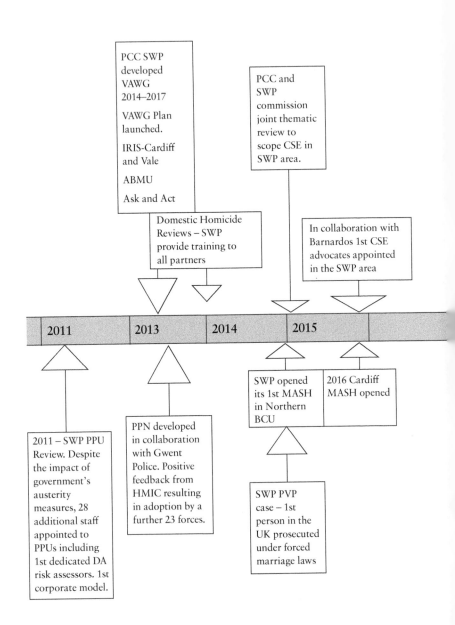

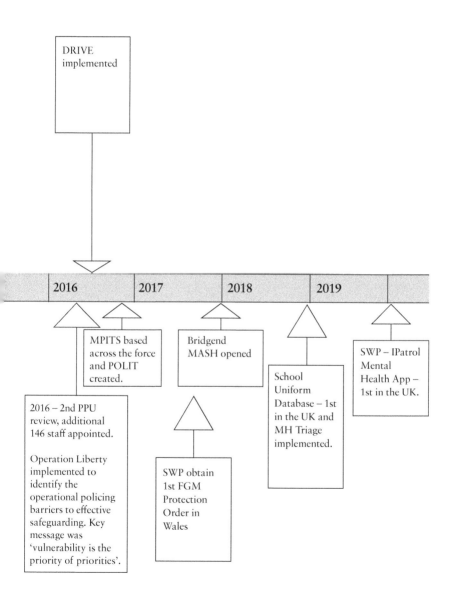

DRIVE implemented

2016 | 2017 | 2018 | 2019

MPITS based across the force and POLIT created.

Bridgend MASH opened

School Uniform Database – 1st in the UK and MH Triage implemented.

SWP – IPatrol Mental Health App – 1st in the UK.

2016 – 2nd PPU review, additional 146 staff appointed.

Operation Liberty implemented to identify the operational policing barriers to effective safeguarding. Key message was 'vulnerability is the priority of priorities'.

SWP obtain 1st FGM Protection Order in Wales

10

POLICING AND THE DILEMMAS OF MEDIA COMMUNICATION

Martin Innes and Catherine Llewellyn-Roberts

Early on the morning of 28 September 2016, officers were called to attend an incident in Queen's Street, Cardiff. When they arrived, they found a man and a woman had tragically been fatally wounded with a knife, and the perpetrator had fled the scene. The first responders took the steps to initiate a murder investigation that would, in due course, lead to the identification and successful prosecution of Andrew Saunders. It transpired that the offender had previously been in a romantic relationship with the female victim, but she had left him and become involved with the second victim, a work colleague. As numerous studies of the aetiology of homicide attest, it was a scenario that is one of the most common motivations for why men kill (Polk 1994).

However, what marked this particular case out as slightly more unusual was that soon after the discovery of the bodies, rumours started to circulate on social media speculating about the cause of the deaths. Specifically, two rumours were acquiring some online traction. Related to significant public awareness and concern about terrorism at that time, the first of these claimed that the Cardiff incident was a terrorist attack. The second rumour was that the victims were members of the homeless community. Thus, in different ways, both had an air of 'surface plausibility' in that they refracted wider public security concerns emanating from a series of prior tensions and incidents.

Moreover, because of this, the rumours were loaded with potential to cause wider and deeper ramifications for community cohesion and public safety.

In an effort to try and proactively manage these potential implications, a decision was taken by the local Basic Command Unit (BCU) Commander and her communications support staff to step outside of the standard routines and rhythms that guide how the police response to fatal violence usually unfolds. This includes an approach whereby initial statements by the police to journalists typically only set out the basic facts of the incident and that an investigation has been launched. The intent being to avoid police giving out misinformation, affording an opportunity for the police crime investigators to confirm what is known, the evidential supports for this, and thus what else needs to be determined if they are to ascertain 'who did what to whom and why?' In this particular case though, it was decided that it was more important to engage in an early debunking of the unfounded rumours before they could acquire too much influence upon public understanding, inducing second order harms upon cohesion and fear. And so it was that the BCU Commander made a press statement to refute and 'squash' the rumours. It worked. With an early official statement, that directly confronted the substance of the unfounded claims, the online trolls, rumour-mongers and speculators desisted. Although it could do nothing to remedy the essential tragedy of two young people having been murdered, it was a communicative act that in all probability mitigated any wider harms and community tensions.

The challenges and dynamics highlighted in the preceding passages exemplify themes about how social media and the new media ecosystem are presenting new complexities and challenges for policing, that have been the subject of several recent academic studies. For instance, in their empirically-led analysis of the immediate aftermath of the terrorist murder of Lee Rigby in 2013, Innes et al. (2020) found that the lack of a coherent strategic communications approach enabled far-right groups to harness social media channels to amplify their messaging and sow discord. Tracking forward a few years to the 2017 UK terror attacks, Innes et al. (2018) report how police had learned their lessons, and were communicating far more rapidly and assertively to reduce opportunities for far-right groups to propagate hate.

Media has always been intimately intertwined with policing. This reflects how much of what the police do – responding to emergencies and crises, and occasions where people have infringed morals and laws – is imbued with the basic ingredients of a drama. In effect, police organisations are a recurring source of dramatic stories that journalists can use to titillate, excite and engage their audiences. Relatedly, fictionalised narratives about crime and criminals, and those who serve to protect from their deeds, have an important role in building a base of public support and legitimacy for the institution of policing more generally (Reiner 2010).

But as hinted at in the story used to open this chapter, reflecting structural shifts in the media ecosystem associated with the disruptive effects of the increasing availability of digital social media channels, the police-media relationship is undergoing some significant and profound revisions. Previous generations of scholars could point to close, mutually supportive, relations between individual police officers and specialist crime correspondents (Chibnall 1977), and how such institutional intertwining 'seeded' an ability to define certain individuals and groups as 'folk devils' and thus targets for the manufacture of 'moral panics' (Cohen 1972). The current state of police-media relations feels substantially different. As captured in the opening story, social media has established a whole series of new channels via which information (both true and untrue) can be transmitted and shared, and it has also significantly increased the pace at which this happens.

Of course, these are not trajectories of development that are exclusive or unique to the police. All social institutions have been disrupted by the compounding effects of the 'information revolution' (Margetts et al. 2016). Indeed, in many ways this is the key point as, somewhat ironically, such impacts have been especially profoundly felt in newsrooms and amongst the practitioners of journalism (Couldry and Hepp 2017). Globally, there has been a dramatic decline in the number of news organisations, and especially local newspapers, providing citizens with reporting on crime and policing in their areas. They have been replaced instead by a plethora of social media channels and platforms via which information (rather than knowledge) can be shared. Those news organisations that do continue, have in turn, been transformed by social media in relation to how their 'content' is produced, transmitted and received by audiences.

That said, for all these changes, stories about crime and policing still retain the essential ingredients for what Altheide (2002) dubs 'media logic'. These are the base ingredients from which media institutions render specific events in the world 'newsworthy', selecting from amongst all the various things that do happen, what is of interest to journalists and their editors to cover, and how this is done. Crime and policing stories are after all, frequently freighted by a sense of moral drama where bad things have been done by 'bad' people, and in respect of which the forces of order need to be restored. Moreover, such narratives often titillate their audiences with scandalous details of wrongdoing.

In this chapter, the aim is to explore these large-scale and sweeping disruptions and developments, and how they manifest in the work of South Wales Police. For communication is central to any public service in terms of how they are subjected to a degree of scrutiny and accountability, and the attempts made to secure and maintain a degree of public confidence and legitimacy. In centring this theme of strategic communications in policing, the chapter does not just cover the kinds of crisis communication that are involved in high-profile emergency response modes, important as they are. Instead, much of the discussion is concerned with the volume and diversity of the more mundane forms of communication that are integral to how a large organisation, providing a range of public services, functions. And where there is an inherent public interest in the work being performed, and a potential for scandal is never far away.

MANAGING MEDIA COMMUNICATIONS

As rehearsed above, in the aftermath of major crimes and incidents police communications work is often especially visible to the public. However, much less is known about the more routine aspects of police strategic communications, and as such, there is value in just mapping out some key patterns and trends in this regard.

In South Wales Police, there is a fundamental threefold division of labour in terms of the organisation of public-facing communications activity. There are corporate communications functions that are performed for and on behalf of the organisation as a whole, undertaken by a central unit of communications professionals. Each Basic Command Unit maintains their own capacity and capability, for more locally-oriented communications with the public, usually channelled through a named press officer. Finally, some of the specialist units have their own assets that they can draw upon. In addition to communicating with the public, it is worth remembering, that in an organisation of over 5,000 staff, spread over a wide geographic area, there is an additional substantial requirement to communicate messages to these people as well. This is in order that they can stay abreast of current organisational strategies, thinking and concerns.

A further layer of complexity derives from bilingualism and the requirement to communicate in Welsh as well as English. The most recent iteration of the Welsh Language Act introduced a statutory duty upon all public services in Wales to ensure their key communications are presented in both languages. This is worth keeping in mind when interpreting much of the data and material presented below, inasmuch as for all their press releases and social media work, South Wales Police generate versions in two languages.

Reflecting the nature of police work, the rhythm and tempo of communications activity can be broadly divided between crisis communications and emergency response, and the more routine kinds of work conducted in 'normal time'. Below the surface of these two principal operational modes though, there has been considerable evolution in how public communications activity via the media is conceived and performed. Historically, it is probably fair to say that there was a far more cautious and controlled approach to the media. Precisely how this manifested at particular moments in time was inflected by the personalities of the senior leaders in the force and how they viewed their media skills, but it was less open and more formal than is usual today.

Equally however, if we scroll back thirty or forty years, the media environment was also markedly different. There were fewer local/regional media outlets operating in South Wales, but they had greater influence, in terms of public reach and political agenda-setting, than their contemporary equivalents possess. Consequently, far greater concern gravitated around any reporting that was to feature in the *Western Mail* or on the BBC Wales evening news. But whilst this description works in terms of conveying broad patterns and trends in police-media relations, this overarching narrative should not obfuscate some of the complexities in terms of how such relations have waxed and waned.

Periodically, and probably similarly to what has happened in many other police forces, South Wales Police has cooperated with 'fly on the wall' documentaries made by broadcast journalists. Through programmes such as *Sierra, Whiskey, Charlie* for the BBC in the 1990s, and *Traffic Cops* more recently, South Wales Police has sought to burnish its reputation by granting access to camera crews to observe their work in close-up detail. On balance, in many such cases, the view from within South Wales Police on the outcomes of participating in such programmes has been mixed. There is certainly value in providing the public with insight into police work, but the footage that makes for good television isn't always that which enhances the reputation of the police. This is over and above the kinds of serious investigative journalism that have contributed to uncovering the kinds of reputationally damaging miscarriages of justice discussed in Allsop (Chapter 7).

Given this backdrop it is difficult to get a good handle on the volume of work that is being performed in terms of communicating with the public by South Wales Police. One indicator though can be derived from looking at the volume of 'media calls' over time. This is useful because it provides a relatively stable metric of activity. For example, Table 10.1 below tracks the number of 'media calls' established by South Wales Police annually between 2015–19.

Table 10.1: South Wales Police annual media calls

Year	Number of media calls
2015	2,757
2016	2,613
2017	2,873
2018	3,713
2019	3,843

From these data it can be discerned that there is a general trend of the volume of media work increasing. This is potentially interesting in light of the aforementioned 'de-specialisation' of crime reporting in media organisations, wherein far fewer journalists now focus exclusively on crime and policing issues, compared to previous decades. However, in terms of its impact upon the overall level of 'demand' for police stories, the decline in specialisation in crime reporting is probably over-ridden by the effects of the multiplication and diversification of media outlets.

Within these figures are embedded a number of regular media campaigns conducted by South Wales Police that are programmed into the calendar, anticipating known seasonally varying crime problems. For example, the Communications Department runs its annual 'Operation Bang' campaign in the run-up to Halloween and bonfire night, in an attempt to dissuade and deter young people from engaging in anti-social behaviour. The 'Operation Bang' brand is now well established in South Wales having been developed over a number of years, and utilises a range of multi-modal communication assets, ranging from social media clips to posters, to try and get its core message across. Similarly, in the period before Christmas every year, campaigns targeting domestic violence and drink-driving are activated.

There is a delicate balance to be struck in media communications by the police, given much of the 'raw' material they are dealing with. This requires navigating between informing and sensationalising, and enhancing public situational awareness of what is happening without it tipping over into prurience. The nature of some of these sensitivities are illustrated by extracts from the following media release published by one of the BCUs in South Wales in June 2015:

Take heed of burglary threat.
Many people in xxxx are failing to heed repeated warnings on the threat of burglars. A spike in burglaries in the xxxx areas has sparked fears that householders are ignoring our security advice and that the message is still not getting through ... In recent weeks we have been upping the ante on appeals to the public right across xxxx to secure their property, whether it's their house, shed, garage or bike, to prevent criminals from making off with personal property, however the message is still not getting through.[1]

The intent behind this message was clear; to warn the public about an increase in burglaries and to try and influence them to engage in protective behaviours. In this regard, it is typical of many similar messages that are communicated by police across England and Wales every year. However, viewed through an alternative lens, it very much adopts a 'fear frame', trying to leverage behaviour change through frightening the audience about the risks they are exposed to. In effect, it is a logic model that involves police increasing fear of crime in an effort to reduce crime rates.

This highlights several of the key tensions and dilemmas invoked when organising police strategic communications with the public. In theory at least, a subsidiarity principle in the construction and communication of messages is probably a good thing. This is because it allows messages to be tailored to local contexts, interests and problems, so that they will be most relevant and impactive. However, police officers are not experts in how to influence public opinion via mediated communication, and the complex issues of cognition, affect and behaviour that have to be negotiated and reconciled when doing so. As a consequence of which, although well-intentioned, some of what they say can have unintended effects – as noted above. But at the same time, the tendency to centralise the authoring of communications can lead to a neglect of the kinds of local texture and nuance that can be crucial in capturing the attention of the intended audience members. Thereby, reducing the likelihood of police strategic communications shaping public cognition, affect and behaviour.

SOCIAL MEDIA COMMUNICATIONS

As with most organisations and institutions, policing has been profoundly influenced by the dynamics and mechanics of the information age, and its internet-based technologies, such as social media. The extent to which the more interactive, informal and responsive style of communication afforded by social media platforms has disrupted long established patterns of organisational communication is now well documented (Margetts et al. 2016). Similarly, a number of studies have attended to how such processes of reform and reconfiguration are being manifested in a policing setting (Crump 2011; Bullock 2018). Allied to which, there is a growing evidence base about how such trajectories of development include new forms of crime harm and risk, that police are having to take responsibility for managing and mitigating a range of cyber-enabled and cyber-dependent offending (Wall 2007; Dupont 2013).

South Wales Police have a presence on Facebook, Twitter, Instagram, YouTube and LinkedIn. Reflecting the organisational structure highlighted above, there are various corporate, divisional and specialist unit accounts operating on both Twitter and Facebook, but only single corporate accounts for Instagram and YouTube. As is made clear in the Force's policy documentation, there are a range of risks and opportunities attached to social media usage, and a balance that has to be struck between encouraging and facilitating public engagement by individual officers and units, and the potential risks to the organisation's reputation and staff safety, if people message content they should not or comment in ways that are inappropriate. As a consequence of which, over time it is possible to observe a bit of movement back and forth between corporate control and regulation, and more of an 'organic' locally driven approach. Related to which, it is apparent that South Wales Police's policy and posture in this regard is not the same as that adopted by some of the other forces in Wales.

Such issues of balance notwithstanding, there is some empirical evidence to suggest that social media is becoming increasingly important to how South Wales Police communicates and engages with its publics. For instance, Figure 10.1 below tracks the number of followers for SWP's corporate and Facebook and Twitter accounts for the past four years:[2]

The trajectory of development is unmistakable. The force estimates that its main corporate Twitter account reaches approximately 11% of the adult population across South Wales, with the equivalent divisional accounts reaching around 6%. By way of contextualising these figures, for England and Wales it is estimated that around 15% of adults used Twitter, and approximately 60% have a Facebook account.

In 2018, the force conducted a survey of a limited number of its Twitter followers, wherein 69% of the respondents stated that they were most interested in using this channel to 'access updates about incidents'. The next highest response was to get 'insights into police work' which was endorsed by 29%. Especially intriguing though is when we compare these data to similar questions

Figure 10.1: South Wales Police main social media account interactions by year (to 30/06)

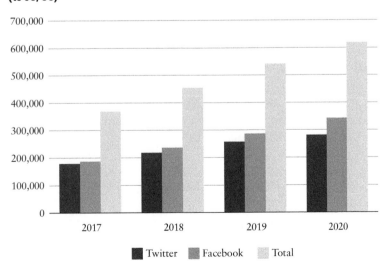

posed to followers of the force's Instagram account, where 80% of the users of that platform said they were using it to get 'insights into police work'. Instagram followers were also far more likely to say they also used WhatsApp and YouTube, than were Facebook and Twitter users.

These patterns are worth highlighting on the grounds that they provide us with an important insight – that different social media platforms enable police to engage with different segments of the public. This is confirmed by looking at other data. For example, of the 11,915 followers of the SWP Instagram account in February 2019, 44% were aged under 24. Whereas, 62% of the 121,717 Facebook followers and 53% of the 127,112 Twitter followers were over 45 years of age.

There is a clear difference in scale across the platforms used by South Wales Police, but all of them are potentially valuable in terms of giving the force an opportunity to communicate directly with at least certain sections of the public, without the additional interests and pressures that journalists reporting on stories bring with them. To a degree, this is a view reciprocated by those who follow South Wales Police accounts. In the aforementioned 2018 survey of Twitter followers, one question asked about trust in different sources of information:

- A total of 95% of those surveyed said they trusted South Wales Police's Twitter feed either 'always' or 'sometimes', and 98% expressed similar sentiments in respect of the Force's website.
- This compares with 64% who trusted Twitter generally, 69% who trusted local news websites, and 24% who felt they could trust information accessed via Facebook.

That said, such data do not tell us much about the content that these different platforms are being used to access. When we turn to investigate such matters, the data are revealing. For instance, in June 2020, two out of the top three Facebook posts made by South Wales Police with the most interactions were stories about police dogs. Similarly, on Twitter, one of the three most liked stories concerned the retirement of a police horse.

As an instrument for public engagement social media can have both positive and negative impacts on public perceptions of policing. One example of this and how it can be used positively by police was the 2014 NATO Summit, which was centred upon the Celtic Manor Hotel in Newport within the Gwent Police area whilst several associated events were held in Cardiff. The number of world leaders attending (from President Obama down) meant it had impact across the whole of Wales and South West England. For South Wales Police, the security operation implemented for it was literally unprecedented, in the proper sense of the word. It involved miles of security fencing being put up around a number of key venues and considerable disruption to residents and commuters over a period of several weeks.

Another highly visible manifestation of the Summit was the appearance of large numbers of armed police officers on the streets of Cardiff in the days leading up to the main event. The combination of a large number of VIPs, alongside heightened concerns about the threat of Islamist-inspired terror attacks, meant that UK policing's mutual aid arrangements had been triggered, with the result that armed officers (and other personnel) from forces across the country were deployed to South Wales. Monitoring public social media at the time identified that the sudden (at least from the public's point of view) appearance of highly visible armed police patrols on the streets of Cardiff had triggered a fair degree of concern and anxiety. But a quick bit of strategic thinking by senior officers managed to turn this into an opportunity. The officers on the streets were told to positively engage with the public, as much as they could, in the lead-up to the summit. As a consequence, pictures of children and their parents posing with armed officers and their armoured vehicles in and around Cardiff started appearing on Twitter, Instagram and Facebook feeds. These grew in volume accompanied with far more positive messages about the police presence.

COVID, COMMUNICATION AND CONTROL

As with so much else, the global coronavirus pandemic has revealed much about the underlying conditions of social order and the police role in its production and reproduction. For amongst many things, the response to the pandemic has figured as a massive natural experiment in the conduct of social control and the role of strategic communications therein. Confronted by an invisible pathogen with a clear capacity to deliver significant public harm, the police were rapidly enrolled in a whole-of-government influence operation, designed to effect profound public behaviour change in an effort to try and reduce the risks of infection and transmission. And where behaviour change campaigns are typically fairly targeted towards particular audience segments and certain individuals, in this case, the intent was to leverage a collective adoption of social distancing measures and associated alterations in patterns of public interaction. Of course, this effort extended significantly beyond policing, but the police were assigned a pivotal role in dealing with those who refused compliance.

Engaging with these developments and in common with other forces, South Wales Police configured their approach around the national '4Es' model advocated by the National Police Chiefs Council of 'engage, explain, encourage, enforce'. The logic being that most people, most of the time, would follow governmental guidelines and stipulations, such that their legal enforcement would only be needed as a 'last resort', for a small minority of individuals who could not be persuaded or cajoled to conform. And for the most part, it appears to have worked as intended, with opinion surveys suggesting high levels of public permission for the police approach.

This notwithstanding, an added wrinkle of complexity for South Wales Police (and the other three forces in Wales) is that responsibility for public health in Wales is devolved and as such, when Welsh Government policy and/or messaging departed from that of the Westminster Government, especially given that policy has been evolving rapidly, this created a lack of clarity.

On occasion, clear tensions between government ministers' expectations and desires, and how police have been seeking to operationalise their role, have been observed. This was particularly on display in mid-December 2020 when, confronted by a variant of the virus affording it with enhanced transmissibility, first the Westminster and then the Cardiff governments rapidly shifted to a lockdown position, less than seven days before Christmas. Understandably unpopular, the ramifications for policing were covered in a BBC Wales article headlined 'Covid: Policing Christmas rule-breakers in Wales "difficult"' (Flint 2020). In the text Welsh Health Minister Vaughan Gething is cited as saying he wants to see an 'enforcement-first approach' to rule-breakers. In response to which, representatives of the Wales Police Federation were quoted describing just how difficult this is, and the fact that their members have already reported multiple instances of being coughed upon and spat at.

These kinds of sentiments were broadly aligned with the corporate messaging put out by South Wales Police, who in a press statement issued on 21/12/20 stressed:

> The last thing any police officer wants to do over the Christmas period is to have to issue fixed penalty notices for breaches of the Coronavirus regulations and I am appealing to the public to do the right thing so we don't have to. The threat posed by Covid-19 to all communities in South Wales is very real and the Welsh Government's regulations exist to save lives and protect our NHS. It has been an extremely difficult year for everyone, including the officers, staff and volunteers of South Wales Police, who have been working tirelessly to support the public health response to Covid-19. Police officers, PCSOs and police staff colleagues will be working throughout the festive period, fighting crime and responding to the needs of some of the most vulnerable in our society. They know how difficult it is to be away from their own families at Christmas, and they do not want to ruin the occasion for anyone. So I'd again appeal for the public's support to do the right thing so we don't have to enforce the legislation.[3]

This extract exemplifies a number of the themes highlighted in the preceding sections. The dominant sentiment is clearly one of trying to encourage people to comply because it is the right thing to do, and to cast the imposition of fixed penalty notices as something that will be undertaken reluctantly by police. Furthermore, in accenting the impact on police officers, police staff and their families, the statement is clearly attempting to articulate the ethos that 'the police are the public and the public are the police.' In adopting this perspective, it is a mode of strategic communications aligned with what Sir Robert Mark, former Commissioner of the Metropolitan Police, dubbed the philosophy of 'winning by appearing to lose'. Mark's profound insight was that public legitimacy and permission for policing sensitive and contentious issues was not necessarily advanced by emphasising 'hard' policing power'. Instead, by stressing how policing was on the back foot and constrained, it is sometimes possible to secure greater public compliance, obedience and support.

Additionally though, the coronavirus pandemic also illustrates the difficulties and challenges for a local policing agency in terms of communicating with its local communities in a 'noisy' information environment. For although South Wales Police can set out their position and approach in the communications they transmit across the media and social media channels they have available to them, this does not mean this is the dominant message received by large numbers of the public. Compelling statements by politicians and indeed other police forces can capture much of the media 'bandwidth' in terms of what stories and lines major news organisations report. These can easily override any local communications and approaches, especially where these are more considered and more complexly constructed.

But this is just one of the many challenges of police media communications work.

Although at the time of writing data was not available, it seems plausible that the Covid-19 global health pandemic will have instantiated and accentuated the broad patterns and trends mapped out above, inasmuch as social media is playing an increasingly influential role in terms of how police engage and interact with members of the public. Layered on top of which, the restructuring of the mass media industry will likely induce added complexities to be negotiated and nuanced. Whilst attending to such techno-political forces and their implications, it is important that we do not over-state the situation, after all much police work is still a very 'analogue' undertaking. That said, in a short period of time, the emergence and diversification of social media has provided new and innovative ways by which police can send messages to the public, and listen to the 'chatter' online to inform their work.

COMMUNICATING THE FUTURE

In turning to think about how the patterns and trends laid out in the preceding section are likely to evolve and develop into the future, there are a couple of general maxims from the academic discipline of science and technology studies worth introducing. The first of these holds that 'first we shape the technology, then the technology shapes us'. The essential idea being that although human operators typically invent and implement new technologies and devices to help meet a need or solve a challenge, they cannot anticipate all the consequences that flow from its introduction. This is especially so when we are talking about complex and contingent social systems such as policing and, as a consequence, there are likely to be an array of intended and unintended effects. The second maxim pivots around the sense that technologies are typically morally and political neutral, and as such, can induce both good and bad outcomes, often at the same time.

Blended together, these maxims certainly provide enhanced understanding of the police relationship to new information communications technologies, such as the internet and social media. For, as rehearsed above, these have afforded new mechanisms via which the police can engage, and talk with and listen to, their communities. But equally, these same technologies are increasingly seen as responsible for an array of harms that are likely to register increasingly strongly on the police's radar. For instance, a number of social media sites, especially those utilising strong end-to-end encryption, have proven potent enablers of child sexual abuse, when in the hands of individuals with such proclivities. Relatedly, they have facilitated a significant increase in the sharing and availability of images of child sexual abuse.

One problem associated with social media that it is predicted will likely become increasingly salient to the future of policing is the management of misinformation and disinformation. This is not a new problem for policing. After all, as Innes (2014) documents in his case study of the triggers of a public disorder incident that occurred in Birmingham in the early 2000s, it is well evidenced that unchecked rumours disseminated by alternative media sources, can result in serious consequences. But what social media do provide is a capacity and capability for disinforming and misinforming messages to take hold at an unprecedented scale and pace.

Research on social media's involvement in constructing and communicating deliberately misleading messages (disinformation) and similar, but unintentionally misleading ones (misinformation), has largely circulated around significant democratic events and elections (Benkler et al. 2018). This reflects how, in the public and political mind, the totemic example of such activities is provided by the influence operation run by the St Petersburg based 'Internet Research Agency' (aka the 'troll factory') and its attempts to interfere with the outcome of the 2016 US Presidential election (Dawson and Innes 2019).

There is evidence that other malign online actors have learned from and adapted some of the tactics and techniques pioneered by the IRA's digital operators. Grinnell et al. (2020) suggest that this can be thought of as a twin-track process of 'normalisation and domestication'. The latter construct focusing upon how similar forms of digital deception are increasingly understood as 'part and parcel' of how political campaigns and negotiations are conducted. Related to which, the notion of 'normalisation' conveying how it is all seen as just an ordinary and unremarkable feature of living life online.

Given that Cardiff is the home of the Welsh Government and Senedd, potentially these processes might have a direct and material impact upon the work of South Wales Police going forward. If allegations of electoral fraud and political corruption, whether founded or unfounded, become a regular feature of the election cycle, then South Wales Police might find itself having to engage far more frequently in the 'policing of politics'. Elements of this are already happening in terms of monitoring the amount of online hate and abuse that is directed at political representatives of all kinds, via online portals. The levels of polarisation and antagonism associated with the Brexit process and other recent European elections, have already signalled the extent to which public figures are subject to increasingly troubling threats and intimidation, requiring police to implement 'soft target protection measures'.

The above is symptomatic of a wider trajectory of development, wherein 'trolling', digital harassment and a myriad of other forms of cyber-enabled harassment have been growing as a form of social problem, that the public seemingly want the police to engage with. This is in addition to the massive volumes of online financial frauds and scams that are recorded each year. In the context of the Coronavirus pandemic and the extended lockdowns that have been made, there is increasing concern about the possible implications of young people spending more and more time online, potentially exposing them to a variety of different extremist ideologies.

Indeed, the scale of these problems is such that demand for policing services across each of these domains far outstrips the police's capacity to supply appropriate resources. Consequently, managing and mitigating the scale and prevalence of these types of crime problem are likely to require more sophisticated strategic communications crime prevention campaigns being designed and delivered by the police, as they seek to influence the behaviour of ordinary citizens to better protect themselves from the growing array of digital risks and threats.

An equally challenging future scenario however, could relate to criminals seeking to 'weaponise' disinformation in pursuit of their own ends. One could imagine a scenario, for example, where a police officer is the target of a smear campaign, alleging corruption or misconduct, motivated by a criminal seeking revenge on officers who have disrupted their activities. These kinds of possible futures come freighted with a range of ethical and normative dilemmas. For example, if by monitoring social media channels police detect signals that an algorithm interprets as indicating an individual might be going down a path of criminality, could they, should they, direct micro-targeted influencing messages towards this individual to try and deter them?

In a not dissimilar fashion, in a highly polluted media eco-system, where disinformation and misinformation is routinely profligate, would it ever be justified for police to use 'reassurance bots' to boost their public messaging, in order to quash a malicious rumour that might be generating fear?

CONCLUSION

Whilst the core work of policing and by extension the whole institution itself is sometimes referred to as 'law enforcement', five decades of academic research on the police has demonstrated that enforcing the law is only one part of what the police do, and is often done as a 'last resort', only when other options have been exhausted. Far more of the social order maintenance that policing supplies is achieved through techniques of influence and persuasion, accepting that they are ultimately underpinned by a legally endowed capacity to invoke coercive force and sanctions to secure compliance.

Framing the social functions and performance of policing in this way, starts to illuminate how and why communication is so important to the mission. For how the public thinks about and perceives the police matters in terms of willingness to follow police issued instructions, and for the levels of support and permission the public provides to the police. Indeed, it is quite plausible to assert that, what the public thinks of the police is far more central to the British policing model, than to the principles and traditions guiding the policing styles adopted in other countries.

It would be naïve to think that everyone is equally receptive to police messaging and communications. Indeed, part of the value of adopting a high-resolution case study of South Wales Police's public communications strategies and practices, is in illuminating some of the complexities and tensions that are routinely being negotiated. For what emerges from this approach is a recognition of just how difficult it is to think comprehensively about the organisation and conduct of policing, without including some analysis of how strategic communications messages about these topics is transmitted and received on an ongoing and recurring basis.

Notes

1. This extract has been edited to remove disclosive data about the locality concerned.
2. The figures for 2020 are only up until June, and for reasons expanded on below can reasonably be expected to have increased.
3. *https://www.south-wales.police.uk/news/south-wales/news/Our-approach-to-policing-over-the-christmas-period/* (accessed 21 December 2020)

References

1993. Welsh Language Act. *1993, c38*. Available at: *https://law.gov.wales/culture/welsh-language/welsh-language-act-1993*

Altheide, D. 2002. *Creating fear: news and the construction of crisis.* New York: Aldine de Gruyter.

Benkler, Y., Faris, Y. and Roberts, H. 2018. *Network propaganda: manipulation, disinformation, and radicalization in American politics.* New York: Oxford University Press.

Bullock, K. 2018. 'The police use of social media: transformation or normalisation?' *Social Policy and Society* 17(2), pp. 245–58. *https://doi.org/10.1017/S1474746417000112*

Chibnall, S. 1977. *Law and order news: an analysis of crime reporting in the British Press.* London: Tavistock Publications.

Cohen, S. 1972. *Folk devils and moral panics: the creation of the mods and rockers.* London: Paladin.

Couldry, N. and Hepp, A. 2017. *The mediated construction of reality.* Basingstoke: Palgrave Macmillan.

Crump, J. 2011. 'What are the police doing on Twitter? Social media, the police and the public'. *Policy & Internet* 3(4), pp. 1–27. *https://doi.org/10.2202/1944-2866.1130*

Dawson, A. and Innes, M. 2019. 'How Russia's Internet Research Agency built its disinformation campaign'. *The Political Quarterly* 90(2), pp. 245–56. *https://doi.org/10.1111/1467-923X.12690*

Dupont, B. 2013. 'Cybersecurity futures: how to regulate current risks'. *Technology Innovation Management Review* 3(7), pp. 6–11.

Flint, R. 2020. 'Covid: policing Christmas rule-breakers in Wales "difficult"'. BBC News. Available at: *https://www.bbc.co.uk/news/uk-wales-55387700* (accessed 20 December 2020).

Grinnell, D., Innes, M., Innes, H., Harmston, D. and Roberts, C. 2020. *Normalisation et domestication de la désinformation numérique : les opérations informationnelles d'interférence et d'influence de l'extrême droite et de l'État russe en Europe*. Heredote. Available at: *https://www.herodote.org/spip.php?article944*

Innes, M. 2014. *Signal crime: social reactions to crime, disorder and control*. Oxford: Oxford University Press.

Innes, M., Innes, H., Dobreva, D., Chermak, S., Huey, L. and McGovern, A. 2018. *From minutes to months*. Cardiff: Cardiff University.

Margetts, H., John, P., Hale, S. and Yassera, T. 2016. *Political turbulence: how social media shape collective action*. Princeton: Princeton University Press.

Polk, K. 1994. *When men kill: scenarios of masculine violence*. Cambridge: Cambridge University Press.

Reiner, R. 2010. *The politics of the police* 4 ed. Oxford: Oxford University Press.

Wall, D. S. 2007. *Cybercrime: the transformation of crime in the information age*. Cambridge: Polity Press.

11

POLICE GOVERNANCE
AND DEVOLUTION

Peter Vaughan

South Wales Police, along with the other police forces in Wales, occupies a unique position in relation to police governance.

On the one hand, it is part of the system that governs territorial police forces in England, where the tripartite arrangement of Home Secretary, police and crime commissioners and chief constables applies. On the other, it is, in practical terms, a key player in the devolved political landscape of Wales where responsibility for the majority of public services, other than policing, rests with the Welsh Government.

Against this backdrop, this chapter will examine the current constitutional and political landscape, and what it means for South Wales Police in the delivery of its services. The chapter also considers what scope there may be for changes in the future.

In doing so the author will draw upon his experience of policing the communities of South Wales over four decades, including a period of eight years as chief constable. Additionally, the author's perspective has been informed by serving as a Commissioner on the Commission for Justice in Wales. This was established by the then First Minister of Wales, Carwyn Jones, and chaired by Lord John Thomas of Cwmgiedd who has agreed that the Commission's findings can be reflected in this chapter.

During his tenure as Chief Constable, the structure of police governance changed significantly, with the introduction of police and crime commissioners. Such changes notwithstanding, the fundamental principles that underpin policing have remained constant: policing with the consent and support of the public, and based on a deep understanding of communities.

POLICE GOVERNANCE

The history of police governance from the nineteenth century to the present day has been extensively covered by Madge (Chapter 2) and so those details will not be repeated in this chapter. Instead, we will briefly consider that background and then summarise the key features of the current governance structure. Whilst these matters are not specific to South Wales Police, they form an important context for the relationship of policing to Welsh devolution, a topic we will consider later.

As was documented by Madge (Chapter 2), there developed during the nineteenth century two separate systems of provincial police governance. There were watch committees in the boroughs and in counties, initially, justices in quarter sessions and, subsequently, standing joint committees of magistrates and county councillors.

The status of chief constables differed too. In the boroughs, the chief constable was regarded as part of the borough administration and there was a lack of clarity as to the relationship between the watch committee and the chief constable. In the counties the chief constable, since the legislation of the nineteenth century, had control over the disposition of the force and in respect of the appointment, promotion and discipline of its members.

The uncertainties regarding the legal position in the boroughs amongst other matters, led to the Royal Commission on the Police from 1960 to 1962 which, in turn, resulted in the Police Act 1964.

This was the most important and influential piece of police legislation since the nineteenth century. In particular it:

(a) Established as police authorities the watch committees of boroughs and cities, and the police committees of county councils in respect of counties. Where forces were joined together through mergers, there would be combined police authorities (as occurred following the amalgamations in South Wales in 1969);

(b) made it clear that the relevant police force was under the direction and control of its chief constable;

(c) set out the role of the Home Secretary, thus establishing the tri-partite relationship with police authorities and chief constables.

The principle of 'direction and control' has been used as the basis for asserting the operational independence of the chief constable. It is not defined in statute and continued to be the subject of debate and legal challenge after 1964. However, it has remained as a cornerstone of policing to this day.

The current framework for the governance of the police is contained in the Police Reform and Social Responsibility Act 2011 and, importantly, the Policing Protocol made under it.[1]

The 2011 Act abolished police authorities and replaced them with elected police and crime commissioners (PCCs). It also re-stated that a police force is under the direction and control of its chief constable. Further to which, under the Act, the PCC and chief constable are declared to be legal entities as corporations sole.

The Protocol sets out in detail the respective roles and responsibilities of PCCs, Chief Constables, Police and Crime Panels and the Home Secretary.

The following is a brief summary of the main aspects in relating to each:

The PCC:

(a) Sets the strategic direction and objectives of the force through the Police and Crime Plan, which must have regard to the Home Secretary's Strategic Policing Requirement (SPR);

(b) scrutinises, supports and challenges the overall performance of the force;

(c) holds the Chief Constable to account for the performance of the force;

(d) decides the budget and sets the precept for the force area;

(e) appoints and removes the Chief Constable;

(f) maintains an efficient and effective police force for the force area;

(g) enters into collaboration agreements with other PCCs and other bodies;

(h) provides a local link between the police and communities;

(i) holds the Chief Constable to account for the performance of the force's functions;

(j) issues an annual report to the Police and Crime Panel;

(k) monitors complaints against members of the force and deals with complaints against the Chief Constable;

(l) has responsibilities beyond those relating to the police force, for example, in the delivery of community safety and crime reduction, and for the enhancement of the delivery of criminal justice in their area.

The Chief Constable:

(a) Has responsibility for maintaining the Queen's Peace and has direction and control of the force's officers and staff;

(b) is accountable to the law and the PCC for the exercise of police powers and for the delivery of efficient and effective policing;

(c) in leading the force acts with impartiality;

(d) appoints the force's officers and staff;

(e) supports the PCC in the delivery of the Police and Crime Plan;

(f) assists the PCC in planning the force's budget;

(g) has regard to the Strategic Policing Requirement;

(h) is the operational voice of policing in the force area;

(i) enters into collaboration agreements with other chief constables and other bodies;

(j) has day-to-day responsibility for the financial management of the force.

The Police and Crime Panel:

(a) Its stated purpose is to provide checks and balances in relation to the PCC by scrutinising and challenging the PCC on the exercise of the latter's statutory functions;

(b) has powers of veto in relation to a proposed precept and the proposed appointment of a chief constable;

(c) has powers of review in relation to the PCC's Annual Plan, and Police and Crime Plan.

(d) can require the PCC to attend the Panel to answer questions;

(e) has the power to appoint an acting PCC if the PCC is incapacitated, resigns or is disqualified;

(f) has responsibility for complaints against the PCC other than those of a serious or conduct nature, which must be referred to the Independent Office for Police Conduct.

The Home Secretary:

(a) The Protocol states that

> the establishment of PCCs has allowed the Home Office to withdraw from day to day policing matters, giving the police greater freedom to fight crime as they see fit, and allowing local communities to hold the police to account.

A point we will return to later in this chapter.

(b) The Home Secretary retains legal powers to intervene in policing and has a specific statutory responsibility to issue a Strategic Policing Requirement.

Finally, in relation to the Protocol it is worth noting that throughout it emphasises the operational independence of chief constables and their forces. Thus, at Paragraph 18 it is stated:

> … the PCC must not fetter the operational independence of the police force and the Chief Constable who leads it.

This is followed up by Paragraph 22, which confirms that

> [a]t all times the Chief Constable, their constables and staff, remain operationally independent in the service of the communities that they serve.

Finally, Paragraph 30 confirms that

> [t]he operational independence of the police is a funda-
> mental principle of British policing. It is expected by the
> Home Secretary that the professional discretion of the
> police service and oath of office give surety to the public
> that this shall not be compromised.

The Protocol goes on to deal with other aspects of operational policing in greater detail. Taken together, this is the background against which policing in the context of devolution will be examined.

DEVOLUTION, THE POLICE, AND THE CRIMINAL JUSTICE SYSTEM

The devolution settlement in Wales has added a further layer of complexity to the governance of policing. The Government of Wales Act 1998 established the National Assembly for Wales (now the Senedd or Welsh Parliament). Since that time the Welsh Government, although not having oversight of policing in Wales, has taken an increased interest in policing and other elements of the criminal justice system. As part of this, it could be said that, in relation to the police, the tri-partite structure has become a four-part or quadripartite structure, with Welsh Government joining the Home Office, PCCs and Chief Constables in the governance of the police service.

In this section, the Criminal Justice System (CJS) and its operation in the Welsh devolved setting will be examined, particularly in relation to the complexity of the system and tensions arising from it.

The overall complexity of criminal justice policy and organisation

The police service operates within the CJS, alongside the Crown Prosecution Service (CPS), courts, prisons and probation services. It is, however, not a system in the ordinary sense of the word, as each body has its specific responsibilities. These responsibilities are complex. For example, Welsh policing policy is set by the Home Office in Westminster, but the public sector environment in which Welsh policing operates with its partners is set by Welsh Government.

The joint responsibilities for criminal justice of the UK Government, the Welsh Government and local authorities, are in the Welsh context, delivered through a vast array of overlapping committees, boards and other groups. Such committees and bodies are primarily concerned with criminal and social justice and social policy matters, and have created a level of complexity that is increasingly hindering effective working.

The role of the UK Government

The Home Office has policy responsibility across both England and Wales for crime prevention and action on all forms of crime. It leads on civil emergencies and counter terrorism. Its main responsibilities with regard to policing are to:

- Maintain a system of local accountability that assures Parliament that forces spend their resources in a way that achieves value for money.
- Assess how much funding forces need, decide how much the policing system receives as a whole, and allocate grants to PCCs.
- Intervene if Chief Constables or PCCs fail to carry out their functions effectively.
- Identify opportunities for forces to work efficiently, support them to do so, and provide statutory guidance in respect of financial matters.

The role of the Home Office has, over time become less influential in a policing context. Since the advent of PCCs it has been described, in a report by the National Audit Office, as involving a 'light touch'. This is something the Home Office itself seems to agree with. In written evidence to the House of Commons Home Affairs Committee they commented that:

> It does not run policing but is supporting the sector to become self-reforming.

The same Home Affairs Committee, concluded that there was a complete failure of leadership from the Home Office.[2]

The role of Welsh Government

Although the criminal justice system remains primarily the responsibility of the UK Government, there are significant overlaps with the policy responsibilities of the Welsh Government in areas such as health and education.

The Welsh Government has developed and implemented policies on community safety, female offending and youth justice, working with both devolved and UK bodies. As the Welsh Government has responsibility for health and social care, it has worked to set criminal justice policies with an emphasis on prevention. Substance misuse policy is one example of this approach. The Violence against Women, Domestic Abuse and Sexual Violence (Wales) Act 2015 placed duties on public bodies regarding prevention, protection and support, although it was unable to place duties on the police, Crown Prosecution Service or courts.

The role of local authorities

Welsh local authorities have a number of responsibilities in relation to justice, including some powers to bring prosecutions, and for Youth Offending Teams. In addition, local authorities are the focus of two bodies:

- Community Safety Partnerships which are the responsibility of local authorities and the police. They were established by Home Office legislation under the Crime and Disorder Act 1998, although half of the required partners are devolved;
- Public Service Boards were established by the Well-being of Future Generations (Wales) Act 2015. They replaced the voluntary Local Service Boards in each of the 22 local authority areas in Wales. The Public Service Boards are responsible for conducting local well-being assessments, creating well-being plans to address key issues and working together to deliver results in the short, medium and long term. There are

currently 15 such bodies in Wales, made up of the following statutory members:

- The local authority;
- The Local Health Board;
- The Fire and Rescue Authority;
- Natural Resources Wales.

In addition, the following are statutory invitees:

- The Welsh Ministers;
- Chief Constables;
- Police and Crime Commissioners;
- Probation;
- At least one body representing relevant voluntary organisations.

Under the current arrangements for Public Service Boards, those working for the Ministry of Justice cannot be required to participate, despite their statutory status. Conversely, there are few legislative levers to enable devolved bodies to be held to account for reducing reoffending and improving rehabilitation outcomes.

The local priorities identified in each Public Service Board plan vary from area to area. However, making communities feel safe and reducing anti-social behaviour, substance misuse, domestic abuse and reoffending, feature particularly strongly in cities and post-industrial areas. Over the past decade there has also been a clear emphasis on early years in all Public Service Boards, including reducing Adverse Childhood Experiences. This is particularly the case with the Public Service Boards in the South Wales Police area.

The role of Chief Constables and Police and Crime Commissioners

The four Welsh police forces of Dyfed Powys, Gwent, North Wales and South Wales, emerged out of a series of amalgamations in the late 1960s. Each is headed by a Chief Constable responsible for operational policing decisions, and the direction and control of police officers and staff.

As mentioned earlier, the Police Reform and Social Responsibility Act 2011 introduced Police and Crime Commissioners (PCCs) to replace Police Authorities. PCCs were modelled for England and this modelling did not fully take into account Welsh devolution and the increasingly important role of the Senedd and Welsh Government. As we have seen in relation to the Policing Protocol, Chief Constables are operationally independent, but otherwise are accountable to their local PCC. Each police force has a single PCC who appoints their own office staff.

Apart from some light oversight from the Home Office, the accountability of PCCs is to the electorate every four years. Since the introduction of PCCs a variety of systems for the governance provided by the role have developed. In London and Manchester, the PCC is a role fulfilled by the Mayor. As more mayoral structures are developed in England, this model may become increasingly familiar. The span of control for Mayors is far greater than that of other PCCs, in that they set the vision for and have oversight of other key public services in an area. A further difference in England is that some PCCs have become the governing body for the Fire and Rescue Service. Neither of these changes applies to Welsh PCCs.

Other bodies involved in policing functions

There are a number of intersecting and external organisations which affect policing in Wales. These include:

- The National Crime Agency (NCA)
- The National Counter Terrorism Security Office
- The National and Regional Counter Terrorism Units
- British Transport Police
- The National Police Air Service
- The National Police Coordination Centre (NPoCC)
- The National Fraud Intelligence Bureau
- HM Revenue and Customs (HMRC)
- The Border Force
- The College of Policing
- The National Police Chiefs' Council (NPCC)
- The Association of Police and Crime Commissioners (APCC)

- The Security Service (MI5)
- The Government Communications Headquarters (GCHQ)
- HM Inspectorate of Constabulary and Fire & Rescue Services (HMICFRS)
- The Independent Office for Police Conduct (IOPC)
- Audit Wales (formerly The Wales Audit Office)

The need for close operational collaboration and interoperability between the police services of Wales and England has been a long-term requirement. History has shown that when it comes to large scale events and incidents, no single police force has the capacity and capability to manage all the various facets.

This, together with the ability of national policing assets to respond has, from time to time, been a concern. It was very apparent as a result of the cuts to policing following the 2010 Comprehensive Spending Review. This period also saw the introduction of PCCs and the emerging concerns from the Home Office that PCCs and Chief Constables would prioritise their spending on 'local' assets, rather than their ability to respond to issues outside their force area. Indeed, the provision of national 'strategic' capabilities was of such concern that, in 2012, the then Home Secretary developed the Strategic Policing Requirement (SPR). The SPR (revised in 2015) sets out the Home Secretary's view of the national threats that the police must prepare for and the appropriate national policing capabilities that are required to counter those threats.

As the previous National Police Chiefs' Council (NPCC) lead on the SPR the author remains convinced that to effectively 'police' significant threats to public safety, unforeseen demands on police resources and internationally significant events such as the Newport and Cardiff NATO Summit of 2014, police forces across Wales and England will always need to complement each other, work closely and have the ability to function interoperably. This is certainly a consideration that guides South Wales Police's relationships with the other forces in Wales.

Close cooperation in policing is not limited to just Wales and England. The police service of Wales and England has also regularly called on the services of the Police Service of

Northern Ireland and Police Scotland. These arrangements have been reciprocal. Policing resources from Wales and England were sent to Northern Ireland and Scotland for events such as the Northern Irish 'Marching Season' and the 2005 G8 conference in Scotland. Thus, clearly evidencing the police service's ability to effectively deploy resources to and from devolved administrative countries.

Attempts to establish better governance and accountability of the police in Wales

Experience has shown that Welsh policing has found itself in a difficult position, in terms of the complexly layered governance and accountability structures it has to navigate. It has to be fully cognisant of Home Office expectations and requirements, yet also ensure that it is orientated towards Welsh Government and its policy direction. As most of the public sector partners of the Welsh police work under the Welsh Government, the connection with them to effectively engage with communities and make a positive difference is crucial. This has, however, been quite a challenge. The Home Office has not always fully taken into account the devolved setting in Wales and whilst policing has had a strong voice with Welsh Government, it is not always high on their agenda. Quite simply, a position has been reached where it could be argued that neither the Home Office, nor the Welsh Government, fully understand policing in Wales.

The need for a coherent approach to policing across Wales was strengthened following the aborted amalgamation proposals of the Westminster Government in 2006. The work carried out to create a single operational and administrative entity provided opportunities to improve the service Welsh Policing delivered. To maximise those opportunities, the All Wales Policing Group, which was established to deliver the requirements of a single Welsh police service, furthered those collaborative opportunities after 2006. This group fed into the regular meetings of Welsh Chief Constables and the Police Authorities of Wales (PAW).

Since 2006, there have been a number of successful collaborative ventures, for example: the South Wales and Gwent Joint Legal Services; the Joint Scientific Investigations Unit; and the

Joint Firearms Unit, which covers South Wales, Gwent and Dyfed Powys. However, successes were hard won and gaining a consensus from the interested parties proved increasingly difficult despite the financial challenges the service faced from 2010 onward.

Steps have also recently been taken to try and improve governance and accountability within the current scheme of devolution. In April 2017, the Chief Constables and Police and Crime Commissioners of Wales re-established the role of the 'All Wales Deputy Chief Constable'. Whilst there were similarities to the previous Wales wide DCC role, the main priorities for the new post were to develop relationships between the four forces, to improve the Welsh Policing perspective (i.e. to better understand the implications of the potential devolution of policing), to focus on the opportunities for collaboration, and to oversee collaborative operational units such as TARIAN (the regional organised crime unit for the South Wales, Dyfed Powys and Gwent police areas) and WECTU (the Wales Extremism and Counter Terrorism Unit).

The Police Liaison Unit (PLU) is funded by the four Welsh Forces and PCCs. It is housed within the Welsh Government buildings and works closely with the Welsh Government's Community Safety Division. It engages on police and community safety related matters with officials from across the Welsh Government and the Senedd.

A Cross-party Group on policing was established in the Assembly (as it was then called) in July 2018. This Group aimed to consider the questions of how policing operates within the devolved and reserved aspects of public services in Wales, what are the current issues facing the service in Wales and how best to engage with the Senedd on policing challenges and on policy and practical issues of common interest. Attendance at this meeting was ad-hoc and never really achieved what it was established to do.

A Policing Board for Wales was established in November 2018 by Alun Davies MS, the then Cabinet Secretary for Local Government and Public Services. The Board, now called the Policing Partnership Board for Wales, brings together a wide range of bodies having an interest in Welsh policing issues.

In addition to the Chief Constables and Police and Crime Commissioners of each of the police forces in Wales, attendees include Welsh Government Cabinet Ministers and officials, the Secretary of State for Wales, the Home Office, HM Prison and Probation Service, NHS Wales and the Welsh Local Government Association. The intention of the Board is to achieve a better understanding amongst partner agencies of policing issues, where the majority of public services are devolved.

In addition to the Board, a group entitled 'Policing in Wales' comprising all four Police and Crime Commissioners and Chief Constables meets regularly to co-ordinate activities between them. The Welsh Chief Constables also convene separately to deal with matters of common interest especially in respect of operational matters.

Whilst such ways of working have helped in trying to make the best of the current complicated system, they do not offer a long-term solution to the tensions caused by the 'quadripartite' governance that operates in Wales. What is clear is that there is no real cohesion between the Welsh and UK Governments, and certainly no 'single line of sight' from their policy or vision to public service delivery in Wales. To be truly effective such clarity of purpose and effective governance are essential to make a positive difference in our communities.

The complexity of funding

Policing in Wales is subtly different from that in England, both in terms of funding sources and also, increasingly, ways of working. The next few paragraphs outline such differences.

The funding for the police forces in Wales is complex; it differs from that in England in that the funding derives from three sources:

a. UK Government funding through a police grant determined by a Home Office funding formula;
b. Welsh Government funding as part of the local government finance settlement;
c. A local police precept set by Police and Crime Commissioners, and collected via Council Tax.

The Welsh Government provides some additional funding every year for policing. This comprises funding for Police Community Support Officers and school liaison programmes. In fact, the majority of the funding for Welsh policing comes from the Welsh Government and through the Welsh local authorities.

A particular concern of the author whilst Chief Constable, and shared by PCC Alun Michael, was that the funding needs for Wales in general, and South Wales Police in particular, had not been addressed (and still have not). There have been repeated attempts to convince the UK Government and Home Office that the funding formula failed to recognise the environment in which South Wales Police operated. They have not responded to repeated representations that Cardiff needs additional funding as a capital city and seat of Welsh Government, and so the funding arrangements have remained unaltered. Cardiff has not, from a policing finance perspective, been recognised in the same way as London or Edinburgh. Edinburgh receives additional funding from Scottish Government that acknowledges its capital city status. When it is considered that the extra costs of policing Cardiff as a capital city have been estimated around £3.5 million each year, this has had a huge impact on the services South Wales Police can offer elsewhere.

Police education

Police education in Wales and England has undergone significant change to meet the increasingly complex demands that policing faces. It is not necessary to explain this change in detail, except in relation to Police Constable Degree Apprenticeships as the forces in Wales have had to develop their own financial arrangements to meet the needs of Wales and because of a difference in the funding of apprenticeships.

The Police Education Qualifications Framework was introduced by the College of Policing. The framework provides three entry routes to join as a Constable:

i.   Police Constable Degree Apprenticeship;
ii. Degree Holder Entry Programme, including fast-track detectives;
iii. Pre-join degree.

The different approaches for funding initial police learning in Wales and England is a clear example of the emergence of different funding arrangements for policing in Wales and England. The University of South Wales delivers the Police Constable Degree Apprenticeships (PCDA) and the Degree Holder Entry Programme (DHEP) for South Wales, Gwent and Dyfed Powys Police in Wales and for the Devon and Cornwall, Dorset, Wiltshire and Gloucestershire police forces in England. For the Welsh forces, it is the individual force that has to fund both the PCDA and DHEP programmes. For English forces the PCDA are fully funded through the English Apprenticeship scheme (although the DHEP similarly is the responsibility of the individual force).

In England, funding for the Police Education Qualifications Framework is provided through the National Apprenticeship Levy. Welsh police forces contribute around £2.5 million per year to the Levy. As policing is a UK Government responsibility under the current scheme of devolution, the Welsh Government is clear that it is not responsible for the long-term funding of the Police Education Qualifications Framework apprenticeships, which do not meet the Welsh Government's assessment of the local economy-based skills deficits. The Home Office however maintains that apprenticeship funding has been passed to the Welsh Government via the Barnett Formula (a formula whereby the UK Government calculates how much funding should be passed to the Welsh Government). Although interim packages have been agreed between the Home Office and Welsh Government, there are concerns that the police forces in Wales are disadvantaged when compared to English forces.

At a time when budgets are stretched, matters such as disagreements over apprenticeship funding create friction and risk putting a strain on working relations. To some extent this was compounded by the withdrawal of Welsh Government funding for TARIAN. Whilst the funding from the Welsh Government for Schools Liaison Officers and Community Support Officers provides a capability that is the envy of English police forces, the future of such funding is also uncertain since it is discretionary.

It could be said that without direct responsibility for policing, any Welsh Government decision to remove or reduce funding is a more straightforward one than for matters that are devolved. However, this does mean that policing in Wales currently finds itself without a coherent strategy for its future from the Welsh Government. Whilst it could be argued that this is the correct position, as policing remains a reserved matter, policing is, however a Welsh public service that is reliant on relationships with other devolved public services and the Welsh Government. The absence of such a strategy is leading to a divergence between funding arrangements for Welsh police forces and their English colleagues. It would be a matter of concern if such a difference led, over time, to a lowering of the level of service South Wales Police and other Welsh police forces are able to offer their communities.

THE FUTURE

The need for an aligned approach

At every operational level policing in Wales involves an interaction with devolved public services, such as education, social care, health or housing. Whilst there are many good examples of initiatives between policing and devolved public services, the approach to joint working is not consistent across Wales, nor across the South Wales Police area. Indeed, where there is effective collaboration, it is usually due to a local desire to improve things, rather than as a result of a coherent national strategy.

Policing is a fundamental part of the justice system and there needs to be alignment of policy and delivery with other bodies involved in delivering criminal justice. It is clear that when different parts of this system work to different policy drivers, as is the case now, unnecessary problems are caused. To be truly effective, the police must be able to work within the CJS and with other public services such as education, health and social welfare. To enable this to happen effectively, there should be a single overarching criminal justice policy framework throughout Wales that is consistent with the policies for health, education and social welfare.

As mentioned above, the current complicated system of devolved and non-devolved agencies and the complex funding arrangements, together with the sometimes conflicting priorities, stand in the way of a coherent and more efficient approach. Devolving responsibility for policing and the wider CJS to Welsh Government would enable a truly 'joined-up' approach between all Welsh public services and improve effectiveness, efficiency and the delivery of a long-term plan that has a positive impact on all our communities.

That policing should become a devolved public service working alongside other local partners and be the responsibility of Welsh Government was a key recommendation of the Commission on Justice in Wales. Such a move would replace the current complex quadripartite governance system with a new tri-partite structure consisting of Welsh Government, Welsh Chief Constables and PCCs. Beyond policing, the Commission also recommended that the entire Welsh Criminal Justice System should be devolved to Welsh Government. This would finally enable the single line of sight from policy or vision, to reality of service delivery in Welsh communities.[3]

The Commission published its findings in October 2019, and it is the author's hope that steps will be taken to recognise the unique position Welsh Policing finds itself in and implement the recommendation to devolve the CJS and policing. History has shown however, that despite successive recommendations, the UK Government has been reluctant to devolve criminal justice and policing to Wales. In the Second Reading debate on the Wales Act 2017 in the House of Lords, Lord Hunt, the Secretary of State for Wales from 1990 to 1993, stated that he had at that time reached agreement with the then Home Secretary Kenneth Clarke about the transfer of policing from the Home Office to the Welsh Office, but that 'it was stopped by the bureaucracy of Whitehall'.

In 2014, the Commission on Public Service and Delivery in Wales (the Williams Commission) commented that if policing were devolved there would be scope for greater and better coordinated joint working between the three emergency services. The Commission on Devolution in Wales (the Silk Commission) was an independent commission established by the Secretary of State for Wales in 2011. This also recommended devolving policing to Wales by 2017. This followed on from the four Welsh PCCs issuing a statement in August 2016, that the devolution of responsibility for policing was inevitable.

CONCLUSION

Policing and the wider criminal justice system should be devolved to the Welsh Government. There are, however, a number of caveats to this position for policing, reflecting several factors. The first of these is the ability of the Welsh police service to work closely with colleagues from England, Scotland and Northern Ireland.

South Wales Police has successfully overseen many major and internationally significant events, for example: the European Summit of 1998, the NATO Summit of 2014 and the Champions League Final of 2017. The ability to call for extra resources from UK wide policing was essential to the effective policing of such occasions. The obligations of the Strategic Policing Requirement (SPR) and the consequential interoperability of UK policing meant the command of different officers from different forces was seamless. It is operationally essential that if policing were to be devolved, the Welsh police service should continue to meet the requirements of the SPR and interoperability arrangements.

This reflects the fact that the UK policing system has been, and continues to be, predicated upon essentially local forces, drawing together to deliver national functions. This seems preferable to the inverse relationship found in some other countries wherein a fundamentally national policing entity is required to disaggregate itself and deliver localised services

The second caveat would be to ensure that the respective roles and responsibilities of the 'new' Welsh tripartite governance system are commensurate with those set out in the current Policing Protocol. The principle of operational independence of the Chief Constable and their resources should be re-asserted and formalised in a corresponding Welsh Policing Protocol.

A third caveat concerns the capacity and capability of Welsh Government to oversee policing. There is currently no department of Welsh Government that has responsibility for the Welsh police service, should policing be devolved, this would therefore mean that the capacity and capability to do so would have to be created.

The final caveat concerns the level of funding Welsh Policing would receive. If policing were to be devolved, then the level of funding transferred to Welsh Government for its oversight of policing is crucial. Should the inequalities and vagaries of the current funding regime persist and be simply moved to Cardiff then the Welsh public will inevitably receive a poorer level of service. Either that or communities here will have to pay disproportionately for their policing services through their local police precepts and business rates.

Should such caveats be met, the consistency and coherence of approach to policy and delivery across all public services in Wales, and the 'single line of sight' that devolution of policing would bring, would transform the environment, making a positive difference to the safety and security of the Welsh public and their communities.

Notes

1. It should be noted that in March 2022, the Home Secretary published a consultation document on revisions to the Protocol. The most significant aspect of it is a revised statement of the role of the Home Secretary, making it explicit that it is for the Home Secretary to set the Government's strategic direction on national policing policy and that it for PCCs and chief constables to reflect and implement that policy at a local level. The details in this chapter regarding the Protocol may, therefore, change in due course. In addition, the Home Secretary has undertaken reviews of the role of PCCs. On 7 March 2022, she made a statement to the House of Commons (Patel 2022) in which there was set out proposed extensions to the role in respect, for example, of offender management, criminal justice boards and violence reduction units.

2. However, as indicated earlier the consultation document on revisions to the Policing Protocol contains a revised statement of the role of the Home Secretary and the Home Office citing the application of 'a stronger strategic grip, and reformed governance and oversight to provide central system leadership' including the creation of the National Policing Board chaired by the Home Secretary.

3. In May 2022, the Welsh Government published 'Delivering Justice for Wales' in which it set out in detail its vision for the devolution of justice services including policing.

References

1964 Police Act. *1964, c. 48*. Available at: *https://www.legislation.gov. uk/ukpga/1964/48/contents*

1998 Crime and Disorder Act. *1998, c. 37*. Available at: *https://www. legislation.gov.uk/ukpga/1998/37/contents*

1998 Government of Wales Act. *1998, c. 38*. Available at: *https://www. legislation.gov.uk/ukpga/1998/38/contents*

2011. The Policing Protocol Order. *SI 2011/2744*. Available at: *https:// www.legislation.gov.uk/uksi/2011/2744/made* (accessed 26 May 2022).

2015 Well-being of Future Generations (Wales) Act. *2015, anaw 2*. Available at: *https://www.legislation.gov.uk/anaw/2015/2/contents/ enacted*

Home Affairs Committee. 2018. *Policing for the future* (HC 515, 2017–2019), [Online]. London: The Stationery Office. Available at: *https:// publications.parliament.uk/pa/cm201719/cmselect/cmhaff/515/515. pdf* (accessed 26 May 2022).

Home Office. 2015. *The strategic policing requirement*. London: The Stationery Office. Available at: *https://assets.publishing.service.gov. uk/government/uploads/system/uploads/attachment_data/file/417116/ The_Strategic_Policing_Requirement.pdf* (accessed 26 May 2022).

Jones, R. and Wyn Jones, R. 2019. *Justice at the jagged edge in Wales*. Cardiff: Wales Governance Centre, Cardiff University. Available at: *https://www.cardiff.ac.uk/__data/assets/pdf_file/0006/1699215/ Justice-at-the-Jagged-Edge.pdf* (accessed 26 May 2022).

National Audit Office. 2018. *Financial sustainability of police forces in England and Wales 2018* (2018). London: The Stationery Office. ISBN: 978-1-78604-211-8. Available at: *https://www.nao.org.uk/wp-content/ uploads/2018/09/Financial-sustainability-of-police-forces-in-England -and-Wales-2018.pdf* (accessed 26 May 2022).

Patel, P. 2022. *Update on part two of the Police and Commissioner Review*. London: UK Parliament. *https://questions-statements.parliament. uk/written-statements/detail/2022-03-07/hcws664*

The Commission on Justice in Wales. 2019. *Justice in Wales for the people of Wales,* Cardiff: The Stationery Office. ISBN: 978-1-83876-822-5. Available at: *https://gov.wales/sites/default/files/publications/2019-10/Justice%20Commission%20ENG%20DIGITAL_2.pdf* (accessed 26 May 2022).

The Welsh Government. 2022. *Delivering justice for Wales.* Cardiff: The Stationery Office. ISBN 978-1-80364-256-7. Available at: *https://www.gov.wales/sites/default/files/publications/2022-06/delivering-justice-for-wales-may-2022-v2.pdf* (accessed 17 June 2022).

12

REFLECTIONS

Martin Innes and Gareth Madge

Each of the preceding chapters that collectively make up this book have been informed by three guiding principles. First, they take South Wales Police and its work as the base unit for analysis. Thus by looking across the individual contributions, it is possible to build a picture of the complexity of a modern police organisation, as it delivers a variety of services to multiple communities. Second, most of the chapters have been jointly authored by academics and practitioners with the aim of blending a deep understanding of the practical issues and challenges involved in delivering policing day in and day out, whilst connecting such insights to a wider spectrum of issues. Finally, albeit to different degrees, a common thread is that all of the discussions seek to situate contemporary considerations within a historical perspective.

Taken together, these three 'core ingredients' enable the book to make a unique contribution to the policing studies literature. In this final chapter, we want to draw out some key recurring themes that span across the individual contributions, using these to reflect upon some of the main current and future challenges for policing.

POLICING COMPLEXITY

Arguably one of the key insights that adopting the perspective outlined above affords, is conveying the complexities of contemporary policing. The individual chapters have mapped out many of the key organisational structures and processes involved in delivering a variety of different policing services to a range of communities, groups and individuals. Some of whom are seeking interaction with the police, but others are not.

Indeed, adopting a historical lens enables us to appreciate how one of the key recent trajectories of development has been the evolution of what might be labelled 'full spectrum policing.' Specifically, this has involved increasing investment in both neighbourhood and national security focused services, in addition to the more well-established crime management and emergency response functions that have traditionally provided the core of the police organisational mission. Following the Islamist-inspired terrorist attacks in the United States in 2001, and then in the UK and Europe in the years following this, the police role in countering terrorism became notably more visible and mainstream.

Intriguingly, whilst these national security developments were taking place, there was a parallel set of adaptations taking place, at a more local level, in the 'neighbourhood security' layer. This involved a drive to tackle anti-social behaviour, physical disorder and other forms of 'low-level' crime through a major national investment in the establishment of Neighbourhood Policing teams. The core idea being to have small groups of officers dedicated to particular geographical units, leading the delivery of services to residents in these areas. A key innovation in terms of these teams in South Wales, as in many other forces, was the introduction of the Police Community Support Officer role. These non-warranted officers were intended to be 'on point' for engaging with communities and helping to diagnose their particular policing and security needs.

Other dimensions of this emergence of full spectrum policing include the types of issues foregrounded in Robinson et al. (Chapter 9) relating to the growing recognition of the importance of policing violence against women and girls. The significance of which, in terms of thinking about 'the spectrum' of police responsibilities, is the increasing involvement in 'private' spaces where forms of non-public harms are occurring. Several decades of research on this area suggest that this is a form of often 'hidden' criminality that police organisations have struggled to work out how to adequately manage, albeit there is a general acceptance that it is a form of violence to which they need to respond.

One further relevant variant in terms of mapping the contours of the emergence of 'full spectrum policing', albeit it was slightly later in its onset, is the analogue-digital shift. Along with very many other dimensions of social life, policing has been profoundly re-shaped by the effects of a range of digital information and communications technologies. The rise of various kinds of cyber-enabled and cyber-dependent crimes, including fraud and hate, alongside the opportunities to capture digital evidence and intelligence from a range of technological devices, have altered the kinds of skills and knowledge that police organisations need within their workforce.

The overarching point though, in terms of understanding the contemporary police mission and the organisations designed to deliver this, is that these pressures have been co-occurring and co-mingling. So the demand for enhanced moral, financial and personnel investment in national-neighbourhood security, public-private space provisions, and analogue and digital services, have all combined in terms of their organisational effects. Put another way, police have retained their primary responsibility for the emergency maintenance of social order and responding to infractions of the criminal law, whilst also taking on the management of a number of related harms.

Modern police organisations consequently comprise multiple moving parts in terms of different departments and units, many of which are engaged in an ongoing need to triage incoming work, as demand for services outstrips the capacity to supply officers to service it. Of particular value in understanding how some of these demands and frictions are negotiated, several of the chapters in this volume have sought to explicitly connect some of the 'backstage' issues of running large, bureaucratic organisations, and how these shape what the public sees in terms of 'frontstage' service provision. The chapter on finances and resources, in particular, illuminates an aspect that is rarely explicitly considered by researchers, but does much to influence the size and shape of the police force in an area.

Similar themes appear in the discussion of police governance. It is striking just how complicated the contemporary provisions for securing police accountability have become over time, and the delicate balance that has to be struck between the roles of the Chief Constable, Police and Crime Commissioner, and the Home Office. At a national level, these complexities are replicated and reinforced, by the growing number of other organisations and roles that are engaged in governing policing, such as HM Inspectorate of Constabulary and Fire & Rescue Services, the College of Policing, National Crime Agency and Independent Office for Police Conduct. Placing these developments in historical context, there does appear to be an ongoing dialogue of trying to find, but never quite achieving, the right weighting of localisation and centralisation. Indeed, at the time of writing, there appears to be a growing perception that things have become too localised and fragmentary, and as such, it seems likely that, there will be some more centralising moves undertaken by the Home Office as it seeks to establish more influence over the strategic direction of police activities.

Issues of governance and accountability, and their complexity, are afforded particular salience in Wales, given the partially devolved nature of the governmental apparatus. As was discussed in some detail in Vaughan (Chapter 11), whilst most public services including health, education and social services are devolved, so that politicians in the Welsh Government set policy and strategy, policing is not and remains under the purview of the Home Office. One consequence of which is that South Wales Police, along with the other Welsh police forces, are routinely having to navigate and negotiate an intricate web of political stakeholders and expectations. This certainly inflects discourses and practices of partnership working.

Within the Welsh political tradition, there is a strong accent upon the importance of partnership work and collaboration. In part, this might well be an artefact of being a relatively small country, meaning that it is relatively easy for key figures in different agencies to establish personal relationships. But equally, these arrangements do mean that the forces in Wales can find themselves subject to different political pressures and expectations than arise for their compatriots in England. This seems to arise with particular regularity when dealing with vulnerable people, who are often multi-service users. As such, police have to retain an awareness that, for effective partnership working to take place, it is important to take into account that their partners may have different standards to comply with, or performance metrics to meet. Especially in an era where, as we will come to discuss more fully shortly, there has been unrelenting pressure to limit public spending.

This sense that there can be similar yet different pressures on English and Welsh police forces, was especially visibly highlighted in terms of the recent coronavirus pandemic, and how public health measures were enacted, especially in relation to social distancing and public gatherings.

More generally though, the response to the pandemic exemplified some worrying developments in terms of the politics of policing. Not least, a tendency for the occurrence of what Innes, Roberts and Lowe (Innes et al. 2017) dubbed 'the legislative reflex'. This describes how, when faced with an acute emergency or crisis, politicians feel that they need to be seen to be doing something. Consequently, they rapidly draw up and introduce new laws, often with little regard given to their practical utility and how these could be implemented by police. But that is not their point. For what such legislative manoeuvres do accomplish, is expressing and giving symbolic form to sentiments of moral outrage and/or popular concern.

Connecting these issues back to the theme of complexity, looking across the various chapters, it is apparent how these pressures and triggers for innovation and reform, are associated with a series of what social scientists term 'exogenous' and 'endogenous' shocks. The latter are the kinds of issues and crises that are internal to, or directly related to policing. In contrast to which, exogenous shocks are external factors, such as dramatic changes to the social, political and economic system, that feed through to shape the work of the police.

The kinds of reforms and adaptations outlined above, are often responses to pressures induced by processes of social, political, cultural and economic change in society. This is something that previous generations of police leaders and scholars of policing were highly alert to, and may be a lesson that needs to be relearnt today. For example, writing in the late-1970s, Commissioner of the Metropolitan Police Robert Mark (1977) entitled one of his books 'Policing a Perplexed Society'. At around the same time, Stuart Hall (1978) and his colleagues published their seminal study 'Policing the Crisis'. Albeit approaching the issue very differently, and with contrasting ideological standpoints, they both recognised how macro-structural forces and currents in society induce compelling pressures for police reform. They also both acknowledged that these pressures trigger forms of reactance and resistance. As Mark pithily recognised, one of the recurring challenges for policing is having to be 'on point' in terms of navigating social change, as social norms, conventions and morals evolve and adapt.

Returning to these 'classics' of the literature on policing is warranted because of how we appear to be situated in a historical moment itself defined by a stream of crisis and scandal events, that both individually and collectively, have undercut public confidence in public institutions and social cohesion, to some degree. Indeed, as they grasp for a way of articulating the state we are in, some social and political commentators have suggested we are living through a period of 'permacrisis'. This is on the grounds that there have been a series of significant political, economic and social shocks, that are continually disturbing and unsettling the institutional order, and unravelling elements of the social fabric.

The global financial crash that started in 2008, had a profound effect on public services, including policing, as many Western governments introduced austerity measures in an attempt to diffuse the financial repercussions. As described in several of the chapters herein, for policing this resulted in a reduction in workforce numbers, including the departure of many of the most experienced officers, in a very condensed period of time. This economic shock had some influence upon the political shock that transpired with Brexit, and the decision of the UK to leave the European Union. In other decades, this in and of itself, would have been seen by policy analysts as a seismic and transformative event. However, before many of the repercussions could be fully worked out, there then followed the coronavirus pandemic and its attendant social, political, economic and cultural effects. And then, even before the pandemic has passed, and still ongoing at the time of writing, there was the outbreak of a major armed conflict in Europe. Albeit it is difficult to anticipate what the result of Russia's invasion of Ukraine will be, it is showing every sign of being a protracted fight, and will almost certainly reconfigure the established European security architecture, in quite dramatic ways for a generation.

The political and economic consequences of the situation in Ukraine will be reinforced by the onset of what is being referred to in the UK as a 'cost of living crisis'. The prospect of declining living standards and an inflationary wage-price spiral, will have a series of 'downstream' effects on policing. Thus any expectations that recent uplifts to real-terms police budgets will be sustained appear optimistic. There are also likely to be increases in demand as the acute economic pressures people are experiencing are translated into the occurrence of both acquisitive and violent crime. This is all before any attempt is made to factor in the consequences of the existential threats posed by climate change, which are already starting to manifest in an increase in flooding events and changes in patterns of population migration.

At first glance, such risks and events can seem to be rather remote from local policing. And, to some degree, police forces will continue to deliver the core services that have traditionally formed their core institutional remit. However, context and atmospherics do matter, and they do make a difference. Both singly and in combination, these kinds of pressures can provide the trigger for community tensions and the degradation of community cohesion that manifests in hate crimes. They are also connected to the emergence of 'new' crime types such as 'human trafficking' and 'human slavery' as immoral, yet entrepreneurial, organised crime actors, offer ways of transporting people away from desperate situations.

The overarching point though is that there are a range of reasons why policing has become increasingly complex. Understanding and mapping these patterns of development and placing them in their historical context is important in terms of being able to forecast what comes next.

POLICING LEGITIMACY

At the time of writing, there has been considerable consternation expressed about how a series of incidents associated with the aforementioned state of 'permacrisis', are causing the institutional legitimacy of the police service to be eroded. There have been a series of serious failings and scandals including the issues raised by the Sarah Everard case, who was raped and murdered by a serving Metropolitan police officer, followed by mistakes made in the public order policing of the public vigil after her death. There were also revelations about the highly misogynistic and sexist culture in Charring Cross Police Station in London, that were implicated in the political decision to ask Cressida Dick, the Commissioner of the Metropolitan Police, to step down from her post.

Arguably, South Wales Police have experienced their own iteration of this phenomenon in the form of the Mayhill disorder. But whereas the aforementioned issues in London were attributable to personal discreditable conduct, the issues in Swansea arguably arose due to organisational failings. The wider analytic point for this book being that there are multiple pathways by which public perceptions of the legitimacy of policing can be degraded. The situation in Mayhill involved a serious breach of public order, when a large group of adults and young people gathered in the Mayhill area of Swansea, on the evening of 20 May 2021, and started attacking the property of local residents in and around Waun Wen Road. This included setting light to cars and rolling them down the large hill that bisects the community, as well as throwing bricks at the windows of houses where residents were sheltering. Despite repeated calls for assistance by those subject to the violence, it appears that the police took a significant amount of time to muster sufficient officers to mount an effective response to the violent mob, and for an extended period they appeared to offer no response.

In the days and weeks following the incident, an inquisition into what had transpired was launched by local journalists, with some coverage also appearing in national media. For a time, the police's strategic communications response was to try and defend their actions and deflect the mounting criticism. However, this did not work in dissipating the political and public concern, and an independent panel of enquiry was established. When it published its findings, the enquiry found that there had been deficiencies in the scale and speed of South Wales Police's response, with the clear implication that an earlier, more assertive posture could have prevented a fair proportion of the destruction that occurred that night.

Developing the strands of argument outlined in the preceding section of this chapter, modern police organisations are complex, multi-faceted entities that are doing multiple things in parallel, and to a certain degree the public understands this. And yet, events such as Mayhill and the scandals that occurred in London, do cast a shadow over public perceptions of the police. This matters because, perhaps more so than in many other jurisdictions, what the public thinks about the police in the UK is held to matter and be an important indicator. In the US for example, discussions of policing tend to be couched far more explicitly in a rhetoric of 'law enforcement'. This is rather different to the tenets of the British police tradition, where the key rhetorical tropes are focused upon the doctrine of 'policing by consent', and the idea that 'the police are the public and the public are the police'. Notwithstanding the active 'myth-making' that such notions involve, they do convey important sentiments about who the police are and how they understand their social functions.

So how should we understand and make sense of these issues? Drawing an analogy with the NHS – an institution that continues to sustain high levels of public legitimacy and regard – might be instructive. The NHS is able to retain high levels of public esteem and support, even though patients regularly experience de facto rationing of a number of services, encounter long waiting times for many treatments, and struggle to get appointments to see a doctor. Such issues notwithstanding, generally people report that in a crisis, when there is an acute need for emergency treatment, the performance of the NHS is often first class. Where its challenges lie, more often relate to managing levels of demand in relation to more routine health matters – for example in terms of securing a GP appointment.

There are parallels with the world of policing, where the critical emergency response is often impressive, but it is in other areas (community facing services or public protection) where capacity and capability often feel significantly mismatched to the levels of demand. As a consequence, adopting the long view of police reform, it often seems that what can be observed is a shift towards and then away from community policing and prevention, vis a vis a more reactive style of policing, dominated by emergency response and crime management tasks. Indeed, over the decades, there have been recurring attempts to try and clarify the core mission of policing, often triggered by concerns that the 'reach' of the police service has been over-extended, straying into areas of public policy and 'social engineering' beyond their primary institutional purpose. It is easy to see how this happens. Particularly when it comes to the preventative functions of policing, moving 'upstream' from a crime or other form of harm, is always alluring because of the promise of being able to interdict causal factors. But all the time, there are a steady stream of incidents and cases that have to be serviced and dealt with. Thus, the recurring challenge for senior police leaders is striking the right balance between proactive and preventative tasks, and reacting to incidents that have not been prevented.

In South Wales, one indicator of this, has been the repeated adjustments to the boundaries between the Basic Command Units or 'Divisions'. Over an extended period of time, the boundaries between these geographic units have been drawn and redrawn, and their numbers have fluctuated. Such reforms are often accompanied by changes to staffing allocations, in terms of the proportion of the workforce dedicated to response, or community policing roles. The key point for this chapter though is that such reform measures are not just internal administrative undertakings. Rather they are inflections of a deeper set of structural pressures about how to reconcile the fact that the demand for policing services almost always outstrips the supply of available resources.

Given all these considerations and factors, it is striking that over the past five years or so there has been a trending decline in public confidence in the police in the UK. The data are patchy, and it appears there are bumps and dips in the various sources of tracking defined crises and events, and the issues seem more pronounced in some regions than others. There are also complex methodological and conceptual issues about the extent to which public perceptions of this kind are influenced by local delivery factors, versus more abstract national and institutional ones. But certainly for a model supposedly predicated upon public consent, the causes and consequences of such a decline warrant attention and investigation.

POLICING CULTURES AND IDENTITIES

How police individually and collectively navigate and negotiate these pressures and challenges will depend a lot upon the 'heart and soul' of the organisation, or what more formally tends to get labelled as values and identity. The anthropologist Clifford Geertz (1973) famously referred to the importance of 'the stories we tell ourselves about ourselves' in terms of how and why particular cultural values and dispositions get produced and reproduced in society. It is an approach that seems to have some value for understanding police organisational culture also. For a theme that has appeared several times across the individual chapters, has been how South Wales Police has frequently sought to craft an organisational identity around its affinity with its communities.

For example, in relation to the policing of the 2014 NATO Summit that was held across the Gwent and South Wales force areas, many senior officers reflected upon how they approached the challenge by encouraging their teams to be approachable and open, set against a backdrop of significant amounts of foreboding physical security infrastructure, and extensive disruption. Similarly, the recollections of South Wales officers being deployed to London to assist with widespread public disorder in 2011, was how they were viewed very positively in terms of their demeanour by Londoners. These are just two examples of the stories that South Wales Police have told themselves about themselves, and conveys how such tales are involved in not just recounting or describing events, but expressing values.

As with all cultures, the work of producing and reproducing an organisational culture occurs through defining both what it is, but also what it is not. Some police forces seek to configure a sense of professional self around competency for public order, or implementing problem-oriented policing, or major crime. In South Wales's case, a lot of the identity work has pivoted around notions of community. Importantly this is not about getting all 'warm and fuzzy' about some mythical notion of community. There are tensions. Not all groups are equally supportive of the police, and in some areas, there are fairly intense pockets of distrust. Progress on race equality has been especially slow and sporadic. Over the years there have been plenty of initiatives and reforms seeking to remedy the situation, both in terms of the internal make-up of the police as well as how ethnically diverse communities are policed, but these appear to have been temporary bursts of activity and concern. Fundamentally, there has been a lack of strategic will to sustain the necessary reforms over an extended period of time such that they can leverage significant change.

Whilst acknowledging the import of such issues and challenges, it remains the case that South Wales Police are attentive to and interested in how they are perceived by and thought about by the communities they serve. Of course, they do not always get things right, and there are some legacy cases that cast quite a shadow over parts of the force's reputation (see Chapter 7, on major crime).

One way in which South Wales Police has sought to engage with and compensate for these stresses, and for the wider disjuncture between levels of demand and supply, is via investments in technology. Through systems such as the command and control infrastructure provided by Niche, or the geo-tracking of patrol cars and officers afforded by IR3, or deployment of facial recognition cameras, it is clear that judicious investment in a range of information technologies has played an increasing part in how the policing of communities gets done, but also the stories that members of South Wales Police tell to themselves about this work.

Switching to a longer historical view, it is clear the relationship with technology is one area where there has been a significant transformation in the disposition of South Wales Police as an organisation. Notwithstanding that policing as an institution does not have a great track record in terms of early adoption of new technologies, by the 1980s, even when compared to their peers, much of South Wales Police's infrastructure was out-dated. That is clearly not the case nowadays.

What some of the key contemporary technologies being implemented by South Wales and their peers afford is enhanced precision. That is, by collecting and processing more and different kinds of data the police have a higher resolution view of matters of interest to them. This includes their capacity and capability to track and trace individuals and groups who both pose a risk, but are also 'at risk' in terms of their vulnerabilities. A similar logic applies also to the ability to track and trace their assets, both in terms of cars and people. So whereas for previous generations of officers, a loosely coupled degree of command and control was provided for by the 'fixed points' on the beat patrols, through geo-location systems such as IR3, patrols can be tasked far more dynamically, with real-time awareness of the multiple competing demands upon them. Taking a forward look, it is likely that these moves towards 'precision policing', across a range of disciplines, are likely to constitute a significant trajectory of development.

However, it is important that we do not 'oversell' the impacts of policing technologies as their effects tend to be complex. So whilst it is common-place to hear reference to 'technological solutions' in how some police talk, particularly when interacting with industrial partners, this is not a language we are seeking to replicate or reproduce herein. For technology is never just a simple 'plug and play' solution when introduced into a policing environment. Rather there are complex interactions between organisational routines and procedures, user behaviours and the physical affordances of the technological system itself, that have to be negotiated and reconciled. This is attested to by South Wales Police's experiences of adopting and then adapting each of the technologies listed above. There were/are important differences in terms of how they have been operationalised on a day-to-day basis, compared with the imagined visions circulating pre-deployment. This is important to acknowledge given how the integration of increasingly sophisticated technological innovations are almost certainly a key structuring influence upon the future trajectory of development of policing in South Wales and beyond. But in forecasting what such developments might look like, it is important to retain a sense of the complexity involved.

Reprising the themes of complexity and legitimacy introduced in the preceding sections, one area where policing technologies have started to have a marked effect is in terms of how accountability and thus legitimacy are negotiated. As Brayne (2021) highlights, some of the most intriguing consequences of police services implementing new technologies has not been the monitoring that they afford of criminals – which is often the intended purpose – but the enhanced surveillance that they provide over officer conduct and behaviour. The most obvious example of which is the widespread and rapid uptake of body-worn video cameras. Originally envisaged as a method of evidence capture to support prosecutions, many officers have found the footage of their encounters with members of the public to be retrospectively useful in demonstrating the professionalism of their conduct, in what are sometimes tense and difficult interactions, and in seeing off vexatious complaints. Conversely, they have also been useful in identifying instances of inappropriate or egregious conduct by officers.

Notably, for the past two decades or so, a persistent narrative in terms of the stories police organisations tell themselves about themselves has been one of 'digital deficit'. That is, about them not having enough officers who are accomplished users of new digital technologies, such as social media, that they can cope with the vast volumes of information, intelligence and evidence that are now routinely available. Undoubtedly, the ongoing 'datafication' of society will continue these pressures. However, at the time of writing, there are the first signs that the perceived problem is starting to tip from a 'digital skills deficit', towards a more 'analogue' form, about officers not having face-to-face, community engagement competencies. This is partly driven by generational demographics, inasmuch as the police are now recruiting from a pool of young people who are 'digital natives', and unlike their predecessors, have grown up surrounded by social media, such that they are entirely familiar with its conventions, uses and abuses.

These are not issues or challenges confined to policing. They articulate with the broader societal impacts that our new media ecosystem is having upon the social ordering of reality, in terms of what and how we know things, and the ways we relate to and interact with each other. And as with assessing these social, political, economic and cultural effects more generally, it is vital to understand how the digital and analogue dimensions of social life are increasingly folded into one another. This is especially true for policing where, because of how its core mission is about engaging with peoples' emergencies and crises, there will always be a need to perform their roles with empathy and sensitivity.

POLICING'S 'SOFT POWER'

Perhaps because they are an agency endowed with state authority to implement coercive force across a range of situations and settings, it is this aspect of policing that is centred in many of the stories told about the activity of policing, both within police organisations and outside of them. However, one of the recurring themes of research on the police, is just how much of their work gets done without explicit recourse to their formal legal powers. It is a tendency pithily summarised by Professor Keith Hawkins (1992) as how 'law' is more often than not, an instrument of 'last resort'. The art and craft of skilled policing involves being able to expertly influence, persuade and cajole people to comply with legal norms and conventions, backed by the invocation of criminal sanctions only if required.

Understanding the conduct of policing in this way, has certain affinities with the political scientist Joseph Nye's work on 'soft power' (1990). Nye differentiates between 'hard power' and 'soft power' as a way of understanding how some actors are able to achieve their objectives through the power of influence, attraction and persuasion, rather than just naked coercion. Transposed into a policing setting, it is a concept that appears helpful in understanding how and why policing gets done in particular ways. This is particularly true when it comes to explaining the perceived power and public value of community policing.

As has been recorded at several points across this volume, as an organisation, South Wales Police have invested much in an identity that centres a closeness and affinity with the communities of South Wales. Whilst there may be a commitment to the values of community policing, that does not mean that it has always been possible to practically sustain and realise these. There is little doubt that to deliver meaningful community policing requires a significant investment of resources. As detailed by Innes et al. (2020), the evidence is clear that when done properly, in terms of having dedicated officers, proactively engaging with local communities, and systematically targeting the concerns that afflict them, a range of both tangible and more intangible outcomes can result. These can include preventing crimes and anti-social behaviour, improving levels of social cohesion and collective efficacy, and driving up public confidence in the police.

Ultimately though, it is down to the decisions of police leaders about whether to invest in such modes of policing in the hope that they generate these outcomes. This appears to be an increasingly difficult choice though, given the increasing range of demands and expectations being made, especially in terms of servicing both traditional types of crime, alongside more digitally enabled forms of harm. Much of the work of contemporary police leadership is then about establishing an appropriate balance between competing demands, and in managing the necessary trade-offs that arise across portfolios. After all, there is no obvious formula for deciding what is the right level of investment to make in a major crime team to ensure that there is enough capacity and capability to ensure that the majority of the 'resource-hungry' murder enquiries that are commissioned identify the perpetrator. As opposed to investing in public order policing assets that ensure most football matches are relatively safe and peaceful events.

It is because of the inevitability of these trade-offs that the institutional soft power of the police becomes important. For what it provides is a basic well of social support for the police from the public, and an acceptance of what policing can practically achieve.

POLICE REFORM, STRUCTURES OF FEELING AND STRATEGIC NARRATIVES

Writing in the 1960s, the cultural analyst Raymond Williams (1961) coined the term 'structures of feeling' to capture how and why prevalent public sentiments and moods evolve and adapt across different historical moments. His central idea was that there are always different ways of interpreting and making sense of the world vying with each other for attention. These cannot necessarily be fully articulated (hence his preference for the notion of a 'feeling', rather than thought), but fundamentally there are conventions for what can be thought and said about particular issues and institutions at particular points in time.

The purpose of introducing Williams's notion of structures of feeling into a discussion of police reform and improvement is that it illuminates some of what is missing in terms of the contemporary world of policing. As individuals who are interested in, but 'outside' of the police, it appears to the authors of this chapter that any sense of a strategic narrative for police reform and improvement is lacking. It is not clear what stories the police want to tell themselves about themselves, and by extension the public, about who they are, and how they are adapting to the pressures of structural, social, political and economic change in society.

It seems that confronted by the array of complex challenges outlined in the preceding sections, recent key police reforms have become largely reactive to and driven by events and scandals, rather than based upon a coherent and compelling sense of how to improve coming from within the service, that can be put positively and proactively. By way of comparison, for example, in the early 2000s, the police reform agenda in terms of practice and delivery was oriented around the implementation of Neighbourhood Policing and also the development of counterterrorism. In previous decades an engine for reform was supplied by thinking around concepts such as 'problem-oriented policing' and 'intelligence-led policing'. There really hasn't been anything comparable to these for the last decade, in terms of how policing is to be organised and conducted to respond to the prevailing conditions and challenges it is tasked to react to.

Assessments and analyses of such concepts and models of policing have, for understandable reasons, largely been grounded in their practical implications and implementation. However, we can also understand their significance and importance in terms of their expressive and symbolic functions. That is, providing explanations and justifications for how and why police structures and processes can and should be revised and amended. It can be plausibly argued, that to a significant extent, this is what ideas such as community policing, intelligence-led policing and problem-oriented policing supplied. As much as they engaged changes in how policing was practically performed, they also gave structure and form to feelings about what policing was for, and how it needed to be reconfigured.

Thinking in such terms is helped by connecting with Innes's (2014) work on signal crimes and control signals. A central idea within his 'Signal Crimes Perspective' is that acts defined as crimes and social control responses to these, always have both a material and expressive component. In respect of the latter dimension in particular, some acts are freighted with enhanced capacity and capability to impact and affect how people think about their safety and security. This applies as much to institutions such as the police, as it does to individuals.

Aligned with these ideas, it is clear that the occurrence of scandals and crises have always played a role in driving the quest for police reform and improvement. What is different about the contemporary moment is the 'presence in absence', induced by the lack of a strategic narrative from within policing, about how to respond to them. In effect, policing feels somewhat 'de-centred' and fragmentary, comprising an array of activities and disciplines that are only 'loosely coupled' to one another.

For example, a key shaping narrative in terms of the contemporary politics of policing, is the need for significant enhancements to the prevention of and response to violence against women and girls. As described in Chapter 9 of this book, this has been a movement underway for several decades now, driven by the potent blend of imperatives of research evidence and activists' campaigns. It is the fulcrum of a wider shift, in terms of how the purview of policing has been progressively shifting from largely being focused upon public spaces, as it was in its nineteenth century incarnation, to being increasingly involved in the regulation of private behaviours.

Whilst there does appear to be increasing recognition of the importance of this aspect of the police role within and beyond the police service, there is also trepidation about precisely how it should be undertaken. Questions are repeatedly posed about what precisely the 'proper' role for police officers in such situations is, and where and when do they need to hand over responsibility to other public service agencies. Perhaps one reason for this uncertainty is a moral question about how to balance equity of policing and the application of law, versus protecting vulnerable people. Traditionally, it has always been posited in theory if not practise, that the police should be independent and act with neither 'fear nor favour', in terms of those subject to their interventions. Yet this seems to induce certain tensions and frictions in terms of their ability and willingness to intrude into private spaces, where they regularly encounter individuals at risk, because they are exposed to multiple overlapping and intersecting vulnerabilities. One consequence of which is that officers are regularly confronted with a dilemma about how much they can and should look to 'compensate' for these individuals circumstances, in terms of the level of protective service they provide, compared with how they might treat other citizens.

Such dilemmas are especially associated with the growing focus upon violence in private as opposed to public spaces, and have been directly connected with the growing visibility of discourses around the adoption of 'public health' approaches to policing. Although there is frequently a lack of definition around what the latter phrase actually means in practice, it generally seems to involve high levels of population surveillance to detect 'outbreaks' of problems of interest, and then partnership interventions to prevent more occurrences, and mitigating the consequences of incidents. Framed in this way, there appears to be strong similarities with the core components of both problem-oriented and intelligence-led policing reform models, albeit they had a far more defined sense of what the role of the police actually is. Moreover, it is appropriate to ask 'what is the evidence base for the success of public health styled interventions more generally?' Certainly, given the recurring political debates about how the NHS is struggling to cope and requires increasing resources 'just to stand still', there is little to suggest that public health methods of intervention can do much to systematically break the cycle of demand created by more structural societal pressures.

A second shaping narrative upon the current police improvement agenda is what we might refer to as 'datafication'. Of course, this is not a phenomena restricted to policing, as the increase in overall volumes of data and their role in influencing the organisation and conduct of life, involves a wider and deeper process of societal transformation (Brayne 2021). However, what policing does need to do is establish a position and story to tell, about how and why various modes of data are being used to inform their policies and practices. Currently, the 'datafication of policing' seems stuck between an 'over-policing' narrative of increasingly penetrative surveillance, versus an 'under-policing' narrative where police organisations are being over-whelmed by the volumes of data they can access. This manifests, for example, in the repeated complaints that police simply cannot cope with the vast volumes of digital intelligence and evidence they are now routinely accessing as part of their investigations. It is also present in the lack of response to the majority of complaints of digitally enabled or digitally dependent frauds, for example.

Datafication though, also creates a potential for other innovations. One such, is the rise of the 'open source' intelligence and investigation movement. The investigative function of police, in terms of the identification, collection, processing and interpretation of information into intelligence and evidence, has always been conceptualised as a core institutional function. But there is a profound question about 'how much of this work actually needs to be done by warranted officers with special legally endowed powers?' Obviously, some of it does. But there are many bits of the investigative process that could be performed by non-police personnel, who possess sufficient technical skills and knowledge that they know how to find information and collate it, so a chain of evidence is established. This happens quite a lot in the investigation of fraud, and has also been a key feature of the work of the open-source journalism organisation Bellingcat (Higgins 2021). They have demonstrated how careful and meticulous use of publicly available 'open-source' material collected via the internet and social media can be used to mount allegations and build cases in relation to murder and war crimes offences. It seems entirely plausible that similar logics and practices could be applied to elements of the police's crime investigation function. Potentially, this might involve much of the initial case building work being conducted by non-police personnel, before the intelligence and evidence that has been collected gets handed over to the police at the point at which decisions to charge are to be taken, or when legal powers are really required to progress the activity.

One further shaping narrative on current debates about the role of the police, has gravitated around the concept of 'evidence-based policing'. This holds that reforms and innovations should only be introduced where there they have been robustly and systematically tested to demonstrate they 'work' as intended, across multiple situations and settings (Sherman 1998). Although there has been some interest from within policing in these ideas, it is fair to say that evidence-based policing's popularity and influence has been located more outside of the police service amongst some academics and think-tanks, than within it. There is certainly little 'evidence' to suggest that it has leveraged a large institutional level effect in terms of transforming how policing routinely gets done on the streets, on a day-to-day basis. Moreover, in an era of 'permacrisis', it is difficult to envisage how space will be created for the long-term, deliberative building of a wide-spread evidence-base, in the face of more immediate and visceral political and economic pressures.

All of these issues need to be incorporated and integrated if we are to try and forecast what the future might hold for policing. For whilst we do not know everything about what is coming next, what we can see, looks profoundly challenging. The blend of growing and overlapping economic, social and political crises that can be observed at the current moment, possess the potential to make the environment for the police very difficult, both in terms of a growth in 'traditional' types of crime and disorder, but also in increasing the prevalence and distribution of some 'new' crimes.

The point about differentiating between 'shaping' and 'strategic narratives' in this discussion has been to articulate how there can be a range of incoherent pressures and challenges that are shaping and influencing the structures of feeling that rise up around an institution such as the police. But a clear and compelling strategic narrative is required to synthesise these and establish a vision for how they can meaningfully be responded to. At the current time, we cannot discern that the UK police service has such a vision and strategic narrative.

In part, this is attributable to the general momentum tracked over the past two decades or so, wherein the governance of policing has become increasingly crowded and complicated. The result being a decentred and fragmented set of arrangements, where there is no single police 'voice'. At a national level, depending on the issue, there is the National Police Chiefs Council, the College of Policing, HM Inspectorate of Constabulary and Fire & Rescue Services, Association of Police and Crime Commissioners, Independent Office for Police Conduct, the Commissioner of the Metropolitan Police, National Crime Agency, as well as the Home Office, all likely to proffer a view. It is unsurprising therefore, that it is difficult for the police service to speak with a coherent and/or consistent perspective.

It is a crowded environment that also makes it difficult at a local level for a Chief Constable to set out a long-term vision for reform given how they have to 'satisfice' the agendas of so many stakeholders and interested parties. Pressure is compounded by the fact that many contemporary Chief Constables' tenures are far shorter than those of their predecessors; the Police Foundation (2022, p. 122) recently asserted the average is now 3.65 years. The summary impression that one gains of how policing has adapted to recent changes and pressures is of a series of 'bolt-ons' and incremental adaptations, rather than any more deliberative and thought through process of what these cumulatively mean for the construction of the police mission, and how this is conveyed to the public.

Looking forward, it is highly likely that the confluence of pressures outlined above will elicit calls for institutional reforms. One variant of this will be to further instantiate suggestions that individual forces amalgamate, to produce economies of scale and thus financial efficiencies. As has been documented in some of the more historical passages of this book (see Madge, Chapter 2), forces such as South Wales have undertaken similar reform processes before, and there are probably lessons to be learned from these examples. More recently, South Wales Police and the other forces in Wales have sought to moderate this amalgamation agenda by establishing mechanisms for increased collaboration. For example, through establishing shared legal services and major crime teams, amongst other reforms that are only partially evident to ordinary members of the public. However, there potentially comes a point where the degree of integration and co-dependency becomes such that a merger looks an increasingly viable and plausible option.

Recent discussions of force mergers and the possibility of shifting to a single (or perhaps only two) Welsh Police Forces, has often become wrapped up in wider political debates about the devolution of policing and the criminal justice system to Wales. Viewed through a Welsh political lens, devolving policing to Wales certainly has its attractions, not least in terms of establishing parity with the situation in Scotland and greater coherence with the agendas of other public services that are already devolved. However, once again there are significant resistances to be overcome. Not least, about how Welsh Government could accrue the capacity and capability to administer this area of responsibility, given it has not been within its purview to date. However, given the scale and intensity of the pressures on the horizon, we cannot dismiss the idea that the devolution of policing may progressively acquire significant political support.

A final institutional reform proposal that can be anticipated is to draw a sharper distinction between national security facing policing functions, and local policing. For example, it seems entirely plausible to suggest the majority of digital policing tasks could be undertaken by a single specialist national agency dedicated to this task, rather than having it distributed across all the current existing forces, alongside their territorial policing responsibilities. This is on the grounds that a single agency could be better placed to establish the expensive technological infrastructure needed for such work, and might also be better placed to secure workers with the requisite skills and expertise. Relatedly, the lead national responsibility for counter-terrorism could be taken away from the Metropolitan Police Service and given to the National Crime Agency. This is certainly an option that has been 'quietly' discussed for a number of years now, and might appear increasingly attractive to a number of key actors as the political and economic pressures mount in the coming years.

More generally, returning to some of the ideas rehearsed above about 'signal crimes', potentially framing a reform agenda in these terms, could provide for a methodology for reconciling some of the fundamental tensions between supply and demand that seem to recurrently bedevil policing. If the fundamental premise is accepted that 'not all crimes are created equal' in terms of their ability to induce both objective and subjective harm, with some incidents having disproportionate effects, then steering police attention and effort towards these signal crimes, rather than less influential events, does possess an undergirding logic.

Any of these options would constitute a 'big' political decision. But what history teaches us is that such significant reconfigurations often become more attractive in periods of turbulence and crisis. After all, when the social order is more settled, the case for reform is less pressing because things appear to be working sufficiently well. Indeed, it is developing precisely this kind of perspective that was one of the key motivations for writing this book. By focusing upon a single police force to explore, amongst other things, how its history has shaped its present and possible future, our aim has been to trace some of these recurring patterns of reform as part of an ongoing quest for improvement.

References

Brayne, S. 2021. *Predict and surveil: data, discretion and the future of policing*. New York: Oxford University Press.

Geertz, C. 1973. *The interpretation of cultures*. New York: Basic Books.

Hall, S., Roberts, B., Clarke, J., Jefferson, T. and Critcher, C. 1978. *Policing the crisis: mugging, the state and law and order*. London: Macmillan.

Hawkins, K. 1992. *The uses of discretion*. Oxford: Clarendon Press.

Higgins, E. 2021. *We are Bellingcat; an intelligence agency for the people.* London: Bloomsbury.

Innes, M. 2014. *Signal crime: social reactions to crime, disorder and control.* Oxford: Oxford University Press.

Innes, M., Roberts, C. and Lowe, T. 2017. 'A disruptive influence? 'Prevent-ing' problems and countering violent extremism policy in practice'. *Law & Society Review* 51(2), pp. 252–81. *https://doi.org/10.1111/lasr.12267*

Innes, M., Roberts, C., Lowe, T. and Innes, H. 2020. *Neighbourhood policing: the rise and fall of a policing model.* Oxford: Clarendon Press.

Mark, R. 1977. *Policing a perplexed society.* London: George Allen & Unwin.

Nye, J. S. 1990. 'Soft power'. *Foreign Policy* (80), pp. 153–71. *https://doi.org/10.2307/1148580*

Police Foundation. 2022. *The strategic review of policing.* Available at: *https://www.policingreview.org.uk* (accessed 15 June 2022).

Sherman, L. 1998. *Evidence-based policing.* Available at: *https://www.policinginstitute.org/wp-content/uploads/2015/06/Sherman-1998-Evidence-Based-Policing.pdf* (accessed 15 June 2022).

Williams, R. 1961. *The long revolution.* London: Chatto & Windus.

BIBLIOGRAPHY

1831. Special Constables Act. 1831, c41.

1835. Municipal Corporations Act. 5 & 6 Will 4, c76.

1839. County Police Act. 2 & 3 Vict, c93.

1888. Local Government Act. 51 & 52 Vict, c41.

1946. The Police Act. 9 & 10 Geo 6, c49.

1964. Police Act. 1964, c48.

1964. Police Act. 1964, c48.

1965. Race Relations Act. 1965, c73.

1969. South Wales Police (Amalgamation) Order. S.I. 1969 no. 484.

1970. Equal Pay Act. 1970, c41.

1974. Health and Safety at Work etc Act. 1974, c37.

1975. Sex Discrimination Act. 1975, c65.

1976. Race Relations Act. 1976, c74.

1984. The Police and Criminal Evidence Act. 1984, c60.

1985. Prosecution of Offences Act. 1985, c23.

1993. Welsh Language Act. 1993, c38.

1994. Police and Magistrates Courts Act. 1994, c29.

1995. The Police Areas (Wales) Order. SI 1995 No 2864.

1996. Criminal Procedure and Investigations Act 1996, c25.

1997. Police (Health and Safety) Act. 1997, c42.

1998. Crime and Disorder Act. 1998, c37.

1998. Crime and Disorder Act. 1998, c8.

1998. Government of Wales Act. 1998, c38.

2002. Police Reform Act. 2002, c30.

2011. The Police Reform and Social Responsibility Act. 2011, c13.

2011. The Policing Protocol Order. SI 2011/2744.

2015. Well-being of Future Generations (Wales) Act.

2015. Well-being of Future Generations (Wales) Act. 2015 anaw 2.

ACPO (Association of Chief Police Officers). 2005. Identifying, assessing and managing risk in the context of policing domestic violence. London: Association of Chief Police Officers.

ACPO (Association of Chief Police Officers). 2006. Practice advice on professionalising the business of neighbourhood policing. Wyboston: Centrex. Available at: *library.college.police.uk/docs/acpo/ Professionalising-NeighbourhoodPolicing.pdf*

Alderson, J. 1979. *Policing freedom*. Plymouth: Macdonald and Evans.

Allsop, C. 2017. 'Cold case homicide reviews'. In: Brookman, F., Maguire, E.R. and Maguire, M. eds. *The handbook of homicide*. Chichester: Wiley Blackwell.

Allsop, C. 2018. *Cold case reviews DNA, detective work and unsolved major crimes*. Oxford: Oxford University Press.

Allsop, C. and Pike, S. 2019. 'Investigating homicide: back to the future'. *Journal of Criminological Research, Policy and Practice 5*, pp. 229–39. *https://doi.org/10.1108/JCRPP-03-2019-0021*

Altheide, D. 2002. *Creating fear: news and the construction of crisis*. New York: Aldine de Gruyter.

Amin, A. and Thrift, N. 2017. *Seeing like a city*. London: Sage.

Baker, E. R. 1965. 'The beginnings of the Glamorgan County Police'. In: Williams, S. (ed.) *Glamorgan Historian*. Cowbridge: D. Brown & Sons.

BBC News. 2013. 'Cardiff "best city" in UK for young adults says poll'. 2 October. Available at: *https://www.bbc.co.uk/news/uk-wales-south-east-wales-24354835*

Bellis, M., Ashton, K., Hughes, K., Ford, K., Bishop, J. and Paranjothy, S. 2016. *Adverse Childhood Experiences and their impact on health-harming behaviours in the Welsh adult population*. Cardiff: Public Health Wales NHS Trust. Available at: *https://www.ljmu.ac.uk/~/ media/phi-reports/pdf/2016_01_adverse_childhood_experiences_ and_their_impact_on_health_harming_behaviours_in_the.pdf*

Benkler, Y., Faris, Y. and Roberts, H. 2018. *Network propaganda: manipulation, disinformation, and radicalization in American politics*. New York: Oxford University Press.

Berlin, I. 1998. *The proper study of mankind: an anthology of essays*. London: Pimlico.

Berry, G., Izat, J., Mawby, R., Walley, L. and Wright, A. 1998. *Practical police management*. London: Police Review Publishing Co.

Bittner, E. 1974. 'Florence Nightingale in pursuit of Willie Sutton: a theory of the police'. In: Jacob, H. (ed.) *The potential for reform of criminal justice*. London: Sage.

Bourlet, A. 1990. *Police intervention in marital violence*. Milton Keynes, UK: Open University Press.

Braga, A. A., Papachristos, A. V. and Hureau, D. M. 2014. 'The effects of hot spots policing on crime: an updated systematic review and meta-analysis'. *Justice Quarterly* 31(4), pp. 633–63. *https://doi.org/10.1080/07418825.2012.673632*

Brain, T. 2010. *A history of policing in England and Wales from 1974: a turbulent journey*. Oxford: Oxford University Press.

Brayne, S. 2021. *Predict and surveil: data, discretion and the future of policing*. New York: Oxford University Press.

Brodeur, J. P. 2010. *The policing web*. Oxford: Oxford University Press.

Brookman, F. and Innes, M. 2013. 'The problem of success: What is a "good" homicide investigation?' *Policing and Society* 23(3), pp. 292–310. *https://doi.org/10.1080/10439463.2013.771538*

Brookman, F., Jones, H., Williams, R. and Fraser, J. 2020. 'Crafting credible homicide narratives: forensic technoscience in contemporary criminal investigations'. *Deviant Behavior* 43(3), pp. 340–66. *https://doi.org/10.1080/01639625.2020.1837692*

Brookman, F., Maguire, E. and Maguire, M. 2018. 'What factors influence whether homicide cases are solved? Insights from qualitative research with detectives in Great Britain and the United States'. *Homicide Studies* 23, p. 108876791879367. *https://doi.org/10.1177/1088767918793678*

Brown, K. M. and Keppel, R. D. 2012. 'Child abduction murder: the impact of forensic evidence on solvability'. *Journal of Forensic Sciences* 57(2), pp. 353–63. *https://doi.org/10.1111/j.1556-4029.2011.01970.x*

Bullock, K. 2014. *Citizens, community and crime control*. Basingstoke: Palgrave Macmillan.

Bullock, K. 2018. 'The police use of social media: transformation or normalisation?' *Social Policy and Society* 17(2), pp. 245–58. *https://doi.org/10.1017/S1474746417000112*

Bureau of Justice Assistance. 2016. The Cardiff Model: strengthening community capacity to reduce violence. US Department of Justice. Available at: *https://bja.ojp.gov/funding/awards/2016-aj-bx-k042*

Cabinet Office. 2017. National Risk Register 2017. Available at: *https://www.gov.uk/government/publications/national-risk-register-of-civil-emergencies-2017-edition* (accessed 5 October 2020).

Cardiff Council. 2018. Cardiff's well-being plan. Cardiff: Available at: *https://www.cardiff.gov.uk/ENG/Your-Council/Strategies-plans-and-policies/Local-Wellbeing-Assessment/Draft-Local-Well-being-Plan/Documents/Wellbeing%20Plan%202017.pdf*

Cattaneo, L. B. and Goodman, L. A. 2005. 'Risk factors for reabuse in intimate partner violence: a cross-disciplinary critical review'. *Trauma, Violence, & Abuse* 6(2), pp. 141–75. doi: 10.1177/1524838005275088

Chibnall, S. 1977. *Law and order news: an analysis of crime reporting in the British Press*. London: Tavistock Publications.

City of Cardiff Council. 2017. Cardiff's well-being plan. Available at: *https://www.cardiff.gov.uk/ENG/Your-Council/Strategies-plans-and-policies/Local-Wellbeing-Assessment/Draft-Local-Well-being-Plan/Documents/Wellbeing%20Plan%202017.pdf*

City of Cardiff Council. 2021. Statement of licensing policy. Cardiff: Shared Regulatory Services. Available at: *https://www.cardiff.gov.uk/ENG/Business/Licences-and-permits/Entertainment-and-alcohol-licences/Documents/Statement%20of%20Licensing%20Act%20Policy.pdf*

Clarkson, C. M. V., Cretney, A., Davis, G. and Shepherd, J. P. 1994. 'Assaults: the relationship between seriousness, criminalisation and punishment'. *Criminal Law Review*, pp. 4–20.

Clements, J. 2020. Policing the COVID-19 lockdown – what the public thinks. Crest Advisory. Available at: *https://www.crestadvisory.com/post/policing-the-covid-19-lockdown-what-the-public-thinks* (accessed 14 May 2021).

Cohen, L. E. and Felson, M. 1979. 'Social change and crime rate trends: a routine activity approach'. *American Sociological Review* 44(4), pp. 588–608. *https://doi.org/10.2307/2094589*

Cohen, S. 1972. *Folk devils and moral panics: the creation of the mods and rockers*. London: Paladin.

Cohen, S. 1985. *Visions of social control*. Oxford: Blackwell.

Cole, S. 2002. *Suspect identities: a history of fingerprinting and criminal identification*. Cambridge, MA: Harvard University Press.

Collins, R. 2008. *Violence: a micro-sociological theory*. Princetion, NJ; Oxford: Princeton University Press.

Commonwealth of Australia. 2015. Domestic violence in Australia. Finance and Public Administration References Committee. Available at: *https://www.aph.gov.au/parliamentary_business/committees/senate/finance_and_public_administration/domestic_violence/report*.

Connell, R. 2009. *Gender*. Cambridge: Polity Press.

Contini, M. and Wilson, B. 2019. Canadian Multi-Agency Risk Assessment Committee (MARAC) Model Program. Guelph, Ontario: University of Guelph. Available at: *http://hdl.handle.net/10214/17415*

Couldry, N. and Hepp, A. 2017. *The mediated construction of reality*. Basingstoke: Palgrave Macmillan.

Cretney, A., Clarkson, C. M. V., Davis, G. and Shepherd, J. P. 1994. 'Criminalising assault: the failure of the "offence against society" model'. *British Journal of Criminology* 34, pp. 15–26.

Crime and Security Research Institute. The Cardiff Model for violence prevention. Cardiff University. Available at: *https://www.cardiff.ac.uk/crime-security-research-institute/publications/research-briefings/the-cardiff-model*

Critchley, T. A. 1967. *A history of police in England and Wales, 900–1966*. London: Constable.

Crump, J. 2011. 'What are the police doing on Twitter? Social media, the police and the public'. *Policy & Internet* 3(4), pp. 1–27. *https://doi.org/10.2202/1944-2866.1130*

Dalgleish, D. and Myhill, A. 2004. Reassuring the public: a review of international policing interventions. London: Available at: *http://citeseerx.ist.psu.edu/viewdoc/download?doi=10.1.1.604.1940&rep=rep1&type=pdf*

Davenport, J. 2019. 'London hospitals "risk lives" by not sharing anti-violence data'. *Evening Standard* 4 February. Available at: *https://www.standard.co.uk/news/health/london-hospitals-risk-lives-by-not-sharing-antiviolence-data-a4056681.html*

Davies, J. 1981. *Cardiff and the Marquesses of Bute*. Cardiff: University of Wales Press.

Davies, J. 1994. *A history of Wales*. London: Penguin.

Dawson, A. and Innes, M. 2019. 'How Russia's Internet Research Agency built its disinformation campaign'. *The Political Quarterly* 90(2), pp. 245–56. *https://doi.org/10.1111/1467-923X.12690*

Delsol, R. and Shiner, M. 2015. *Stop and search: the anatomy of a police power*. Basingstoke: Palgrave Macmillan.

Department of Health and Home Office. 2008. *Safe. Sensible. Social.* London: Home Office. Available at: *https://ranzetta.typepad.com/files/sss-toolkit.pdf*

Department of Health and Social Care. 2014. *A&Es and police will share information to help tackle violence*. London: DHSC. Available at: *https://www.gov.uk/government/news/aes-and-police-to-share-information-to-help-tackle-violence*

Devroe, E., Edwards, A. and Ponsaers, P. 2017. *Policing European metropolises: the politics of security in city-regions*. Abingdon: Routledge.

Draisma, C., Stam, C., Toet, H. and Blatter, B. 2016. Pilot 'Preventieve aanpak geweld' Amsterdam-Amstelland. Amsterdam.

Droste, N., Miller, P. and Baker, T. 2014. Review article: 'Emergency department data sharing to reduce alcohol-related violence: A systematic review of the feasibility and effectiveness of community-level interventions'. *Emergency Medicine Australasia* 26(4), pp. 326–35. *https://doi.org/10.1111/1742-6723.12247*

Drury, I. 2015. '"This crying wolf HAS to stop": Furious Home Secretary Theresa May attacks police officers for "scaremongering" over budget cuts'. *Daily Mail* 20 May. Available at: *https://www.dailymail.co.uk/news/article-3089363/This-crying-wolf-stop-Furious-Theresa-attacks-police-officers-scaremongering-budget-cuts.html*

Dupont, B. 2013. 'Cybersecurity futures: how to regulate current risks'. *Technology Innovation Management Review* 3(7), pp. 6–11.

Edwards, A. 2010. Working paper 133: evaluation of the Cardiff Night-Time Economy Co-ordinator (NTEC) post. Cardiff: Available at: *https://orca.cardiff.ac.uk/78193/1/wp133.pdf*

Edwards, S. 1989. *Policing 'domestic' violence: women, the law and the state*. London: Sage.

EIGE (European Institute for Gender Equality). 2019. *A guide to risk assessment and risk management of intimate partner violence against women for police*. Luxembourg: Publications Office of the European.

Available at: *https://eige.europa.eu/gender-based-violence/risk-assessment-risk-management*

Eisner, M. 2016. 'Homicide rates in major UK cities'. In: Shepherd, J. P., Avery, V. and Rahman, S. (eds) *Targeted policing*. Police Professional, pp. 14–16.

Emsley, C. 1996. *The English police: a social and political history* 2nd edn. Harlow: Longman.

Ericson, R. and Haggerty, K. 1997. *Policing the risk society*. Oxford: Clarendon Press.

Ericson, R. V. 1982. *Reproducing order: study of police patrol work*. Toronto: University of Toronto Press.

Ericson, R. V. 1993. *Making crime: a study of detective work*. Toronto: University of Toronto Press.

Evans, N. 1980. 'The South Wales race riots of 1919'. *The Journal of Welsh Labour History* 3(1), pp. 5–29.

Evans, N. 1983. 'The South Wales race riots of 1919: a documentary postscript'. *The Journal of Welsh Labour History* 3(4), pp. 76–87.

Fielding, N. 1995. *Community policing*. Oxford: Clarendon Press.

Flint, R. 2020. 'Covid: policing Christmas rule-breakers in Wales "difficult"'. BBC News. Available at: *https://www.bbc.co.uk/news/uk-wales-55387700* (accessed 20 December 2020).

Florence, C., Shepherd, J. P., Brennan, I. and Simon, T. 2011. 'Effectiveness of anonymised information sharing and use in health service, police, and local government partnership for preventing violence related injury: experimental study and time series analysis'. *BMJ* 342, p. d3313. *https://doi.org/10.1136/bmj.d3313*

Florence, C., Shepherd, J. P., Brennan, I. and Simon, T. R. 2014. 'An economic evaluation of anonymised information sharing in a partnership between health services, police and local government for preventing violence-related injury'. *Injury Prevention* 20(2), pp. 108–14. *https://doi.org/10.1136/injuryprev-2012-040622*

Ford, K., Barton, E. R., Newbury, A., Hughes, K., Bezeczky, Z., Roderick, J. and Bellis, M. A. 2018. Understanding the prevalence of adverse childhood experiences (ACEs) in a male offender population in Wales: The Prisoner ACE Survey. Available at: *https://phw.nhs. wales/files/aces/the-prisoner-ace-survey/*

Foucault, M. 1977. *Discipline and punish: the birth of the prison*. New York: Vintage.

Fox, J. 2014. 'Is there room for flair in a police major crime investigation?' *The Journal of Homicide and Major Crime Investigation* 19(1), pp. 2–19.

Geertz, C. 1973. *The interpretation of cultures*. New York: Basic Books.

Gill, M. and Mawby, R. 1990. *A Special Constable: a study of the police reserve*. Aldershot: Avebury.

Goffman, E. 1967. *Interaction ritual: essays in face to face behaviour*. New York, NY: Pantheon.

Goldstein, H. 1990. *Problem-oriented policing*. New York: McGraw-Hill.

Greene, J. 2000. 'Community policing in America: changing the nature, structure and function of the police'. In: Horney, J. (ed.) *Criminal Justice 2000: policies, processes, and decisions of the criminal justice system*. Washington DC: US Department of Justice.

Grinnell, D., Innes, M., Innes, H., Harmston, D. and Roberts, C. 2020. 'Normalisation et domestication de la désinformation numérique : les opérations informationnelles d'interférence et d'influence de l'extrême droite et de l'État russe en Europe'. *Heredote*. Available at: *https:// www.herodote.org/spip.php?article944*

Hall, S., Roberts, B., Clarke, J., Jefferson, T. and Critcher, C. 1978. *Policing the crisis: mugging, the state and law and order*. London: Macmillan.

Harrison, M. 2020. *A case study analysis of how public order policing is interpreted and practised in South Wales*. University of South Wales.

Hawkins, K. 1992. *The uses of discretion*. Oxford: Clarendon Press.

Higgins, E. 2021. *We are Bellingcat; an intelligence agency for the people*. London: Bloomsbury.

HMIC. 2001. *Open all hours: a thematic inspection report on the role of police visibility and accessibility in public reassurance*. London: Her Majesty's Chief Inspector of Constabulary.

HMIC. 2006. *South Wales Police: baseline assessment*. Her Majesty's Chief Inspector of Constabulary. Available at: *https://www.justice inspectorates.gov.uk/hmicfrs/media/south-wales-baseline-assessment-20060929.pdf*

HMIC. 2008. *The thematic inspection of major crime*. London: Her Majesty's Chief Inspector of Constabulary. Available at: *https://www.justiceinspectorates.gov.uk/hmicfrs/media/major-challenge-20090630.pdf*

HMICFRS. 2019. *PEEL: Police effectiveness, efficiency and legitimacy 2018/19: An inspection of South Wales Police*. Available at: *https://www.justiceinspectorates.gov.uk/hmicfrs/wp-content/uploads/peel-assessment-2018-19-south-wales.pdf* (accessed 28 July 2023).

HMICFRS. 2021. Policing in the pandemic – the police response to the coronavirus pandemic during 2020. HM Inspectorate of Constabulary Fire and Rescue. Available at: *https://www.justiceinspectorates.gov.uk/hmicfrs/publication-html/the-police-response-to-the-coronavirus-pandemic-during-2020/#foreword*

HMICFRS. 2022. Value for money dashboards. Available at: *https://www.justiceinspectorates.gov.uk/hmicfrs/our-work/article/value-for-money-inspections/value-for-money-profiles/value-for-money-dashboards*.

HM Treasury, Office of the Secretary State for Wales, Rt Hon Stephen Crabb MP, Rt Hon Greg Hands MP and Rt Hon George Osborne. 2016. *City deal: Cardiff capital region*. Available at: *https://assets.publishing.service.gov.uk/government/uploads/system/uploads/attachment_data/file/508268/Cardiff_Capital_Region_City_Deal.pdf*

Home Affairs Committee. 2018. *Policing for the future*. London: The Stationery Office. Available at: *https://publications.parliament.uk/pa/cm201719/cmselect/cmhaff/515/515.pdf* (accessed 26 May 2022).

Home Office. 1984. *Joint departmental circular on crime prevention*. Home Office, Department of Education and Science, Department of Health and Social Security and Department of the Environment. Available at: *https://depositedpapers.parliament.uk/depositedpaper/2201265/details*

Home Office. 2006. *Crime and cohesive communities: research, development and statistics*. London: The Stationery Office. Available at: *http://citeseerx.ist.psu.edu/viewdoc/download?doi=10.1.1.510.6857&rep=rep1&type=pdf*

Home Office. 2015. *The strategic policing requirement*. London: The Stationery Office. Available at: *https://assets.publishing.service.gov.uk/government/uploads/system/uploads/attachment_data/file/417116/The_Strategic_Policing_Requirement.pdf* (accessed 26 May 2022).

Home Office. 2019. Police workforce, England and Wales. Available at: *https://assets.publishing.service.gov.uk/government/uploads/system/uploads/attachment_data/file/831726/police-workforce-mar19-hosb1119.pdf* (accessed 5 October 2020).

Home Office. 2019. 'Home Office allocates £51 million to police forces for increased action on knife crime ahead of Easter weekend'. Available at: *https://www.gov.uk/government/news/home-office-allocates-51-million-to-police-forces-for-increased-action-on-knife-crime-ahead-of-easter-weekend*

Home Office. 2020. Police workforce, England and Wales. Available at: *https://assets.publishing.service.gov.uk/government/uploads/system/uploads/attachment_data/file/955182/police-workforce-mar20-hosb2020.pdf* (accessed 8 July 2022).

Hunt, W. W. 1957. *'To guard my people': an account of the origin and history of the Swansea police.* Swansea: [Jones, pr.].

Innes, M. 2003. *Investigating murder. Detective work and the police response to criminal homicide.* London: Oxford University Press.

Innes, M. 2007. 'Investigation order and major crime investigations'. In: Newburn, T., Williamson, T. and Wright, A. eds. *Handbook of criminal investigations.* Cullompton: Willan Publishing.

Innes, M. 2014. *Signal crime: social reactions to crime, disorder and control.* Oxford: Oxford University Press.

Innes, M., Abbott, L., Lowe, T., Roberts, C. and Weston, N. 2007. *Signal events, neighbourhood security, order and reassurance in Cardiff.* Cardiff: Cardiff University.

Innes, M. and Fielding, N. 2002. 'From community to communicative policing: "Signal crimes" and the problem of public reassurance'. *Sociological Research Online* 7(2). Available at: *http://www.socres online.org.uk/7/2/Innes.htm*

Innes, M., Innes, H., Dobreva, D., Chermak, S., Huey, L. and McGovern, A. 2018. *From minutes to months.* Cardiff: Cardiff University.

Innes, M., Roberts, C. and Lowe, T. 2017. 'A disruptive influence? "Prevent-ing" problems and countering violent extremism policy in practice'. *Law & Society Review* 51(2), pp. 252–81. *https://doi.org/10.1111/lasr.12267*

Innes, M., Roberts, C., Lowe, T. and Innes, H. 2020. *Neighbourhood policing: the rise and fall of a policing model.* Oxford: Clarendon Press.

Innes, M., Roberts, C., Lowe, T. and Innes, H. 2020. *Neighbourhood policing: the rise and fall of a policing model.* Oxford: Oxford University Press.

Innes, M., Roberts, C., Preece, A. and Rogers, D. 2018. 'Ten "Rs" of social reaction: using social media to analyse the "post-event" impacts of the murder of Lee Rigby'. *Terrorism and Political Violence* 30(3), pp. 454–74. *https://doi.org/10.1080/09546553.2016.1180289*

Jabar, A., Fong, F., Chavira, M., Cerqueira, M. T., Barth, D., Matzopoulos, R. and Engel, M. E. 2019. 'Is the introduction of violence and injury observatories associated with a reduction in violence-related injury in adult populations? A systematic review and meta-analysis'. *BMJ Open* 9(7), p. e027977. *https://doi.org/10.1136/bmjopen-2018-027977*

James, A. 2013. *Examining intelligence-led policing: developments in research, policy and practice.* Hampshire: Palgrave Macmillan.

Jolin, A. and Moose, C. A. 1997. 'Evaluating a domestic violence program in a community policing environment: research implementation issues'. *Crime & Delinquency* 43(3), pp. 279–97. *https://doi.org/10.1177/0011128797043003003*

Jones, D. J. V. 1990. 'Where did it all go wrong? Crime in Swansea 1938–1968'. *Welsh History Review* 15, pp. 240–74.

Jones, D. J. V. 1996. *Crime and policing in the twentieth century: the South Wales experience.* Cardiff: University of Wales Press.

Jones, R. and Jones, R. W. 2022. *The Welsh Criminal Justice System: On the Jagged Edge.* Cardiff: University of Wales Press.

Jones, R. and Wyn Jones, R. 2019. *Justice at the jagged edge in Wales.* Cardiff: Wales Governance Centre, Cardiff University. Available at: *https://www.cardiff.ac.uk/__data/assets/pdf_file/0006/1699215/Justice-at-the-Jagged-Edge.pdf* (accessed 26 May 2022).

Jones, T. 2008. *Handbook of policing.* Cullompton: Willan.

Kemshall, H. and Wood, J. 2007. 'Beyond public protection: an examination of community protection and public health approaches to high-risk offenders'. *Criminology & Criminal Justice* 7(3), pp. 203–22. *https://doi.org/10.1177/1748895807078860*

Krug, E. G., Mercy, J. A., Dahlberg, L. L. and Zwi, A. B. 2002. 'The world report on violence and health'. *Lancet* 360(9339), pp. 1083–8. *https://doi.org/10.1016/s0140-6736(02)11133-0*

Lloyd-Evans, M. and Bethell, P. 2009. 'Review of undetected serious historic crime: why bother?' *Journal of Homicide and Major Incident Investigation* 5(2), pp. 3–16.

Loader, I. and Mulcahy, A. 2003. *Policing and the condition of England: memory, politics and culture.* Oxford: Clarendon Press.

Loftus, B. 2009. *Police culture in a changing world*. Oxford: Clarendon Press.

Lord Scarman. 1981. *The Scarman report*. Harmondsworth: Penguin.

Lowe, T., Innes, H., Innes, M. and Grinnell, D. 2015. The work of Welsh Government funded Community Support Officers. Cardiff: Welsh Government. Available at: *https://orca.cardiff.ac.uk/id/eprint/88880/1/150226-wg-funded-community-support-officers-en.pdf*

Macpherson, W. 1999. *The Stephen Lawrence Inquiry*. London: Stationery Office.

Maguire, M., Morgan, R. and Nettleton, H. 2001. Early lessons from the crime reduction programme: tackling alcohol related street crime in Cardiff (TASC Project). Available at: *https://citeseerx.ist.psu.edu/viewdoc/download?doi=10.1.1.499.1819&rep=rep1&type=pdf*

Manning, P. 1997. *Police work: the social organisation of policing* 2nd edn. Prospect Heights, Illinois: Waveland Press, Inc.

Manning, P. 2010. *Democratic policing in a changing world*. London: Routledge.

Margetts, H., John, P., Hale, S. and Yassera, T. 2016. *Political turbulence: how social media shape collective action*. Princeton: Princeton University Press.

Mark, R. 1977. *Policing a perplexed society*. London: George Allen & Unwin.

Marx, G. 2016. *Windows into the soul: surveillance and society in an age of high technology*. Chicago: Chicago University Press.

Mayor of London. 2019. *ISTV – History of Information Sharing to Tackle Violence*. Available at: *https://data.london.gov.uk/information-sharing-to-tackle-violence/istv-history-of-information-sharing-to-tackle-violence/*

McCartney, C. 2006. 'The DNA Expansion Programme and criminal investigation'. *British Journal of Criminology* 46(2), pp. 175–92. *https://doi.org/10.1093/BJC/AZI094*

McCord, J. 2003. 'Cures that harm: unanticipated outcomes of crime prevention programs'. *The ANNALS of the American Academy of Political and Social Science* 587(1), pp. 16–30. *https://doi.org/10.1177/0002716202250781*

McCulloch, J., Maher, J., Fitz-Gibbon, K., Segrave, M. and Roffee, J. 2016. *Review of the Family Violence Risk Assessment and Risk Management Framework (CRAF)*. Melbourne: Monash University.

Mercer Kollar, L. M. and Sumner, S. A. 2018. *Cardiff Model Toolkit: community guidance for violence prevention*. Atlanta: Centers for Disease Control and Prevention. Available at: *www.cdc.gov/violenceprevention/publichealthissue/fundedprograms/cardiffmodel/toolkit.html*

Mercer Kollar, L. M. et al. 2020. 'Building capacity for injury prevention: a process evaluation of a replication of the Cardiff Violence Prevention Programme in the Southeastern USA'. *Injury Prevention* 26(3), pp. 221–8. *https://doi.org/10.1136/injuryprev-2018-043127*

Michaelson, S., Kelling, G. and Wasserman, R. 1988. *Toward a working definition of community policing*. Cambridge, MA: John F. Kennedy School of Government.

Miller, P. et al. 2019. 'Driving change: a partnership study protocol using shared emergency department data to reduce alcohol-related harm'. *Emergency Medicine Australasia* 31(6), pp. 942–7. *https://doi.org/10.1111/1742-6723.13266*

Miller, S. L. 1998. 'Rocking the rank and file: gender issues and community policing'. *Journal of Contemporary Criminal Justice* 14(2), pp. 156–72. *https://doi.org/10.1177/1043986298014002004*

Morgan, J. 1987. *Conflict and order: the police and labour disputes in England and Wales 1900–1939*. Oxford: Oxford University Press.

Morgan, N. et al. 2020. Trends and drivers of homicide main findings London: Home Office. Available at: *https://assets.publishing.service.gov.uk/government/uploads/system/uploads/attachment_data/file/870188/trends-and-drivers-of-homicide-main-findings-horr113.pdf*

Nash, M. and Williams, A. 2008. *The anatomy of serious further offending*. Oxford: Oxford University Press.

Nash, M. and Williams, A. 2010. *Handbook of public protection*. Willan Publishing.

National Audit Office. 2018. *Financial sustainability of police forces in England and Wales 2018* (2018). London: The Stationery Office. ISBN: 978-1-78604-211-8. Available at: *https://www.nao.org.uk/wp-content/uploads/2018/09/Financial-sustainability-of-police-forces-in-England-and-Wales-2018.pdf* (accessed 26 May 2022).

National Crime Agency. 2019. County lines. London: NCA. Available at: *https://www.nationalcrimeagency.gov.uk/what-we-do/crime-threats/drug-trafficking/county-lines* (accessed 28 July 2023).

Newbury, A. 2020. Serious youth violence in South Wales: strategic needs assessment. Cardiff: Violence Prevention Unit. Available at: *https://www.violencepreventionwales.co.uk/cms-assets/research/ FINAL_Strategic-needs-assessment-highlight-report-compressed.pdf*

NHS Digital. 2014. Information sharing to tackle violence minimum dataset. NHS Digital. Available at: *https://digital.nhs.uk/data-and-information/information-standards/information-standards-and-data-collections-including-extractions/publications-and-notifications/ standards-and-collections/isb1594-information-sharing-to-tackle-violence-minimum-dataset*

NPIA. 2008. *Guidance on investigating domestic abuse.* London: National Policing Improvement Agency.

Nye, J. S. 1990. 'Soft power'. *Foreign Policy* (80), pp. 153–71. *https:// doi.org/10.2307/1148580*

O'Neill, M. 2018. *Key challenges in criminal investigation.* Bristol: Policy Press.

Office for National Statistics. 2020. *Coronavirus and crime in England and Wales: August 2020.* Available at: *https://www.ons. gov.uk/peoplepopulationandcommunity/crimeandjustice/bulletins/ coronavirusandcrimeinenglandandwales/august2020* (accessed 14 May 2021).

Office for National Statistics. 2022. Appendix tables: homicide in England and Wales.

Office, N. A. 2018. Financial sustainability of police forces in England and Wales 2018. London: The Stationery Office. Available at: *https://www. nao.org.uk/wp-content/uploads/2018/09/Financial-sustainability-of-police-forces-in-England-and-Wales-2018.pdf*

Orde, H. 2006. 'Policing the past to police the future'. *International review of law, computers & technology* 20(1–2), pp. 37–48. *https:// doi.org/10.1080/13600860600699445*

PA Consulting Group. 2001. *Diary of a police officer, Home Office research report.* London: Home Office.

Patel, P. 2022. Update on part two of the Police and Commissioner Review. London: The Stationery Office. Available at: *https://questions-statements.parliament.uk/written-statements/detail/2022-03-07/ hcws664*

Police Foundation. 2022. The strategic review of policing. Available at: *https://www.policingreview.org.uk* (accessed 15 June 2022).

Police Standards Unit. 2005. Good practice guide – cold case reviews of rape and serious sexual assault. London: Police Standards Unit.

Polk, K. 1994. *When men kill: scenarios of masculine violence.* Cambridge: Cambridge University Press.

Pollock, I. 2019. 'Child poverty: Wales is the only UK nation to see increase'. BBC News. Available at: *https://www.bbc.co.uk/news/uk-wales-48259327* (accessed 29 July 2023).

President's Task Force on 21st Century Policing. 2015. Final report of the President's Task Force on 21st century policing. Washington D.C.: Office of Community Oriented Policing Services. Available at: *https://cops.usdoj.gov/pdf/taskforce/taskforce_finalreport.pdf*

Quinton, P. and Morris, J. 2008. *Neighbourhood policing: the impact of piloting and early national implementation.* London: Home Office. Available at: *https://www.bl.uk/collection-items/neighbourhood-policing-the-impact-of-piloting-and-early-national-implementation*

Reiner, R. 1978. *The blue-coated worker: a sociological study of police unionism.* Cambridge: Cambridge University Press.

Reiner, R. 1991. *Chief Constables.* Oxford: Oxford University Press.

Reiner, R. 1992. *The politics of the police* 2nd edn. London: Harvester Wheatsheaf.

Reiner, R. 2010. *The politics of the police* 4th edn. Oxford: Oxford University Press.

Repetto, T. 1978. The detective task – state of the art, science, craft? *Police Studies* 1(3), pp. 5–10. Available at: *https://www.ojp.gov/ncjrs/virtual-library/abstracts/detective-task-state-art-science-craft* (accessed 13 September 2023).

Richards, L. 2003. *MPS domestic violence risk assessment model.* London: Metropolitan Police Service.

Robinson, A. L. 2003. *The Cardiff Women's Safety Unit: a multi-agency approach to domestic violence.* School of Social Sciences: Cardiff University. Available at: *https://www.researchgate.net/publication/251416613_The_Cardiff_Women's_Safety_Unit_A_Multi-Agency_Approach_to_Domestic_Violence* (accessed 29 July 2023).

Robinson A. L. 2004. *Domestic violence MARACs (Multi-Agency Risk Assessment Conferences) for very high-risk victims in Cardiff: a process and outcome evaluation.* School of Social Sciences: Cardiff University. Available at: *https://www.researchgate.net/publication/237442284_Domestic_Violence_MARACs_Multi-Agency_Risk_*

Assessment_Conferences_for_Very_High-Risk_Victims_in_Cardiff_
Wales_A_Process_and_Outcome_Evaluation (accessed 29 July 2023).

Robinson, A. L. 2010. 'Risk and intimate partner violence'. In: Kemshall, H. and Wilkinson, B. eds. *Good practice in risk assessment and risk management* 3rd edn. London: Jessica Kingsley Publishers, pp. 119–38.

Rock, P. 2004. *Constructing victims' rights: the Home Office, New Labour, and victims.* Oxford: Oxford University Press.

Rogers, C. 2004. 'From Dixon to Z Cars-the introduction of unit beat policing in England and Wales'. *Police History Journal* (19), pp. 10–14.

Rogers, C. 2007. *Policing the miners' strike. The crime of our lives.* BBC Radio 4.

Roycroft, M. 2007. 'What solves hard to solve murders? Identifying the solving factors for Category A and Category B murders. Does the SIO's decision making make a difference?' *The Journal of Homicide and Major Incident Investigation* 3(1), pp. 93–107.

Rubinstein, J. 1973. *City police.* London: Macmillan.

SafeLives. 2021. *Latest UK Marac data.* Available at: *https://safelives. org.uk/practice-support/resources-marac-meetings/latest-marac-data* (accessed 29 July 2023).

Shepherd, J. P. 1988. *Assaults: characteristics of injuries and injured.* University of Bristol.

Shepherd, J. P. 2005. 'Victim services in the National Health Service (NHS): combining treatment with violence prevention'. *Criminal Behaviour and Mental Health* 15(2), pp. 75–81. *https://doi.org/10.1002/ cbm.38*

Shepherd, J. P. 2019. 'Data and crime'. *The Times* 2 July.

Shepherd, J. P., Avery, V. and Rahman, S. 2016. *Targeted policing.* Police Professional.

Shepherd, J. P., Farrington, D. and Potts, J. 2002. 'Relations between offending, injury and illness'. *Journal of the Royal Society of Medicine* 95(11), pp. 539–44. *https://doi.org/10.1258/jrsm.95.11.539*

Shepherd, J. P., Farrington, D. and Potts, J. 2004. 'Impact of antisocial lifestyle on health'. *Journal of Public Health* (Oxford) 26(4), pp. 347–52. *https://doi.org/10.1093/pubmed/fdh169*

Shepherd, J. P. and Farrington, D. P. 1993. 'Assault as a public health problem: discussion paper'. *Journal of the Royal Society of Medicine* 86(2), pp. 89–92.

Shepherd, J. P., Peak, J. D., Haria, S. and Sleeman, F. 1995. 'Characteristic illness behaviour in assault patients: DATES syndrome'. *Journal of the Royal Society of Medicine* 88(2), pp. 85–7.

Shepherd, J. P., Shapland, M. and Scully, C. 1989. 'Recording by the police of violent offences; an Accident and Emergency Department perspective'. *Medicine, Science and the Law* 29(3), pp. 251–7. *https:// doi.org/10.1177/002580248902900311*

Shepherd, J. P. and Sumner, S. A. 2017. 'Policing and Public Health-Strategies for Collaboration'. *Jama* 317(15), pp. 1525–6. *https://doi.org/10.1001/ jama.2017.1854*

Shepherd, J. P., Tuthill, D., Parry, B. and Dowd, H. 2010. 'An audit of emergency medicine responses to children injured in violence'. *Emergency Medical Journal* 27(2), pp. 125–7. *https://doi.org/10.1136/ emj.2008.069526*

Sherman, L. 1998. Evidence-based policing. Available at: *https://www. policinginstitute.org/wp-content/uploads/2015/06/Sherman-1998- Evidence-Based-Policing.pdf* (accessed 15 June 2022).

Sherman, L. W. 1992. *Policing domestic violence: experiments and dilemmas.* New York: The Free Press.

Sivarajasingam, V., Page, N., Wells, J., Morgan, P., Matthews, K., Moore, S. and Shepherd, J. P. 2016. 'Trends in violence in England and Wales 2010–2014'. *Journal of Epidemiol Community Health* 70(6), pp. 616–21. *https://doi.org/10.1136/jech-2015-206598*

Sivarajasingam, V., Shepherd, J. P. and Matthews, K. 2004. 'Effect of urban closed circuit television on assault injury and violence detection'. *Injury prevention: journal of the International Society for Child and Adolescent Injury Prevention* 9, pp. 312–16. *https://doi. org/10.1136/ip.9.4.312*

Skolnick, J. 1966. *Justice without trial.* New York: John Wiley & Sons.

Smith, E. M. 1989. Merthyr Tydfil Borough Police 1908–1938, a brief history. *Merthyr Historian* 4, pp. 71–86.

Smith, N. and Flanaghan, C. 2000. *The effective detective: identifying the skills of an effective SIO.* London: Home Office.

Social Care, Local Government and Care Partnerships Directorate Analytical Unit. 2015. Information sharing to tackle violence: audit of progress. London: Department of Health. Available at: *https://assets. publishing.service.gov.uk/government/uploads/system/uploads/ attachment_data/file/478613/Information_sharing_audit.pdf*

South Wales Constabulary. 1984–5. Annual Report of the Chief Constable 1984 and Annual Report of the Chief Constable 1985. Glamorgan Archives. Available at: *http://calmview.cardiff.gov.uk/TreeBrowse. aspx?src=CalmView.Catalog&field=RefNo&key=DSWP%2f16*

South Wales Constabulary. 1990. *Splash 90*, programme of events. Bridgend: South Wales Police.

South Wales Police. 1991. *Communicating with youth: schools liaison officers*. Bridgend: South Wales Police.

South Wales Police. 2020. *Working towards a representative workforce.* Available at: *https://www.South-Wales.police.uk/en/join-us/working-towards-a-representative-workforce/* (accessed 28 July 2020).

Sparrow, M. K. 2016. *Handcuffed: what holds policing back, and the keys to reform*. Washington DC: Brookings Institution Press.

Sparrow, M. K., Moore, M. H. and Kennedy, D. M. 1990. *Beyond 911: a new era for policing*. New York: Basic Books.

Stallion, M. and Wall, D. S. 2011. *The British police-forces and chief officers 1829–2012* 2nd edn. Police History Society.

Stelfox, P. 2009. *Criminal investigation: an introduction to principles and practice*. Devon: Willan Publishing.

Sutherland, I., Sivarajasingam, V. and Shepherd, J. P. 2002. 'Recording of community violence by medical and police services'. *Injury prevention: Journal of the International Society for Child and Adolescent Injury Prevention* 8, pp. 246–7. *https://doi.org/10.1136/ip.8.3.246*

Taylor, I. 1999. *Crime in context*. Cambridge: Polity Press.

Taylor, L. J. 1989. *The Hillsborough Stadium disaster inquiry, final report*. London: HMSO.

The Commission on Justice in Wales. 2019. Justice in Wales for the people of Wales. Cardiff: The Stationery Office. Available at: *https://gov.wales/sites/default/files/publications/2019-10/Justice%20Commission%20ENG%20DIGITAL_2.pdf* (accessed: 26 May 2022).

The Welsh Government. 2022. Delivering justice for Wales. Cardiff: The Stationery Office. Available at: *https://www.gov.wales/sites/default/files/publications/2022-06/delivering-justice-for-wales-may-2022-v2. pdf* (accessed 17 June 2022).

Thomas, M. 1969. Annual Report of the Chief Constable. Glamorgan Archives. Available at: *https://glamarchives.wordpress.com/2019/06/*

Tilley, N. 2008. 'Community policing'. In: Newburn, T. and Neyroud, P. (eds) *Dictionary of policing*. Cullompton: Willan.

Tiratelli, M., Quinton, P. and Bradford, B. 2018. 'Does stop and search deter crime? Evidence from ten years of London-wide data'. *The British Journal of Criminology* 58(5), pp. 1212–31. *https://doi.org/10.1093/bjc/azx085*

Tong, S., Bryant, R. P. and Horvath, M. A. H. 2009. *Understanding criminal investigation*. Chichester: John Wiley and Sons Ltd.

Trojanowicz, R. C. 1983. 'An evaluation of a neighbourhood foot patrol programme'. *Journal of Police Science and Administration* 11(4), pp. 410–19.

Trojanowicz, R. C. 1986. 'Evaluating a neighbourhood foot patrol programme: The Flint Michigan Project'. In: Rosenbaum, D. P. (ed.) *Community crime prevention*. Beverley Hills: Sage, pp. 157–78.

Tuffin, R., Morris, J. and Poole, A. 2006. An evaluation of the impact of the National Reassurance Policing Programme. London: Home Office. Available at: *http://doc.ukdataservice.ac.uk/doc/7450/mrdoc/pdf/7450_hors296.pdf*

Violence Prevention Alliance. 2019. National Plan of Action officially launched. *The Peace Guardian*, 3: October–December.

Wall, D. S. 2007. *Cybercrime: The transformation of crime in the information age*. Cambridge: Polity Press.

Warburton, A. and Shepherd, J. P. 2004. 'Development, utilisation, and importance of accident and emergency department derived assault data in violence management'. *Emergency Medicine Journal* 21, pp. 473–7. *https://doi.org/10.1136/emj.2003.004978*

Warburton, A. L. and Shepherd, J. P. 2006. 'Tackling alcohol related violence in city centres: effect of emergency medicine and police intervention'. *Emergency Medicine Journal* 23(1), pp. 12–17. *https://doi.org/10.1136/emj.2004.023028*

Weisburd, D., Wyckoff, L. A., Ready, J., Eck, J. E., Hinkle, J. C. and Gajewski, F. 2006. 'Does crime just move around the corner? A controlled study of spatial displacement and diffusion of crime control benefits'. *Criminology* 44, pp. 549–92. *https://doi.org/10.1111/J.1745-9125.2006.00057.X*

Welsh Audit Office. 2010. Sustaining value for money in the police service. Audit Commission. Available at: *https://www.audit.wales/sites/default/files/Sustaining_value_for_money_in_the_police_service_in_Wales_English_2010_14.pdf*

Whitzman, C. 2008. *Handbook of community safety, gender and violence prevention*. London: Routledge.

Williams, R. 1961. *The long revolution*. London: Chatto & Windus.

World Health Organization. 2016. INSPIRE: seven strategies for ending violence against children. Geneva: World Health Organization. Available at: *https://apps.who.int/iris/handle/10665/78176*

Wright, R. 2018. 'On the frontline of London's surge in fatal gang violence: Hackney Integrated Gangs Unit is tackling violence by treating it as a public health issue'. *Financial Times* 10 May. Available at: *https://www.ft.com/content/661e8750-4f01-11e8-a7a9-37318e776bab*

Wu, D. T., Moore, J. C., Bowen, D. A., Mercer Kollar, L. M., Mays, E. W., Simon, T. R. and Sumner, S. A. 2019. 'Proportion of Violent Injuries Unreported to Law Enforcement'. *JAMA Internal Medicine* 179(1), pp. 111–12. *https://doi.org/10.1001/jamainternmed.2018.5139*.

Young, J. 1999. *The exclusive society*. London: Sage.

Zuboff, S. 2018. *The age of surveillance capitalism*. New York: Profile Books.

INDEX